The Bible of Humanity,

Standard Humanism

&

Worldwide Standard Human Society

(The bright & brilliant world of 3rd millennium)

We need the best world
Because we are the best human beings
(7 billion human beings)

Written by
Dariush Ghasemian Dastjerdi

The Bible of Humanity,
Standard Humanism
&
Worldwide Standard Human Society

Written by **Dariush Ghasemian Dastjerdi**

First Amazon Edition: 2017

333+14 pages

Price: 15 US Dollars

ISBN: 9781520306704

Mysore / India

Translated to English by Ms. Dordaneh Aalivandi

WWW.STANDARDHUMANISM.ORG

info@standardhumanism.org

https://sites.google.com/site/standardhumanism/

In the name of nourisher of the universe and the creator and maker of existence;

In the name of nourisher of the universe and the creator and maker of man;

In the name of nourisher of the universe and the creator and maker of wisdom and heart, who gave the mankind the opportunity to find salvation with his wisdom and heart and through his spiritual connection with the absolute truth, and reach the goal of his life in this world and the world after and become prosperous and happy.

I dedicate this book to all the children, girls, women, boys and men who have been oppressed in the course of history and have suffered and have been killed; I dedicate this book with the ultimate feeling of its truth seeking, tyranny fighting and justice seeking to all those who have lived in the darkest days of human history and suffered through the tyranny of the oppressors, the selfish and the hated and there was no justice to pay attention to their right and make them happy; I dedicate this book to them to make them happy, with the hope that God eradicates and cleanses all the pain and sorrow they have suffered from their souls with the joy they feel and may they be happy forever, and know that there is the possibility for mankind to reach a human unity by accepting a new method and retrieve the control of his world from the ignoramus, the selfish, the extortionists and power seekers, and eradicate tyranny and darkness forever and take everything under their own control and create a humane life worthy of mankind and fair for all human beings.

Contents

Introduction

CHAPTER 1

CHAPTER 2

CHAPTER 3

Introduction

Mankind is a highly sophisticated and capable creature; he has this strength, talent and characteristic to adapt himself to the environment in different circumstances or adapt the environment with his needs and conditions, and or adjust with different cultures and races and languages, and or implement different regulations in his society and pass his life by obeying those rules; this capability of mankind has been proven on the earth time and again and has been manifested in different ways; Mankind has been able to take advantage of this incredible capability and guide his life step by step towards more social growth; also through his religions and beliefs and political views he has tried hard to create a human unity and concentrate his energy in a more correct way in the route towards salvation and public goals, even though his achievements have been negligible and primitive! In fact in the realm of human unity and successful universal management in his life mankind has been very weak and feeble and his efforts in the past century in the road to globalization and establishing international understanding in spite of its huge achievements - thru foundation of international organizations for development of law abidance, and or development of science and knowledge, and or international hygiene and prevention of spread of dangerous diseases, and or in the field of improving the condition of global economy and labor and human life, prevention of spread of international terrorism, smuggle of drugs and numerous other substances - is still primitive and young!

Without doubt and certainly mankind is still active and steps towards creating a world suitable for his human life; but the question is whether his path is really towards the welfare of the entire human beings and or in the path towards the good of a group of human beings? Is his path is in line with humanity and or in line with power seeking and extortion? Is his path and direction a smooth and level one towards pure truth and human felicity or it is a road full of ditches which leads to nowhere? And eventually if his path is what the evidence shows, it is not a path worth of human beings and it is still carrying the past shortcomings and goes through the devious roads of the past, how can it go through the main path which is worthy of him?

All the human beings know and believe that the path and the goal of mankind, is a life worthy of him along with peace, friendship and mutual respect, a proper and purposeful life which leads towards material and spiritual sublimity, a proper and purposeful life towards sublimity and welfare in this world and the world hereafter; ... But here the question arises as what really is the better and approved solution among all human school of thoughts which can observe the rights of everyone and implement universal justice?! If we are supposed to present a solution which is approved by a part of the world and disapproved by another part, that solution, naturally will not be logical or legitimate and problem-solving! A solution which can't attract the satisfaction of all human beings with different human, cultural and ideological desires can't have legitimacy and eventually it will become devious and or become obsolete and old! As a result we must find a solution which first of all meets the rights of everyone and the satisfaction of all human beings and secondly it is so powerful, dynamic and practical through which mankind can reach what he deserves and experience human bliss, happiness, peace, devotion, brotherhood and equality and on path towards it, he has thought for centuries and thousands of years and tolerated a lot of hardship ....

Standard Humanism through establishing Worldwide Standard Human Society is following such a scope!

Standard Humanism and Worldwide Standard Human Society suggests a system and principles based on which the human life is changed in a simple, fundamental and dynamic way and will be reformed, and will reach its own truth, and a human peace and joy, and salvation and bliss in this world and the world after which is what all the thoughts and beliefs and doctrines and religions of the world have in mind; the thought and way of life of Standard Human forms the life and advanced administration of the third millennium of mankind.

As the discussion of Standard Humanism is a new one, so it has been tried to be presented in a simple and concise manner so that the elite readers can take advantage of the principles of this school of thought in a general survey and understand it; it is obvious that after it has found enough credibility among the people of the world, we will have more chance to discuss and scrutinize the topics of the book in more precise surveys.

Dariush Ghasemian Dastjerdi

Mysore, India - September 15, 2010

Standard Humanism
&
Worldwide Standard Human Society

CHAPTER 1

Preface and start of the contestation

Who is the man who can present peace and a humane life suitable for all human beings (by their different religions, beliefs, thoughts, cultures, nationalities, languages and races) in an equal and alike way?!

Which religion, school of politics or culture there is to salvage the life of the man from conflicts and dissension, poverty and oppression, and create a humanistic world for him, suitable for peaceful life, and mingled with materialistic and spiritual progress?

Up to now, have there been any ideology, religion and political thought which has been able to gather all human beings under its umbrella, and observe the right of everyone in an equal way in real world?! - Not just by discussions, postulations, and theories - Of course this has never been happened and implemented ….

Then (In this way) the mankind should be in a constant and never-ending fight & tension, and in belief and political supremacy?! Shouldn't there come a time when the mankind can live in peace and calm and have a blissful life?! Isn't it his right to live in peace and tranquility, enjoying the necessary and rightful needs and bounties in his life?! ....

Which man, religion, belief, school of politics and culture there is that has been able or can guarantee the peace and content of mankind completely? Fundamentally is it possible for a man, a religion, a school of politics etc. to carry out this task despite the great variety in human tastes and desires?!

All philosophies, beliefs, religions and schools of politics to thrive and reach to the target of ideal life (From their own point of view) claim that the entire world has to be like them so that human peace and salvation is achieved! But are you ready to set aside your thought, your culture, and religion and political point of view, and just rely on the claim of the followers of another school of thought (Which say if you become like us and accept our school of thought the world will be filled with peace and become ideal) forgo your school of thought and follow their belief?! And if you are not willing to forgo your school of thought, culture, belief and school of politics, how do you expect others to do so! It means that they are willing to forgo their belief and come unified under your umbrella of beliefs! Of course not only them, but also thousands of other religions and beliefs and thoughts! ... Will the entire world accept to become like you with the hope of guaranteeing global peace?!!! This is a raw and primitive imagination, and to prove so it suffices to draw your attention to the fact that you yourself will never consent to forgo your belief and thought, and religion and political point of view and blindly accept the thoughts of others; hence and as a result the human world translates into constant war and tension, and the need for never-ending supremacy; this state of tension mingled with the need for supremacy has always hindered creation of the ideal circumstances for human life and will continue to be so; this has been the case of human life from the day of creation! So shall man always be in a state of war and tension and need for supremacy?! Isn't he supposed to live in peace and tranquility and prosperity?! ....

The mankind is doomed to live in poverty and enmity, ignorance and hegemony and power-seeking, because the only road to salvation which is avoiding cultural, ideological and political war and conflicts has never been fulfilled; not by wars and struggles and conflicts, not by dialogues and discussions, and not by any other means! ....

The only possible way to get rid of conflicts and dominance **based on the yardsticks of today's world** *and the claims of different schools of thought,* is the unification of mankind as the followers of a specific religion and school of politics, or a belief or culture, which fortunately or un-fortunately this dream, is an unimaginable and impossible one (Unless by amusing in the virtual world); If man was supposed to go under the umbrella of a single belief, school of politics and thought in a unified manner, maybe there was the hope of reaching peace as the issue of conflicts and hegemony based on *I am right and others are wrong,* or *my ideology and school of thought is better and preferable and the ideology and school of* *politics of others is incomplete and wrong,* was removed, but history has proved that this is an impossible thing to happen! Which neither with discussion and dialogue, nor with wars and conflicts it has become possible, and will not become so! So again we come to the conclusion that due to the ideological need for supremacy and power the mankind has no choice but to remain in a state of war and conflict and enmity and schism! And this is the reality of the world of humans today which makes the dream of a peaceful, blissful and calm life along with work and wealth and tranquility for all mankind in an equal and fair manner becomes impossible.

So I repeat my question again: Is **peace** ever achievable? Is this - condition - the limit of human life on the Earth, and this huge human world, with the abundance of wealth, ability and power?! Is this the result of all the knowledge, politics, spirituality and culture where the mankind can't provide a healthy human life for himself?! Or with all the material wealth, he has a large portion of the mankind lives under the poverty line and suffers from agony and death and ailments?! In spite of the most powerful political and religious ideologies isn't mankind capable of creating and managing a life worthy of his humane values?! It doesn't seem that mankind in spite of his immense capabilities is so weak that isn't able to manage his life in an ideal and worthy manner; so where does this stem from? Why mankind has not been able and can't organize his life in a humane, complete and proper manner? Why can't man guide and control his life with a humane competence and in the road to observing complete human rights? What has kept mankind so weak and incompetent that in spite of enjoying the best religions and beliefs and political schools, and all types of material and spiritual facilities in his life, he has a slow movement towards establishment of a complete life worthy of his humane status? *A complete life suitable for all the people, and not only for a part or parts of the human society!* ....

The religion of the world is spiritual and elite to the extent that it is able to beautify the spirit of human world in spite of the variety it has and bring it to the state of calm; The world politics is so strong and robust that it is able to organize and administrate its world in the best and most advanced manner; the world has so much riches that provided if it is managed properly all the people can enjoy a healthy and well off life; the science of the world is able to discover and solve all human queries in the fields of his growth, development and progress; and the aspects of human culture are more beautiful and varied than the boring machine life; ....

But under current circumstances of the world, and the religious, political and cultural thirst for power, weak administration in development of third world countries, the growth of terrorism, drug and arms smuggling, and the other problems and dilemmas that have afflicted mankind, it is not possible to have a calm and proper human life; the problem of the world is fundamental; **power-seeking**, **supremacy** and **illiteracy**; supremacy in all aspects of life; ignoring the rights of others and thus oppression which leads to awakening of the spirit of justice-seeking among human societies, and leads to the insistence of the powers to repression of righteous people, which draws the world towards more oppression and chaos; a situation which makes reaching peace an unachievable and impossible dream; a situation which grieves the human spirit and saddens the mankind and hurts him; as situation which leads to the sorrow of women and children and men, and all human beings and the Creator of the universe ….

A part of the claim of humane thoughts and religions and schools of politics are right - where they say: If all the world give in to a single religion and thought unified, the world will go towards an overall peace and progress - this way the conflicts will be reduced and naturally life will be calmer and the human world will go towards more peace and unity and friendship; but another part of this claim isn't that pleasant, and that is the part where there is insistence on supremacy and dominance over others and their belongings! This way when a new thought and religion emerges, after a group of honorable and naïve people come to the conclusion to follow it and enjoy a better and more complete environment, it has been proven that another group of the main and first followers of that school of thought will use their prime stance as a weapon to oppress the new followers and try to bring the new followers under their own umbrella from political angle, in fact they will take advantage of the new religion to implement their supremacy over others; as a result this behavior of them results in a kind of retreat and stance keeping among others and other areas (Where the new belief and thought had not been adopted yet) which basically brings doubt to the righteousness and supremacy of that thought which should have been the main rule in its acceptance and reduces its priority, this strengthens the belief that if we accept the new school of thought (Whether it is better or not) we will be considered as a group of losers in the eyes of the main followers of that school of thought from *political and status point of view,* and as a result if we accept the new school of thought we will in fact be defeated by the main supporters of that school of thought; ... So generally this situation will lead to denial in human mind in accepting the new school of thought and any school of thought that will emerge later, in a way that he will never accept to lose his thought and put himself under the mental and political oppression and control of others and as a result lose his sovereignty and freedom; ....

This situation essentially will put a shadow of doubt on the fundamentals of a school of thought which promotes choosing a better way for life which will lead to unity and friendship among mankind through acceptance of a superior way of thinking which in turn turns it to a political issue, in a way that under these circumstances no one will consent to let go of his school of thought and accept another one on the sheer pretext of: *our suggested school of thought is better!;* This is because by accepting that he will be considered as loser from political and social point of view; so he will decide to bid farewell to it and respectfully refrain from accepting the new alleged school of thought; this way in the course of history there has been rare instances where we witness a nation easily accepting the thoughts or schools of thinking of another nation - be it religious, political or cultural - unless there has been through wars, conflicts and massacres and not through belief and overall consent and decision; ....

This is the bitter phenomena whose negative impact has affected these thoughts more than anything else! In a way that, when a group force you to accept their thought and belief with killing and massacre, fear and terror and as a result you come under their dominance, it is natural that you which would not want to be under their control and yoke, would do any effort and would invent any politics to free yourself from them; ... the most prominent and clearest policy of the defeated in the course of history and always has been making changes - in the fundamentals of that pure and dynamic and savior thought - they will take revenge of the school of thought because of which they have become captive (And try to tarnish it in any possible way by immersing it in lies and impurity and deliver a dark image of it) and also by creating innovations and changes try to make it their own and create a new belief and thought from it! So this way through political control by the conqueror group they will free themselves, and with this trick they will free themselves and become separate, independent and autonomous; obviously in the midst of this all, the honest philosophers and thinkers, or the partial ones and the superstitious public and the ig-noramus will weave stories around the pure truth of their diverging thought and in praise of their man made thought, and consider themselves as the best in the world and others as the wrong and unjustifiable; this is while they are nothing but a political and historical branch and not an absolute truth and the superior solution, whose only beneficial and positive achievement has been the fact that they have been able to individualize themselves this way! This process has been true about most of the old and new historical thoughts and beliefs and still is; (With the exception of some religious and phi-losophical and dynamic cultures and thoughts ...).

The conclusion is no human being, and or thought and religion and policy to this date and in real world has not been able to convince mankind *in a suitable way* that it is the best way towards salvation and this has led to the fact that all mankind without exception has turned towards it and accepted it; this has never materialized and it doesn't seem to do so in the future, as the history has recorded the depth of schism and enmity among different schools of thought from the beginning to this date, day by day and in detail, the negative growth has been so deep that any thought in the direction of unifying the mankind under the umbrella of a single culture, policy and or religion, with the goal of reaching a peaceful human life is an unrealistic naivety; naivety and unrealistic from man's point of view and not from the viewpoint of a particular school of thought which claims it can convince the mankind that his school of thought is superior and can observe the rights of others in a fair and even manner! It is natural that the followers of every thought always seriously have the claim that they are the only ones that can save the world and guarantee the peace and salvation of mankind! But from the point of view of the mankind (World wisdom) this is naivety, because if not so then someday all the thousands of beliefs of the world would bring thousands of human thoughts and beliefs under their own umbrella!!! Because as you believe, or know, or are certain, and or have a proof that one day the whole world will come under the umbrella of your belief, then another person with another belief or thought too imagines, or knows and or is certain that one day your belief and all the other beliefs will come under the umbrella of his belief!!! ... and as you are not willing and will not be ready in the future to refrain from your belief and accept his belief with no questions asked, be sure that he too isn't and won't give in to your belief in the future; so this will not happen till eternity; neither through dialogue, nor through war and killing and crime; as *history* have proved this is not possible! Even if you really are superior he (The mankind) will never be ready to accept your superiority; as eventually he will see himself as your slave and will not accept your superiority; if needed he will give his life for the cause of his belief not to fall slave to you and tolerate this humility; unless you claim that you will kill everyone in a war to keep your belief the only one existing in the world! So this is the way he will think too and will claim that in order to impose his belief to you and the entire world, he will kill you and all the mankind so that only his belief is dominant in the world! ….

Thus this is nothing but the futile attempt of the ignoramus and those thirsty for power, and their world and life and preoccupation which has tarnished the life of the mankind from the beginning of the world to this date and filled it with agony and pain! This has been the belief and destiny of mankind from the beginning of his life on Earth which has turned peace and a life worthy of mankind an unreachable dream! Do you think under such circumstances there is any hope for establishing a healthy world and an environment which is worthy of mankind to live in?!

Is there a better solution to solve this problem, and or basically can we make a change in the world of these ignoramus power-seekers and towards the salvation of mankind in this world and the world after? How can mankind create his own happiness? Which man, idea, belief and or philosophy and policy can create peace and a life worthy of mankind in an equal manner for all the human beings all across the world with thousands of religions and beliefs and thoughts and meet their right and need and contentment?!

All religious and political thoughts and beliefs etc. - Righteously - declare that: If you accept and adopt our belief and fundamentals, and way and methods the world will reach its optimal peace and the mankind will reach salvation and happiness; this claim is surely right, as in the discussion of religion and beliefs this claim has been guaranteed by God and through revelations and divine books etc. but how tedious that the evil of puerility and ignorance with duality and blasphemy and schism and superstitions that have entered religions have diverged them and the result of religions is more enmity, need for superiority among their followers and schism rather than reforming the world! And as a result they have never been able to fulfill their humane and worthy mission (...); and philosophical and political and social theories are also right, as they are the result of the thoughts of spiritual and or smart or wise men who have searched for the happiness of mankind in their mental and or ethereal theories; but even their theories have some shortcomings and lack the required executive guarantees and or fundamentally they have not been designed in a way that they can meet all humane needs, as a result they lack universal acceptability from all humane beliefs and thoughts, and also they lack the required suitability to establish a universal management; so we must find something new! A solution which overrides religion and politics and is accepted and noticed by all human beings and meets the rights of all in an even and equal manner! ....

Here we reach the ***Standard Human philosophy and thought and solution*** in solving the problems of human world! ***It is incredible that the thought of standard human is a different thing!!!*** Most of the existing thoughts, doctrines and beliefs say and claim that if the entire world believes in the fundamentals, laws, methods and solutions of ours in a united manner peace and happiness of mankind will be guaranteed! (Some to the price of suppression of their opposition); but the **Standard Human** states if all the human thoughts and beliefs reach their best, purest and most complete shape, and they become just like themselves, peace and happiness of mankind will be guaranteed! (This claim is incredible and special).

Existing beliefs, invite mankind to accept and adopt their religion and fundamentals, so they start defining peace and happiness of mankind and guarantee it! But Standard Human asks you to be yourself in the best and most complete manner so that the peace and happiness of mankind is guaranteed!

Standard Human suggests a system and fundamentals based on which human life is changed in a simple manner from the root and is reformed, reaches its truth, human peace and happiness, salvation and bliss in this world and the world after, which is the desired element in all thoughts and beliefs and religions in the world; the belief and method of Standard Human forms the advanced life of the third millennium of the mankind.

The belief of Standard Human isn't a thought and belief beside the existing ones, but a strong humane belief which is cleaner, refiner and purifier and has a role that is over and beyond religion and politics; the belief of Standard Human is a beyond religion or politics philosophy which leads to cleansing and purifying all thoughts and beliefs, and takes ignorance, superstition and oppression away from human life and deletes them; the belief of Standard Human is called over politics and religion because it respects all beliefs and thoughts and policies and think of progress, peace and happiness of the human world; ***Standard Human pictures a complete human entity;*** Standard Human is supernatural because of completeness of his philosophy and belief and has the role of supervision and cleansing of all human affairs! So the issue of Standard Human is not about opposition and superiority with other beliefs, but it is the issue of supervision, control, guidance and correction of human affairs and belongings! Otherwise it won't be super human.

When the people in the world gradually got to know the belief of Standard Human and the world got ready to accept this huge human reform from the darkness of ignorance and suppression to the light of wisdom and justice, the time will arrive for ***Worldwide Standard Human Society*** to take shape; the Worldwide Standard Human Society is the final goal of Standard Human and an international and universal system which keeps safe the sovereignty of countries, cultures, religions and beliefs and manages and leads the human world in a humane, dynamic and complete manner with the cooperation of the representatives of all the countries of the world; The worldwide Standard Human Society with a special system in the given fundamental parts of life (Based on the belief and philosophy of Standard Human) including: religion & belief, culture, politics, science, and economy, and with the presence of representatives from all the countries in the world will lead and manage human world, and guarantee the peace and progress of the world in all aspects of human life forever, and eradicate penetration of negative, power seeking, oppressive, exploitive and satanic forces from human life.

Today's world with all its unique characteristics, with its technology, science and wealth, with democracy and universal rule abidance, … has become a little boring and small and weak for modern man; ***mankind needs a greater human mutation,*** otherwise with the weak managerial system and the international control, and the power-seeking system of rich countries and their dominance over the world and naturally their oppression, conditions will be created in which a great reaction will form among the right-seeking groups who are against arrogance, oppression and universal injustice, which will increase the risk in which during a defeat or a sudden change in the world (Due to any natural or unnatural cause) the powers against order and the current system in the world make a more serious uprising against the current situation, and with severe reactions jeopardize the peace and stability of the world and all the positive achievements of it in order to implement their own system; and this means annihilation for humanity and the painful and oppressive new beginning; the world is not in need of a revolution so in the hope of a dream sacrifices all his valuable achievements in the zeal for reaching that! Instead, he needs a positive mutation and a positive change towards a better position; a revolution will destroy all human achievements, but a completive and reforming movement will take him to a higher level; if the current human problems in the areas of religion & belief, politics, culture, economy and science etc. are not solved, and justice and the right to enjoy a healthy human life for all human beings and in a just manner isn't visualized, the mankind will face much greater dilemmas in the future of his life.

The Worldwide Standard Human Society forms a universal and complete human life which is shaped with the help of all countries and thoughts and beliefs of human world, and because of having a powerful management system it has guaranteed the human peace forever and eradicates the risk of creation of any kind of problems in the stability of the word from the root, because it is managed and led by all the nations in the world in a unified manner! ***Standard Humanism and the Worldwide Standard Human Society*** lead to the unity of all the positive forces and energies of the human beings with any religion, belief, nationality, race and culture! The belief of Standard Human with the aid of modern technology and especially via the internet can develop in a huge way and show its positive impact in establishing human unity and make its dynamic role! The unity of positive energies through ***Standard Humanism*** will create a huge shield against any oppression and injustice where all human beings will stay in this common and dynamic human environment and ward off any oppression and shortcoming and confirms any positive move which is in line with good and well-being of mankind.

The advantage of Standard Human belief is that it induces more friendship and sincerity, health and spirituality! And it leads to universal religious, political, cultural and scientific and economical cleansing of the world! And forms management and life of mankind in the third millennium of his life; in the Worldwide Standard Human Society the wisdom of mankind, the riches of mankind, the culture of mankind, leadership and politics and spirituality of mankind will be used in line of preserving the benefits and enjoying the entire mankind from it which leads to a beautiful human life.

Standard Humanism is a human belief and a modern managerial system which is way beyond governments and religions, in a way that it covers all religions and beliefs and cultures and the right of everyone is considered.

The Belief of Standard Human is the minimum of distinguishable standard and the minimum of necessity and the present need of the human beings and the human world under the current circumstances of the world, which we should assess and accept this opportunity and the probability to create a movement and make a move towards what is worthy of mankind and make the most of it under current unsuitable circumstances.

(The followers of) thoughts and beliefs of the world each build houses and live in the best parts of it and invite others to follow and obey them so that they implement peace and justice, but this method has not only ever convinced human beings but it has also intensified tensions and schism among human societies! But Standard Humanism is a glass and very bright and transparent prism which reflects the light of truth of the world over the life of the man and over human beliefs in order to open the eyes of the world towards the light of truth, and by cleansing and shedding light to human beliefs, cultures and politics the right of everyone is considered so that everyone creates his suitable life in the world and starts it next to each other with mutual understanding, justice, equality and peace ....

The Concept and Objective of Standard Humanism

Standard Humanism seeks an ideal world perfect of human life; a proper world, which is the wish of billions of people in the course of thousands of years of human life on this earth; *this is the world that all thoughts and beliefs and religions have pictured and made mankind enthusiastic to reach it; a world with a permanent peace and justice, along with public welfare and with the least agony, poverty and oppression!*

Going through human life Standard Humanism has concluded that reaching the ideal and expected life bearing in mind the existing nature and essence and circumstances ruling the human world is not possible and it calls for different circumstances to be implemented, for this apparent reason that mankind has never to this date been able to create a world worthy of his human life in a way that is the wish and goal of all thoughts and beliefs in a correct and acceptable and stable way! As according to Standard Humanism the problem doesn't lie in thoughts and beliefs but the problem is the nature of human world which no thought and reflection arises successful and proud and triumphant from it!

Based on the philosophy and thought of Standard Human man's life and the nature and the circumstances governing it is in a way that visualizing human goals in it is never possible and changes have to be made in the nature of human life, so that men after thousands of years of gaining experience and thought and bearing hardships and endless pains can start their real life which is worthy of them in this world.

The real goal and purpose of Standard Humanism is change and circumference from the primitive nature and essence of current life, to nature and essence and system of "<u>Standard type growth</u>" (To get out of the cycle of primitive life of the current supremacy and entering <u>the world of gradual and progressive growth</u> towards higher stages and discovering more human capabilities and human life).

Unlike the basic deterrence from the term *"Standard"* and contrary to what most human thoughts and beliefs seek in the line of unifying the thoughts and cultures of mankind, through management and the huge human system and complete Worldwide Standard Human Society, Standard Humanism thinks of the wonderful and beautiful and varied human world with its different cultures and beliefs and thoughts, a world where all people have the right of equal life, and cultural and ideological growth along with social security and justice, and in the most beautiful and humane possible way away from the influence and dominance of ignoramus and the selfish and power seekers, a world where all the cultures, religions, beliefs and nations while keeping their originality and differences in a standard and ideal level will shine.

By adopting the five principles of Standard Humanism and establishment of Worldwide Standard Human Society, human life will enter a new world with a different nature and essence where mankind will experience wonderful leaps and changes and reforms worthy of his life in the third millennium in an exciting and successful manner in all political, religious, cultural, scientific and economical aspects and will think of superior goals!

Philosophy and Thought of Standard Human

CHAPTER 2

Philosophy and Thought of Standard Human
(*Standard Humanism*)

Standard humanism is a new school of thought based on respect of beliefs of others, with the goal of international life based on peace and international human unity.

This school of thought has two main and basic parts:

1/ The philosophy and the principles of human unity and being a standard human (This will be discussed in the third part of the stages and levels of human life).

2/ New world administration through a new system of Worldwide Standard Human Society (This will be discussed in the fourth part of the stages and levels of human life).

Standard Humanism is a new school of thought based on respecting the personality, culture, wisdom, race, nationality, language, thought, religion, identity and beliefs of others; beliefs play a fundamental and great role in the life of human beings; belief gives identity and personality to a man and society, identity and personality through which he forms his life and builds it; people will even give their life for their beliefs.

From a general viewpoint of the world, there is a huge difference between gaining a belief and keeping it! Gaining a belief in human societies apart from the intellectual and truth seeking fraction (Who reach the superior belief and thought in life through study and research) is usually hereditary and runs in the family! People are usually born with a belief in their family or their society, without any research or choice, and in a total random manner and live, but when it comes to defending that belief they defend it in such a way as of losing it is equal to losing the entire human identity and social credibility and even their life; ... due to the importance of belief in human life, most of the challenges in human life are formed in this area! It doesn't matter if it is in the area of religious beliefs and thoughts, or in political, cultural, racial and other areas.

The second part of the motto of Standard Humanism emphasizes on international life based on peace and international human unity; it is natural that when man has been saved from the stage of ignoramus, selfish and superiority-seeking in the realm of beliefs and politics he will reach to a stage of growth and wisdom and knowledge that he will respect the right of living for others with their different beliefs in this world; this wisdom gives him the chance to salvage himself from tensions created because of politics and beliefs and start his peaceful life; in this stage man gets the chance to give a humane order to his life with a new management and design; in this area *Standard Humanism* presents a worldwide system which heralds ideal human life mingled with understanding and cooperation and worldwide peace.

In discussing "Belief" special factors are considered and can be analyzed:

1/ Human beliefs usually manifest in the form of rules and regulations governing religions and or political, philosophical, social, cultural, racial systems etc. and all of them without exception claim that they deliver the best solution for human problems and guide him towards a complete and ideal human life!

2/ Different beliefs, consider thoughts and philosophy, and correct and man reforming and society reforming principles of themselves superior to the beliefs of others, and in defense of their own belief they will go from discussion and dialogue to war and massacre!

From a positive point of view - As the followers of different beliefs have reached this idea or conclusion that their man reforming and society reforming beliefs and principles and regulations are superior and better than the beliefs of others, hence out of benevolence and humanism they try to propagate their belief and convince others in accepting it, and to make others enjoy the benefits and values of their beliefs they might even exaggerate in propagating and presenting the benefits of their beliefs! Of course this is out of benevolence and humanity, just to make their belief look better and make others enthusiastic and convinced to accept their belief.

From a negative point of view - The followers of different beliefs due to their sense of superiority and governance on others, in propagating their belief will debate, insist and persist, and in acute cases will even tend to fight and war and commit massacre! It is because due to their prejudice and selfishness and power seeking and eventually satisfying their savage animal nature they can't consider any place for anyone else in this world! They want to use their belief to have an overall ideological and political and universal governance and make all there is in the world for themselves, as they see themselves superior to everyone else and want to be the only governing power of the world; They defend the belief they have gained accidentally and hereditary and in their family with their blood, because they will lose their identity and become a slave by losing it; so they defend it and fight for it to enslave others and bring them under their yoke and govern over them - and oppress them!

Political and social dominance and power-seeking through beliefs has been the biggest challenge of human life which has eradicated the possibility for a healthy human life and replaced it with fights and violence and aggression; in this regard the power seeking and avaricious followers have done their best and are still trying to use all kinds of positive and negative methods to weaken the beliefs of the opponent or other beliefs and make them seem unreal, incompetent and or even sinuous.

3/ As concepts such as power, riches and fame have the potential of concentration of negative energies in an extensive manner, the selfish mentality of a group of people is stimulated strongly this way and they will do any inhumane act to reach these goals (Power, riches and fame) so they can dominate others and govern over them, and satisfy their greed and avarice; this is why power seekers will do what they can in the line of guile, wile and enmity and dissension and inhuman acts to reach a stance where they can dominate the situation of their world; in this path they are not willing to leave any space empty for others so they can attend to their own world; and as this greed and avarice is in the nature of human world hence this type of power seeking men exist in all societies and among all the fans of world beliefs - more or less - and they are always trying to use anything and more importantly the pure and genuine thoughts of humans to reach superiority over others! This sense of superiority leads to a constant struggle among the supporters of different beliefs in the course of history of human life and has turned peaceful human life through pure human thoughts and beliefs into an unachievable dream.

4/ Human beliefs in the course of the history of human life have never been able to manifest in an ideal manner due to the dominance of negative and power seeking powers and their selfishness and totality, only in rare cases and rare places; in fact elite human beliefs have become a toll in the hands of those seeking power, the oppressors and the ignoramus who follow them; power seekers and the selfish have used the beliefs as a tool to dominate others, hence they have ruined their purity and tarnished them to all kind of ignorance and superstition so in this way they can create schism - among the thoughts of the honest followers of it - weaken the thoughts and take advantage of this unsettled situation and spread their dominance; to make beliefs become divided is nothing but to ruin them and or try to make them ineffective ....

5/ In the discussion of defending beliefs, those honest followers of beliefs who use their beliefs to establish a healthy and limited society devoid of power seeking thoughts and don't seek any goal but those that are in line of peace and a life worthy of human beings, when it comes to defending their beliefs - and not from the angle of attacking the beliefs of others - they put their life on the line truly; this group, are pure and competent men who seek and want welfare and peace of human beings.

Beliefs are the best achievements of human life; beliefs are the law and order and identity in human societies, whether those which have direct divine roots and whether those which stem from thought and wisdom, and the thought of humanitarian, peace loving and justice seeking people; human life without thought and law is equal to an animal's life! All human beliefs have been formed in special time periods and during special stages and necessities governing its time and place and found their identity, as a result all of them are logical and respectable; beliefs are to be respected as in special circumstances they have saved mankind from anarchy and chaos; Each belief has been the necessity of its own time and should be strongly considered respected and credited, and its followers should be considered respected and credited, as a result *the issue of superiority with the goal of selfish ascendancy has no human credibility.*

As beliefs are formed based on special social and cultural circumstances of each region, and its geographical position and finds its identity hence it can't be perceived that one belief can cover the whole world with its endless variety of tastes, customs, cultures and different religions successfully, and in a logical way make all human beings forgo their own beliefs and accept that belief; in the discussion of changing religion and belief and politics too there is only one logic acceptable and logical and that is the fact that the person or persons by logically and wisely surveillance, devoid of environmental pressures each come to the conclusion that another belief and policy is better and superior and as a result choose that.

Power seeking of the selfish and the oppressors, along with the support, following and side taking of the ignorant from them has darkened the life of mankind and tired him and made some hate the idea of having an idea and even run away from it! Who are these selfish, power seekers and the ignorant who follow them who have darkened the history of mankind and made happiness and human peace an unachievable dream! **To recognize them we first need to study and research the stages and levels of human life and nature of human world.**

The stages and levels of human life

From the very beginning of its creation and life on this earth, the mankind has always and simultaneously lived in two stages and levels or better to say lived in two worlds which are as follows:

1/ The real stage and world of human life - Which is made up of human life in all times and ages of his history on earth with all its ups and downs, good and bad, variety in its governments and cultures ….

2/ The visionary stage and world of human life - Which he builds in an ideal and visionary shape simultaneous with his life in real world because of the oppression and pain he suffers and has suffered on earth and in the world of reality, he is submerged deep in that dream and lives in it ….

These two stages are the reality and truth of human life; from the beginning of his creation on this earth mankind has always lived in these two stages and levels of life and passed his sweet and bitter days!

<u>There are third and fourth stages too, which Standard Human philosophy and thought presents and suggests them as a solution for salvation of human beings from the current shortcomings of the world</u>, and we will discuss them in the discussion of stages and levels of human life! The third and fourth stages and levels will save mankind from the current great and depleted vicious circle, filled with ignorance and infirmity and incompetence, and power seeking and supremacy and will pave the way for a real life worthy of mankind in a simple and clear and practical way.

Step and the first level
Real world of human life

Step and the first level,
Real world of human life!

Who can deny the historical wars and oppressions that have darkened and tarnished human life to safe keep the benefits of a few?! The history has always been witness to the pain of mankind and ascendency of the selfish and the despot which by any means have tried to rule over the life of human beings and deprive them from having a clean and healthy life! That historical power seeking and selfishness still exists and we are well witnessing it and in the real world we see that in today's modern time many parts of the world are still under the yoke and oppression of a group of incubus and power seekers, whether in the form of super powers or through groups that give themselves this inhumane right to decide for others; they easily give themselves the right to kill innocent people and introduce themselves as the reformers of the world! ... Maybe today's world more than ever is witness to power seeking and oppression; mankind has always and constantly lived in pain and insecurity and has never been able to build a safe and stable world worthy of him!

Since the beginning of his birth and life on this earth mankind has moved a long way, and stage by stage with the thoughts of scientists, philosophers, prophets and also tolerating many hardships he has been able to form his social progress until he has reached the stage of his current social progress in all aspects of his life; mankind has been through many dark and light periods to reach today, but the main problems of his life based on the great progress he has made have still remained unsolved and even taken much more dangerous and vaster forms! Problems such as the risk of chemical and atomic wars, terrorism, smuggling of drugs and arms ... and worse of all power seeking of big governments and ignorant justice seeking of small groups through terror and panic and massacre, which has taken the world towards dictatorship and chaos!

In the realm of politics only in the past 100 years, mankind has been witness to two tragic World Wars! Which followed no goal but mastery and power seeking; just like the past centuries when looking for power and mastery over the world people went through thousands of big and small wars; so we come to the conclusion that these oppressors and power seekers take every chance to rule over the world; though after World War I, world countries came to this knowledge that by establishing international organizations - which keep world peace - they can annihilate the risk of another war happening, but after a short while another huge war occurred which showed man's inability to control and halter that; following that, newer and more powerful organization was established, but since that organization had its own shortcomings it was not able to prevent Cold War and the great and unprecedented world entrenchment between the East and the West, which had that great political and military clash and universal power seeking and supremacy ended up in war, considering the atomic arsenals of both wings, the world would have moved towards total ruin; a risk which still exists in another form and by terrorist threats! ....

In the course of history, and each time an empire has taken form, due to the oppression and ignoring the rights of a great majority of people, justice seeking protests have been formed which has led to the overthrowing off that apparently eternal empire! Since power comes with pride and excess and oppression, hence the groups that came later on and established the next empires never learned a lesson from the mistakes of their predecessors and just like them they used oppression to reach their goals, hence the justice seeking mentality emerged again and since righteousness and justice are superior, the oppressors have always toppled down, but what a pity that the despot will never change and in each chance they get they want to rule over the destiny of mankind and create another instance of oppression; the demon of ignorance and stupidity and excess seeking doesn't want to leave mankind; hence the story of oppression followed by justice seeking will always continue, it goes on at present time too, and it may be in the near future that current superpowers, when faced with worldwide justice-seeking protests (Fortunately or un-fortunately) will topple down; ....

The positive achievements of super powers are very valuable and it is not fair for them to fall victim to the oppression and supremacy of them; if they think of the rights of others a little, in a realistic way it may decrease their oppression and justice might rule over; though worldwide society should stand vigil about the groups that amidst justice seeking protests, they are trying to dominate others through protests and terrorist attacks; this situation has created a condition in human world which makes it look as if the law governing it is more **the law of jungle!** ....

This position (Eternal and everlasting) of mankind is in the first stage and level of his life, and based on the current circumstances and until the time that he lives under *the law of jungle* he will never be free of it and we will still witness the oppression and negligence of the rights of others and which will result in justice seeking of human groups and ultimately total destruction of super powers.

In this atmosphere of oppression and injustice, and full of chaos and illegality, in the course of human history and in each period of time religion and philosophy and a thought had emerged, to make rulers and oppressors understand that they should establish justice in order to reach salvation and become happy and be able to have an ideal and worthy life of mankind and enjoy a calm life; pure and healthy religions and beliefs of humankind have tried their best each to guide people in each period of time and in each special time and place and with the current language of the people, and show them the best route based on their circumstances, some have been guided and some have stayed in their ignorance, but mankind has never been able to dominate over the circumstances of his world and amend his world in spite of the presence of oppressors and power seekers in the world.

Anyway, in this turbulence and contrast, and in the constant war between light and darkness, justice seeking and oppression, war and peace ... mankind has had no choice but to continue his life, and by creating his beautiful culture and customs has been busy with his life, even though penetration of satanic ignorance here too has tarnished his colorful and happy life with superstition and swept away its purity and beauty! Ignorance and satanic dominance has entered in the realm of science too and by keeping mankind poor by robbing him away from his riches he has been imprisoned in the darkness of ignorance and made mankind its slave, so that he can oppress him as much as he can! ... *As the Satan of ignorance is the enemy of mankind,* and is jealous of his wisdom, intelligence, spirituality, purity, innocence and tranquility, as darkness is enemy of light, and as ignorance is competitor and enemy and anti-wisdom.

This bitter and inauspicious situation, is the reality of human life, and he has never been able to set free himself from it and will not be able to do so unless he pays attention to what all human religions and beliefs have told him, and that is nothing but human unity against oppression and supremacy and satanic ignorance; and can be implemented only through a responsible and great and strong universal organization which will be established by the entire world and for the benefit of all the world, otherwise this cycle will go on and on.

Mankind has to see and create vaster horizons for himself through solving his problems and correct management of his world! A happy and healthy life along with spiritual and materialistic health will have more value than the current useless and life wrecking struggle, there are still many materialistic and spiritual horizons for mankind and it is not worthy of mankind to stay in the troublesome situation he has created for himself and deprive himself and those who will come in the future from a dynamic and achievable human life.

In analyzing why the world of human beings from the beginning until now has been inflicted by oppression, power seeking, supremacy, war and killings and imposing of religion and belief and thought of one in any humane or inhumane manner, and he has never been able to save himself from this eternal vicious cycle, needs we will go through and analyze Standard Humanism's version of **Human nature.**

Human Nature

Researching human nature is important from two points of view, first from the angle of a general look towards the personality and nature of human world, and second from the angle of outlook and survey and analyzing the personality and nature of each and every member of human beings.

The personality and nature of human world

Based on Standard Human philosophy and thought and world ideology, mankind (In general terms) in the course of history and always, and in all eras has been oppressed and has lived in a simple and healthy manner; 70% of world population have always been good (This is a general and symbolic statistics); honest, hale, hardworking and noble persons; men and women, children, girls and boys; good, sincere and hale families; friends and neighbors and ...; this group are the group of the good, the good who are hardworking, peace seeking, honest and humanitarian who will respect their fellowmen under any circumstances and respect the right of life for all people equally; all the benevolence and beneficence, and good and humanitarian acts are the result of the behavior of this group of people; these are the people who deserve the best, as by their act they create the best of human acts; what translates into humanity, wisdom, logic and law is the result of thought and act of this group of people; what emits from their mind and heart and soul is nothing but light, benevolence, understanding, justice and wisdom; they have all the good and ideal human attributes and think of nothing but goodness, peace, composure, felicity, and growth and positive growth of human world; all the idealism, luminosity, peace, serenity and purity of human religions and beliefs has been seen through the wisdom, heart and soul of this group and found meaning; all man has achieved in the field of science and politics and the beautiful cultural manifestations and also growth and development, splendor and economical and social and other welfare is the result of the wisdom, science and behavior of this group of human beings; if the world has been able to keep its stability in spite of all the problems, it is because of the contrivance, mentality, management, politics and thought of this group of esteemed and positive, healthy, frank and humanitarian people ....

Opposite this group of competent, righteous, human-itarian and frank and honest people there is another group of people; this is the group that makes up 10% of human population! (This is a general and symbolic statistics); the 10% of human beings are those whose heart and soul and mind is the haven for all the bad, darkness, bad omens, bitterness, and selfishness, supremacy and power seeking; this negative group are those greedy for wealth and power and fame (Political and power seeking fame) and want to own everything! This ominous, ignorant, power seeking and supremacy seeker group knows no limit for themselves and the route to fulfill their animal and ominous needs! On their route to reach power, riches and fame they will do anything, from lying and guile and tricks and violence to massacre and killing and oppression and any other black act! This group is scattered all across the Earth and are busy carrying out their ignorant and oppressive small and big acts! Their scope of actions is a vast and complicated one, from being bad tempered and oppression towards women and children and girls and boys to not paying the wages and salary of workers and hard workers, or chairing positions which they don't have the ability and competence to manage and as the result of the weak management they hold back the progress of their societies, and or villainy and rebellion and terror and fright, and or disobedience of law, or selling goods at a higher price or down selling, and or ...; through thousands of their small and big inhumane acts they follow a goal which is nothing but enmity towards human beings and humanity! If you ask them to help a poor man they feel so suffocated as if someone has asked for their life, as they know if the problem of a human being is solved he will become happy and they can't see this happiness, as their goal is not the happiness of mankind rather they want to see their pain; even if they have billions of riches you still can't see them helping others as helping is the way of humans and they are not humans ....

This ominous group is a negative group, so the 10% negative are the enemy to 70% positive! This ominous group is an ignorant one, so ignorance and stupidity is enemy to wisdom and knowledge; this ominous group is an incorrect one, so incorrectness and deviousness is enemy to honesty and correctness; this ominous group is a group of liars, so lying and swindling is enemy to honesty and truthfulness; this ominous group is a Satanic group, so the darkness of Satan is enemy to human bliss; ... Hence it is totally clear that in the course of the history from the beginning till now they tend to be enemy to peace and stability, calmness, religion, politics, culture, science, economy and human life, and by dominance and supremacy over all these they take away the possibility from mankind to take advantage of these!

This ominous and negative group is enemy to humanity and his peace and happiness and prosperity, and by any means, thought, trick and act try to hurt mankind and torment him! They are not committed or believe in any belief and tenet and law! By any possible and unethical and illegal act they throw their claws over the property and facilities of human beings to expand their dominance and create more pain and oppression for human beings; they try to dominate religions and by expanding schism among their true believers they replace friendship with enmity! They dominate politics and parties to make their own party victorious, and by dominance over sources of power and riches of their societies they create more ways to oppress mankind! They put hand on the sources of riches of the world and by storing them in their resources they deprive mankind and make him poor and torment him! They bring in ignoramus rituals into beautiful and happy human cultures to drag mankind towards superstition and mental retard! … Everything in this world is just a tool in their hands through which they continue their enmity towards humanity and keep him away from his humane peace and happiness; this ominous and satanic group are enemies to mankind and for thousands of years they have not allowed him to reach what is worthy of him; this ominous and satanic group have control over the world of humans due to the dominance they have over human property, and the 70% good and healthy have always been defeated by them and under these circumstances they have never been able to free themselves from their dominance and take the world to its ideal form; ….

What we mean by Satan and the Satanic 10 percent is the animal nature dominating over prejudiced, ignorant, selfish, avaricious and power-seeking group who have caused schism, pain and poverty, and plight and human retard because of their dominance over all human property; **development of science and knowledge, and strong and multilateral management of human world are among the most important solutions to eradicate the dominance and control of these ignorant and avaricious and power-seeking group.**

The attributes stemming from the animal nature latent or dominant in these people (The Satanic 10%) is divided into two main branches: **The first branch** is made up of all the ignorance …, and unawareness and prejudices and superstitions, which can be seen mostly in illiterate Satanic people, and **the second branch** is made up of all the avarice, selfishness and oppressive power seeking, which can mostly be seen in leaders and governors of human societies; the combination of these two different spectra in one group will have an effect like a nuclear fusion on human societies which can be very dangerous and destructive ….

Following this discussion there is 20% left, the 20% left have a neutral and pallid effect; under any circumstances they have the tendency to incline towards either the good or bad group and stand in their line! Naturally this 20% are followers; when positive circumstances are dominant they incline towards the 70% positive, and when negative circumstances are ruling they incline towards the 10% negative and manifest in the form of the ignorant as the army of darkness of the Satanic negative front; ….

The personality and nature of human beings

Mankind is a compound creature, made up of body and soul!
And from objective point of view towards the personality of
mankind (Based on Standard Human philosophy and thought)
there are two main personality attributes in each human being
plus two ruling energies both of which have roots in his nature
and spirit!

Human spirit has roots in the absolute truth of the world,
and here the interference of ego which has roots in the natural
animal nature of the man and is the reason why attributes stemming from that natural animal nature (In the form of ignorance,
avarice, power seeking and ...) in general cause two main
characteristics: 1/ wisdom and sentiments, and 2/ ignorance and
oppression form in human beings; ....

In fact whatever has roots in the ***absolute truth of the
world*** and flows in human beings through his soul turns him
human (By adorning him with human attributes) and whatever
has roots in the hidden ***natural animal nature*** and or dominant
over the nature of this creature (Mankind) - and manifests in a
natural way and without the control of wisdom or sentiments -
keeps him at the level of a beast (With all the natural and innate
attributes which can be imagined for an animal such as
ignorance, violence, power seeking etc.); ... as a result ***two
main element i.e. wisdom and sentiments stems from the spirit
and the main element stemming from the natural animal
nature and or dominant over human nature is ignorance ...,***
each of which include many subsets; ....

So this creature (Mankind) is a beast which has turned into a human because of the wisdom and human sentiments that are hidden in his soul! Without wisdom and human sentiments mankind is just a beast like other creatures that live based on their natural animal nature and essence ... Hence wherever human wisdom and sentiments don't rule we are faced with a beast which can go to the limit of dangerous lunacy and violence and rapacity where no beast can compete with him! *And this senseless man who has no sentiment is what named "the Satanic 10%" by Standard Humanism ....*

Wisdom is in the head area, and sentiments and feelings and goodness in the heart and chest; ... and the spirit is coordination from the source of energy and truth of the world to give life to human beings! ... Also conscience is the agent of truth in the world to help man and keep an eye on him and be vigilant so that he doesn't lose the right path; ... and wisdom, talent and ingenuity are the varied and abundant gifts of nourisher of the universe through which he can make better use of his wisdom in the path to building a beautiful and worthy and complete life; ... And thought will give his wisdom the memorandum for life in each phase so with a program and goal he can take his life forward; ... and will-power is a decision that with the help of positive or negative energies carries out its tasks; ... and memory is a reservoir which keeps an eye on all that has been learnt and gained; ... but the mind is an environment which like pure air should be devoid of any kind of pollution! As long as wisdom works well the mind will be healthy but when wisdom loses its continuous function the mind lacks oxygen and the man turns into a mental patient with all types of lethargy, depression, superstition, hallucinations, ignorance and ....

Two main characteristic attributes are:

1- **Wisdom and sentiments,** which is made up of five characteristics and five main points; in fact *from wisdom and sentiments* five characteristics and five main and superior life facts stem, which are:1/ Management and politics. 2/ religion and belief and thought. 3/ Culture and art. 4/ Science and knowledge. 5/ Economy and commerce.

2- **Ignorance,** which is made up of all the badness, and in fact all that is bad is in the realm of ignorance whose result is nothing but pain and sadness of human beings! ….

Mental and Sentimental goodness make up 5 superior facts of human life, whose importance are equal, and you can and shouldn't weaken the role of one in front of another, and or consider one superior to the other, as the imbalance among them will have destructive and negative impact on the positive energies which rule human life and disrupt the balance and health of human life, and the result of it will be lack of tranquility and the peace which is worthy of mankind; all that stems from wisdom, logic, science and sentiments and is the result of human thought and ponder and positive and to the benefit of mankind and his correct and humane content is part of these 5 superior facts and its branches; … (These branches will be explained at the fourth stage and level of human life).

Whatever which translates into selfishness, avarice, power-seeking, greed, enmity and oppression, superstition and ignorance, treason, breaking the law, selling goods at a higher price and down selling and … which results in more unhappiness and anarchy for mankind, and these are all reflections of ignorance; what is considered as badness and leads to trampling over the rights of mankind, and injustice about honest and frank children and girls and women and boys and men, and oppression towards mankind and spirit of mankind, are reflections of ignorance and ultimately enmity towards humanity, which is strongly despicable and abhorred; all the blackness and pain and ache and retard of human history is result of ignorance and ineptitude ….

Two energies ruling over mankind are: 1- Positive energy, 2-Negative energy.

1- **Positive energy** pushes mankind towards all that is good
   ….
2- **Negative energy** pushes mankind towards all that is bad
   ….

In explanation and logic behind the negative and positive energies and their impact on the behavior and conduct of mankind there are different philosophies and explanations offered by religions and or different human beliefs; what is apparent and agreed by all is these two energies have proven their presence in human life time and again and in different shapes! ….

For what is defined as goodness there is a source, and for what is badness there is a source too! It doesn't matter if they feed from one single source or have two different sources! Even if there is a group that doesn't accept the presence of these two and call it hallucinations and deny it, for sure they can't deny the presence of good and bad, so as a result we should consider a source for these two, as they exist and they are real and genuine and have an impact on the behavior and conduct of mankind!

Among the interpretations for the source of all the good and positive energies in the world, there is *nourisher and the creator of the world and the power which has created the world,* from whom all the good and righteousness comes from; and the source of all the bad and darkness and oppressions and enmities is the *Satan of ignorance,* who **by some interpretation** considers himself superior to mankind and as a result by any means tries to create pain and torment mankind! ….

In one place positive energies (Which flows in healthy societies through the behavior and conduct of positive people) prevent mankind from doing anything wrong and help him to prevent doing anything bad, or help him complete a good deed; in other instances negative energy or energies (Which is around due to the abundance of a negative atmosphere in places and confinements which are under the control of the Satanic 10%) drag mankind towards themselves to create a negative mentality and drag him towards doing something wrong and put him into trouble; negative energies which are reflected by the Satan of ignorance! Attract some of the weak men towards oppression and badness and will create bitterness and darkness in the life of human beings ….

Degrees of human personality

The weakness and strength percentage of the five superior facts and mental and sentimental attribute and characteristic in each one of us plus the combination of it with the negative attributes stemming from ignorance such as selfishness and avarice etc. create a wide spectrum of degrees of human personality ...; Here *the effort and willpower of each of us in the positive path and wisdom and humanity, will bring support and aid of positive energies, also our downward fall towards negative attributes and ignorance, will attract negative energies towards us and will drag us towards them and sink us in darkness and obliquity, ...*

The combination and incorporation of the negative attributes and characteristics stemming from ignorance in the mind and heart, and body and soul of the 70% positive even though very weak, but its existence and their combination with the attributes and characteristics stemming from wisdom and sentiments creates a wide variety of human personalities which is a reason why human beings have an abundance of sentiments and capabilities and talents.

The percentage of weakness and strength and the varied combination attributes, characteristics and capabilities of the mind and sentiments and ignorance, and the impact and the pressures of the positive and negative energies in each one of us is a reason why some people have more spiritual tendencies (While they have other tendencies in different levels as well but in a weaker degree) some will have more political and management tendencies, some cultural and or scientific and or economical (Business and work) and ...; the reason why 20% of human beings are in a neutral position and in different circumstances will incline towards the ruling situation is that the attributes of wisdom and sentiments and ignorance are weaker in them, and as a result this will make them have a neutral and follower personality! ....

Finally based on the variety in the combination of wisdom and sentiments and ignorance characteristics in the mind and heart and soul and thought of mankind, among human beings 10% of them will be incubus, power seeking, evil and oppressive and ignorant in whom a large percentage of their mind and heart and soul and thoughts is filled with badness, even though there may exist very weak and ineffective percentages of positive attributes! And 20% of human beings have a weak and neutral and follower personality! And the main 70% of human world is made up of good and positive people, who have a variety of personality characteristics, all of whom are healthy, apt and positive thinking men; though because of combination of weak percentages of negative attributes in the personality of these people at times they might do something wrong, but these mistakes are superficial, and negligible and correctable; all good men: women and men, and girls and boys ... and employees and workers, and bosses and good managers ... and the genius and scientists, and philosophers and prophets and ... belong to this group, no matter to which race and nationality and religion and belief and school of thought and country they belong, they are part of the group of worthy people of an ideal human life and they are totally equal with each other, as they are all *human beings.*

(I have explained the discussion of degrees of human personality in **Standard Human** book! But as a summary it can be mentioned that from Standard Humanism point of view four groups of human personality can be distinguished: 1. The standard transcendental human; 2. The standard social human; 3. The standard growing human; 4. The third grade people and or what we call the Satanic 10%! ... The first three groups in spite of all types of differences and social or cultural level and from any religion, belief and nationality are purely equal and identical to one another .../ The Satanic 10% after adopting Standard Human Thought would be equal to others).

List of correct and incorrect actions of humans

Correct and incorrect human actions and behavior are widespread and variable, and in different religious, political and social cultures they have different manifestations and shapes *(Please check pages 286, 287 & 288/ Section: Values)*; It might be difficult to give a list of all of those in a page or discussion, but getting to know a brief of them can be interesting; *these behaviors and actions are as follows:*

A / Right actions and behavior of man:

Every truth and correctness... (1/ Manners and respect 2/ Veracity 3/ Affability 4/ Perspective and wisdom 5/ Observing the right and justice and equanimity 6/ Rule abidance 7/ Honesty and sincerity 8/ Cooperation with others 9/ Honesty and correctness 10/ Tidiness and cleanliness 11/ Shame and prudence 12/ Generosity and mercy 13/ Discipline and system 14/ Study and learning science 15/ To keep the nature clean 16/ Amnesty and taking things simple 17/ Reticence and serenity 18/ Respecting the parents and elders 19/ ...).

B/ False and inaccurate actions of man:

Any inaccuracy... (1/ Tormenting and annoying and teasing children and girls and women and boys, ... 2/ lying 3/ Violence and bad temper 4/ Prejudice and ignorance and illiteracy 5/ Being ungrateful and showing ingratitude 6/ Avarice, greed and loving the material world 7/ Damaging nature, and irritating and suffering all the creatures, birds and animals 10/ Debauchery and not being loyal to family morals 11/ Backbiting and defamation 12/ Impoliteness and lacking respect 13/ Betraying the trust of others 14/ Laziness and lethargy 15/ Jealousy and grudge 16/ Disorder and untidiness and disarray in life 17/ Treason and unfaithfulness 18/ Oppression and cruelty 19/ Breaking the law 20/ ...).

Man

Man is a combined creature, a combination of body and soul; human beings are creatures and like all the other creatures live in this world and pass their life; other creatures on the surface - and from man's point of view - don't understand anything and spend a continuous and innate life, without having any goal in it! The question is if human beings have been created like other creatures without any goal to just live on this earth?! ... Man has wisdom and can think and can choose between good and bad; man's wisdom (The whole human beings) can recognize that he is capable of carrying out great deeds on the earth and have a glorious life, and at times he thinks of his soul and realizes that he has a relation with an extraterrestrial world, his heart attests this relation and his soul shows him the truth that life is not limited to this earth! Man thinks harder and – whether deep and extraterrestrial or through logical and mental analysis – he accepts and attests that his world is something over the world of the animals (On the surface) and as a result he sees his life bigger and more meaningful ...; finally the man comes to the conclusion that he is a special creature on the earth! And can create great materialistic and spiritual wonders through combination of his spiritual and carnal capabilities, also he comes to the conclusion that there might be a life after which is not limited to his life on earth ....

Man is made up of the combination of body and soul, his body - apparently and based on existing evidence - is mortal! Body is earthen and the characteristic of material is changing shape and alteration, and soul - on the surface - is not material and of course we don't know if it changes shape or not? But since Standard Humanism gives special value to mankind and his personality and his identity as a result it believes that the soul of each mankind after his death - the superficial and materialistic death of mankind on the earth - keeps living, so a man's life span might be more than his limited and physical life on earth, i.e. as a spirit, by reincarnation in his body or another body (Whether in this world or other materialistic worlds) goes on and in the route of a goal of which we have no reliable news of! ....

So mankind is a combined and special creature, and can and has the right to create a worthy life for him in this big world, and at the same time having a look at vaster and bigger outlooks he can make himself ready for a more special life! Why a more special life? Because the world is moving and going forward and one can't imagine that the next situation is one worse than what is now (It might be so for some and or it can't be so) <u>The world is moving forward, so for worthy and positive human beings the next position will surely will be a better one</u> ....

Now this discussion will arise as why mankind is supposed to move towards another world he is highly pre-occupied in this world and it seems that forever and in a painful way he is stuck to this materialistic world?! The answer to this question can be explained like this that you can imagine a classroom where a group of students are studying in it, they should pass this course and class (In spite of all its difficulties) to be qualified to go to the next class, with staying at the same class - in this world - there will be no chance to go to a higher level! In human life there is a lot of ups and downs too so that man can reach a higher level of materialistic or spiritual growth in each level so eventually he can commence the world or the other worlds which are more superior in a hale and successful manner! ... Up to the time that mankind has kept himself in the non-dynamic current world he will not have the suitable growth towards the upper levels of his life; ....

The same situation rules over human world too, in the way that in the human world too if it is limited to the unworthy current life and can't create its pervasive and multilateral growth through a universal programming, it can't be able to rise to the upper levels of its human life and as a result in the current world with its innumerable human shortcomings he will be preoccupied and captive forever.

This thought, and generally believing in the fact that life is dynamic and ultra-materialistic and something over this world, brings about other philosophies which fundamentally makes human life more meaningful; philosophy and thoughts such as believing in the retaliation of what you do, believing in heaven and hell and belief in life in other worlds; ….

Human life can only be complete and meaningful and great through total benefit from wisdom and heart and soul, and in the line towards complete spiritual and materialistic life, and a universal outlook.

Fate and destiny

Each of human beings has their own moral and spiritual characteristics and his way of life is different with another man, there might be tremendous differences among the members of a family which creates different lives for them! This man in the course of his life which will be along with his wisdom and control and programming will face events which are out of his control or willpower! These events, whether good or bad happen all of a sudden and man has no control over them, and as a result will have to give in to them! We call them *fate and destiny* (decree)! … Mankind was passing his natural life but was afflicted with unwanted events in which he had no choice or control! Some call it accident and luck! But as man is a great and special creature and all the details of his life just the great order of human nature is sensitive and accurate so luck and accident is not worthy of him but he must and it is necessary to follow a special meaning in case of events (Whether good or bad)! When something bad occurs some lose their endurance and get afflicted by mental weakness and mental defeat! <u>If these people increase their tolerance based on their mental and spiritual and supernatural leanings they will become the ones that come out successful from the test of their meaningful life (Not a mere materialistic, empty and causeless life) and by their spiritual upgrading they will take themselves one level further, and by getting slaked and their spiritual upgrading they become ready to pass the level and class of the world to the stage of their next better life</u> ….

Fate and destiny, and decree are the educational program of human life; Taking advantage of his mental and heart and spiritual capacity and by passing the tests and difficulties of his fate and destiny he gets ready to go to the next class and his superior and better world; … *spiritual upgrade gives the man this power to find the capacity for his next superior life!*

(*Fate … is made up of three parts:* **1**/ what has been written from before – thru the influence of the "energy" ruling universe (The fate of Creator of universe); If we just learn how in the calm run our soul with this energy (God) all our life affairs would run in its easiest way and our success in life would be guaranteed … **2**/ the impact of the behavior of others on our destiny … **3**/ the reflection of our behavior and conduct on our life).

In order to believe the probability of the continuation of human life and existence of other worlds, I invite you to review below examples which prove the vastness and greatness of the universe:

The vastness and greatness of the universe

The universe is vast and infinite; imagine six spacecraft traveling at the speed of light from a single point in six directions, with the goal and mission of reaching the point and end of the world! They spend hours and days and in each moment you expect receiving news from these spacecraft stating that they have reached the end of the world! Days and months and years pass! And centuries and thousands of years and millions of years pass! ... Those space-crafts are moving at the speed of light, but no message will ever be received from them to say that they have reached the end of the world! They must keep on going! There is no end! This is the size of God and the size of the universe where man lives!!! This is the universe of men and it is big and infinite; so how can one have a limited view of human life and imagine his life being accidental and by chance, and simple and materialistic! Even if the truth is that we have a limited life it is wiser to think of a superior life, which will at least have this advantage that we will do better human deeds so as a result we will be hopeful towards the soothing spiritual reflections of it in the universe and our other life ...; the essence of our thinking and the vastness of our thought proves that we are great! And there is the possibility to experience and witness more wonderful worlds in this everlasting infinity!

There is this possibility that other universes might exist and we might be able to see them and live in them, as the creator of the world has created us and has willed to show us Its universe and Its greatness and made us happy and honored by Its friendship and companionship; so as a result by believing in the coming superior lives we will live with better incentive, a dynamic life with a goal which is going forward, and not a limited mortal life which has no goal and is diminutive; ....

Atom and Galaxy Equality

One can have another perception of the universe which can be interesting! That is the theory of Equality of Atom and Galaxy!!! We know that everything in this universe is relative; the truths and realities in face of different location and time circumstances manifest in different ways and find meanings! ... when we look up in the sky we see billions of stars and galaxies which are located far away from each other and are reflecting light; but when we look at them from afar we see them as a concentrated coherent stone mass which has a special shape; also when we look at the stone mass we see it as a coherent shape! ... Now if we lessen our distance to the stone and get nearer to the extent that we become a *particle* compared to the stone, there is the possibility that we can penetrate it and see it from within! Based on the theory of relativity, we make our relation to the stone smaller to the extent that we gradually notice spaces in the texture and parts of it; we make this relativity so small so that we can see a huge space in between the particles that have made up the stone and in between the molecules and atoms; ... we continue our journey and gradually in our *inside the stone journey* we notice that we are getting far away from one atom and get nearer to another one and land on it! This journey has not come to an end yet and we are still moving ahead and change the space and the world of the atom based on our own dimensions and measurements to the extent that we realize that there exists a great universe within the atom! At the same time at the other end of the universe we come further from the galaxies and gradually realize that there is a coherency in their shape and essence! We continue our journey and increase our relativity and dimension towards the galaxies and suddenly to our surprise we come across a pebble! ... We have entered another world whose dimensions are un-imaginable based on our current dimensions! But anyway we can see it! So by distancing ourselves and changing our relativity with the galaxies we have seen their mass in a more coherent shape and witnessed them as a pebble which a little boy (Which compared to our current size is the size of billions of giants) has thrown into the sky while shooting his ball in a football court and we are inside the atoms of that pebble and inside the galaxy of that pebble, living and spending our holiday!!! ....

That giant great world itself might exist inside another giant great world! Inside each pebble around us too there are billions of galaxies and other human lives! ....

This perception can to some extent give an idea of the vastness of the world to us, and for sure no one can say: The universe is not that big that such theories can come true in it; ... man lives in a great universe and the wonders of the world too will surely be as big and vast; ... (*We should only be patient*).

Result of discussion

In the different courses of his life man has tried hard to free himself from the dark situations and from oppression and poverty and all kinds of shortcomings of his life and through all kinds of policies and different international and regional and other programs, but never and by using all methods he has never been able to overcome the oppression and shortcomings ruling over their life and eradicate them; and even if he has become successful in some instances, new problems have arisen in another spot and constantly has kept man in pain and dis-comfort! … Because never and at no time man has been able to focus on the problems of his universe and conquer them, hence his calamities have changed shape and remained with him always! … Because always and under all circumstances the 10% Satanic and ignorant (The animal nature dominant over wisdom, heart and soul of part of mankind) has been active through his tricks and have controlled his life with his enmity! … Because man has not concentrated on eradicating the darkness of ignorance and prejudice, and supremacy and oppression (The satanic kind); … Because man still doesn't know the root of the problems of his universe which have always accompanied him always from the first day he has set foot on the Earth and acts as if his problems are limited to present time! Man has never been able to understand the root of his problems correctly and conquer over it *(What we mean by man is not part of mankind and in a limited time and place, we mean the whole mankind and mentality and universe of mankind, and the function of the man's universe, we mean man's wisdom);* this doesn't mean that man has not had the right tools, but it means that he has not been able to make use of his tools, his knowledge, his policy and management, the guiding and perceptive and warning religions in a correct way and by right application of them amend his world and build it; ....

Wherever penetration of the ignorant has harmed his religion and politics he has not been able to unite the bits and pieces of his religion and politics, and hence he has lost their benefit; wherever he has been oppressed he has not been able to defend himself by universal unity; wherever there has been a war he has not been able to guarantee world peace and has been afflicted with another war; man has very strong tools at hand but he is not able to manage his world in a proper manner as he has never been able to apply his strong humane powers for disarmament of the Satanic 10%! ....

It is under these circumstances that mankind becomes depressed and goes deep in dreams ....

Step and the second level
Dreamworld of human life

Step and the second level,
Dreamworld of human life!

As the 70% positive is cheated and is under the control of the 10% negative and their ignorant followers (The 20%) in the real world and universe, and as a result they can't see the ideal and model world which is worthy of them in this world and in the world of reality, and live in it, and enjoy its beauties and its endless bounties and take advantage of its persistent peace and friendship, and at the same time as they know that there exists a better and superior truth, as a result to see that ideal situation of which they see themselves worthy, they start daydreaming!

This situation creates a fictional and unreal world which noblemen of this real universe build for themselves far away from the eyes and presence of the ignorant and satanic ob-noxious and - parallel to their presence in the real world - they live in it; they are prisoners who have no choice but to imagine the sweet dream of liberty in their mind and picture it.

Knowing the bitter situation of human life in the real world and universe and his life has saddened any compassionate man and makes him try to find a solution, now think of the time that the catastrophe is when children are struggling in poverty and hunger and their parents give them hope that things will get better, they have the hope that things will get better and they will get rid of poverty and hunger, and of course and for sure this will happen; But will poverty and hunger leave human life forever! Or this is our dream in our unreal and dreamworld; knowing that man is suffering in the real world and is under a never ending oppression is really painful, but knowing that he can't do anything to get rid of this pain but to think and dream, is even more painful and agonizing.

A group of human beings pass their lives in peace, happiness and quiet, but another large group only live in the dream of reaching the situation that is worthy of them ...; our problem and our question is the problem of mankind to find a way that all mankind can experience a happy, healthy, leisured life along with peace and tranquility, and the fact that part or parts of the universe is leisured doesn't solve the problem of mankind.

The second stage and level, has been the constant dream and universe of mankind! Mankind facing the unsuitable situations of his life, whether a simple inconvenience and shortcoming and problem to bigger human problems and dilemmas (Depending on how bigger his problem gets) created bigger and more successful dreams for himself; in his dream world there is no trace of oppression and crime, there is no poverty and illiteracy and illness and everything goes on well and in a correct manner; all that is bad fades away in this dream and all that is good appears; the followers of religions are all friends and equal and brothers and there is no schism among them; the rich give away their riches to the needy poor and provide suitable work and living conditions for them; world politicians use all their power and leadership in the route for the benefit and benevolence and public welfare devoid of any power seeking, ... but the Satan of darkness and ignorance and oppression and superstition and schism and enmity is ambushing behind this imaginary balloon to make his attack; in fact the Satan himself gives the chance of daydreaming to man so while he is immersed in the sweet dream imagining happy days, in the peak of hope and joy of man he appears and disappoints him and makes him realize that by daydreaming he can't get rid of him (The Satan of ignorance, oppression and selfishness); he appears and by creating and imposing another pain he repeats his revenge and enmity towards mankind! Poor man ....

Utopia or ideal city

In the history of human social thoughts and beliefs the theory of ideal city has had a special stance, this theory which is famous as *the ideal city* or *Utopia*, is based on optimistic beliefs towards the possibility of creating cities which are systemized from all points of view and are under the precise surveillance of the government and or special religious and or political and legal organizations, and are governed by philosophers, the sage, and or righteous politicians; in this dream world the philosophers and scientists and religious groups have a longer record, all with their own method and for showing that their belief is better and more superior have pictured the dream of a better life in front of the eyes of mankind; all the philosophers and the sage build the ideal city and the utopia based on their own belief in which everything is right and correct! Justice is ruling and there is no trace of poverty, hunger, war and oppression and even groups and beliefs and religions that are against them to prevent their universe making! It seems that philosophers think simpler than normal people!

The library of the imaginary world of human life has a collection made up of millions of ideal and idealistic thesis and beliefs and philosophies which have never been realized or visualized; *Plato in his Republic, Aristotle in his Politics, Etienne Kabhi in Journey to Ikari, Khawaja Nassir Tūsī in Akhlagh-ol-Molook, Campanella in The City of the Sun, Francis Bacon in the New Organ and The New Atlantis, Will Durant in the Joys of Philosophy, also other philosophers such as Kant, Hegel, Russell, Alpharabius, ...* are among the people who have tried to set criteria for the ideal utopia for humans and design and draw it; ….

List of utopian novels
(From Wikipedia, the free encyclopedia, 03/09/2010).

Pre-20th century:

The City of God (written 413–426 AD), by Augustine of Hippo, describes an ideal city, the "eternal" Jerusalem, the archetype of all Christian utopias.
Tao Hua Yuan (421), is a utopia for Chinese intellects.
Utopia (1516), by Thomas More.
Christianopolis (1619), by Johann Valentin Andreæ, describes a Christian utopia inhabited by a community of scholar-artisans and run as a democracy.

The City of the Sun (1623), by Tommaso Campanella, depicts a theocratic and egalitarian society.

New Atlantis (1627), by Francis Bacon.

Erewhon (1872), by Samuel Butler, constitute a satiric romp through a hidden utopia (with dystopian elements) in the mountains of New Zealand.

News from Nowhere (1892), by William Morris, Shows "Nowhere", a place without politics, a future society based on common ownership and democratic control of the means of production.

Looking Backward (1888), by Edward Bellamy.

Gloriana, or the Revolution of 1900 (1890), by Lady Florence Dixie, The female protagonist poses as a man, Hector l'Estrange, is elected to the House of Commons, and wins women the vote. The book ends in the year 1999, with a description of a prosperous and peaceful Britain governed by women.

20th century:

A Modern Utopia (1905), by H. G. Wells.

Islandia (1942), by Austin Tappan Wright, an imaginary island in the Southern Hemisphere, a utopia containing many Arcadian elements, including a policy of isolation from the outside world and a rejection of industrialism. (In a sequel by Mark Saxton - the Islar, 1969 -, the Islandians develop a modern air force to fend off hostile communist-allied neighbors, and debate whether to join the UN).

Walden Two (1948), by B. F. Skinner.

Big Planet (1957), by Jack Vance, depicts a world in which attempts by utopian misfits to set up new societies have gone haywire after many revert to savagery and violence. But one city, Kirstendale, sets up a successful order in which citizens constantly shift their status, titles and duties (from servant to aristocrat and back again) according to an elaborate schedule.

Island (1962), by Aldous Huxley, follows the story of Will Farnaby, a cynical journalist, who shipwrecks on the fictional island of Pala and experiences their unique culture and traditions which create a utopian society.

Ecotopia (1975), by Ernest Callenbach, The Notebooks and Reports of William Weston ecological utopia in which the Pacific Northwest has seceded from the union to set up a new society.

Woman on the Edge of Time (1976), by Marge Piercy, the story of a middle-aged Hispanic woman who has visions of two alternative futures, one utopian and the other dystopian.

The Probability Broach (1980), by L. Neil Smith, presents both utopian and dystopian views of present day North America, through alternative outcomes of the American War for Independence.
Always Coming Home (1985), by Ursula K. Le Guin, a combination of fiction and fictional anthropology about a society in California in the distant future.
The Giver (1993), by Lois Lowry, a story about a community in the future where everything is the same; there are no choices, but no pain.
Uglies (series) (2005), by Scott Westerfield.
....

The goals and pictures of the dreamy world of human life and his dreams are not realistic and will never be visualized (Unless in a short period of time and only for a small group of people), as they don't have the practical and real tools to reach that, as mankind has never and in none of the stages of his life, in spite of all the struggles and efforts has not been able to reach his goals and notions, if he had reached them today he was living in peace and tranquility; if we imagine that under current circumstances and existing provisions his dreams are to come true, this same supposition proves the fact that we are not living in the world of reality and we are surveying the circumstances of mankind in the world of dreams, as the conditions ruling the human world and the nature and essence of it has not changed a bit with his past and the only thing that has changed is the appearance of human life!!!

To visualize the dreams of human life we need tools, we need to know the solutions; human beings (The human world) has never been able to distinguish his road to salvation, if he had he would have used it in the past! Of course there are thousands of solutions! But none of them have solved the problem of mankind in the real world, unless in a limited way and in limited times and for a limited group and not for all human beings and forever; ... Of course the majority of these solutions have been able to solve human problems in the world of dreams! Some through peaceful ways and some by killing their opponents in their mind ....

Mankind has not yet been able to provide the minimum needs for a simple and healthy human life for men! Enjoying a roof, educational and sports facilities, suitable job, appropriate nutrition ... are among the minimum needs of each man and human family (As the minimum requirements for all the people in the world); Mankind has been so weak in distinguishing this and managing his facilities in the route to reaching these needs that under current circumstances and with the present world leadership he has to go a long way to reach it.

A suitable solution should include a complete co-llection which covers the rights and needs of all mankind; such solution should be designed in a way that each human being with any religion, belief, thought and taste in that human world lives in a happy and content manner, and enjoy all the materialistic and spiritual rights that are worthy of him and live in utmost health, fitness and righteousness, and see the humane spiritual and materialistic route and also greater goals in front of him and follow them.

Man has not been able to find his salvation because if he had he would have acted upon it and as a result he would have been rescued and would have reached all the happiness and success that he deserves! If he had found the solution to his problems today we would not witness any trace of oppression, enmity, political frictions and ideological superiority, war, corruption, terrorism, drug and arms smuggling and thousands of other problems and dilemmas; man has not even been able to control them, because if he had succeeded to control and halter them he would have been able to eradicate them for sure; man has not been able to delete these great dilemmas as the Satanic 10% has always been active and the 70% oppressed and good and positive has been manipulated and put into pain and their positive achievements have gone up into thin air ….

If man can't recognize the unstable and acute circumstances of his life he will face this great universal danger that he might lose all his achievements; it is very naïve and primitive if we imagine that through some international pacts and or the leadership and management and universal control of great world powers world stability will stay and will remain so! There have been greater powers and bigger Emperors of whom no trace has been left and they have been eradicated from the face of the earth forever; and not only they have not been able to keep the stability of the world, they have never been able to keep their own stability either! As Satan is bigger, more diplomat, and more powerful than them! The Satan of ignorance and lack of knowledge, the Satan of selfishness and self-worship, Satan of I am right and others are not right, Satan of lying, Satan of illiteracy, … and powers and the corps of righteous men and justice-seekers too put the last and final stroke to their body and delete them forever; *but what's the use* as the mankind has not been saved and the story has started again with the ascendency of the Satanic 10% and has been repeated thousands of time and will be repeated again, until the time that mankind finds his road to salvation and controls his life and starts the main level of his complete human life! ….

If man does not come to realize the unstable and acute situation of his life he will be facing this great universal danger that he might lose all the valuable things he has gained in his life! Currently, there is no real and reliable guarantee to secure the stability of human life! The accumulation of energies and the negative circumstances ruling over human universe is stronger than before; the atomic danger and threat, terrorism and smuggling and inaptitude of the Third World in management of their affairs (When the people of those countries witness the growth and progress of other countries due to the growth and development of the communication facilities and mass media and they envy them and as result they become disappointed and criticize and protests about the inaptitude of the authorities of their own countries and this leads towards more protests and instabilities) are all threats towards the stability of the universe which increase the universal tensions and endanger world peace; in the midst terrorist groups and or armed groups that are looking for rights and only think of their own benefit and think that the whole universe should become like them are among the regional and universal threats which threat the security of human life in a dangerous and tension making manner! Human life is not of priority, interest or importance for these groups! These groups are only after fighting with the part of universal oppression which endangers their group and belief and needs; as a result their behavior and their methods create universal insecurity.

Result of discussion

The atmosphere of the dream world of human life is unrefined and unreachable, as he doesn't have the real and practical tools to reach his dream goals, because each of human groups see their own dream and there is no unity and cooperation between that group and other human groups; ... until the time that the 10% Satanic are active among the 70% positive of humans and they disperse the 70% positive of humans and keep them apart there will be no unity; human beings (70+20%...) are under the control of the Satanic 10%, and this 10% has the best tools in his control: **The tool of schism and power-seeking** and as a result creating enmity; the 10% with the cooperation of the 20% make the materialistic atmosphere through all types of tricks and scams hot and feverish that as a result the weak and latent characteristics inside the personality of some of the 70% is stimulated and makes them interested in materialistic interests, and through these interests inkling towards property and wealth, more jobbery increases and or they create religious and dogmatic prejudice, and this way the ideological boundaries and selfishness and power seeking increases, and as a result as much as possible schism among human societies happens, and finally the spirit of seeking superiority and selfishness and power seeking is reinforced to reach their goal which is creating irregularities in human life ....

The spirit of selfishness and superiority makes your religion, which is a human rule and humane and from its point of view everyone is equal, makes it yours, and you think that you own the religion and are responsible for it and understand it better than others! And this *"ignorance"* forces you to believe that your beliefs and understandings from religion are real and what others understand from it are wrong, and this *ignorance of yours* will increase the schism and tension, and the presence of *"Satan of ignorance"* is proved here who has been able to deceive you easily through his tools (Superiority and creating schism) to take religion towards division through you and weaken it! … **From religion and beliefs the only thing that belongs to you is your deed and nothing else** ….

Hence it is clear that the main tool of the Satanic 10% is creating schism and the greatest tool of the 70% to save themselves from all their pains is human unity; even though consenting to such a unity is very difficult for mankind, as it is the only thing that he has never experienced in the course of his many thousand-year-old life! So reaching it is very strange, wonderful and at the same time very difficult for him! But man with the help of wisdom, heart and through deep spiritual connection with the absolute truth of universal existence knows that this unity is the only way to solve his problems and his only road to salvation, as a result by concentrating all his human capabilities and by asking help from the positive energy of nourisher of the universe he has the hope to reach human unity and as a result happiness and salvation which is worthy of him;
….

Without the unity of positive energies, it is impossible to conquer over the negative energies, the Satanic 10% in the real world of first stage has made human mind so pessimistic towards their thoughts and beliefs towards each other that even in his dreams mankind has never imagined or built a world based on human unity!!! Though now that he thinks of this unity and friendship he is elated, and is eager to know how he can reach friendship and total understanding with other human beings and expand *the realm of the world of friends* and *the world-mates* and reach total and stable humane peace and happiness.

As a solution to save human beings from this bitter, painful and endless situation of the first level and stage which is the real world of human life, and realizing all the dreams of mankind and reaching all of them from the first day of his creation to this day on this earth (Which includes all the wishes and ideals of human beings, philosophers, scientists and politicians, nations, cultures and all the religions and human beliefs!) Standard Human and Standard Humanism create the third level and stage of human life.

Step and the third level
Principles of Standard Humanism

Step and the third level,
Principles of Standard Humanism!

(The principles of human unity against negative and satanic powers of human life and, as a result, Standard Human and his becoming a model human based on the philosophy and thought of Standard Human)

As a solution and a way out to save mankind from the bitter and painful and endless situation of the first world of the life of human beings, and also to visualize all the dreams of mankind from the first day of his creation to this date on the Earth - which includes all the wishes and ideals of human beings, philosophers, scientists, politicians, cultures, nations, and also the goals of all human religions and beliefs! - Standard Human and Standard Humanism have created the third level and stage of human life.

The term ***Standard*** is a universal and well-known word and concept for the whole human beings; people all across the world are familiar with the term and concept of *Standard;* for example, when we say a standard product or merchandise we all realize it means that product or merchandise has the suitable and accepted level and has required privileges and characteristics and the health of a useable and safe product for human use and one can consume it with total assurance; this is a totally understandable and universal concept and people all across the world are familiar with it and understand it; but what concept does the new combination of **Standard Human** and **Standard Humanism** induce?! This combination is very strange, wonderful and interesting; how can human world be standard! What is its yardstick! And basically, what is **Standard Humanism?!** The varied human life with different nationalities, races, languages, cultures and religions and beliefs are scattered in this world and how can the man who lives in different geographical areas become standard or how can we make his life standard! *(Please refer to the page 20).*

The word and concept of **Standard Human** first came to my mind 27 years ago, when I was 23 years old! At the time I was thinking of truth, mankind, the stance of mankind in this world, and the goal of human life and the reason behind his creation, and what are and should the characteristics of an ideal and perfect human being be; at a time that I was purely thinking of mankind! Not about a Christian or Muslim or Hindu or Secular etc. and not about a European or African or Asian or American and …; *just and only and purely about mankind, and just and only and purely about the truth of mankind and truth of the universe.*

The attributes and characteristics I had imagined for an ideal and perfect man and following that for a life worthy of mankind has become more complete in the course of years through thinking and pondering and after the publishing of my first book - named *My Originality* in the year 2000 - and I published my second book titled *Standard Human* in 2002, and then I started the website *StandardHuman.org* in the years 2005-2006 and today (2010) I am penning down the book *Standard Humanism and Worldwide Standard Human Society,* which is the result of all that I have gained in the thoughts and beliefs of an ideal and Standard Human being and also presenting solutions for suitable and universal leadership by "Universal Society of Standard Human" made up of representatives of all the countries across the world.

All these efforts was to find a way to reach *the suitable and appropriate level of human life;* to reach principles and solutions through which we can equip human world and save it from the dead end of slavery and the domination of negative forces and make the dream of the life worthy of human being come true! To build a world where the people of the universe, men, women and children live in it with peace and security, and growth and progress and riches and salvation, a solution is found through which mankind can eradicate poverty and oppression and enmity etc. and the animal nature dominant over human life is deleted forever and he reaches the peace that is worthy of him and builds a human world, a world which is ruled with human wisdom not with oppression and power seeking and selfishness! All the people in the universe take their fair share of world riches, and the minimum of human needs including: housing, education, hygiene and suitable nutrition, job, recreation and sports and ... are there for all the people in the world as a minimum!

This is the pain and preoccupation of all of us who are living in the first and second stage and level of human universe!

And we are looking for a fundamental solution to eradicate the shortcomings in our life; mankind should and has no choice but to find a way to his salvation, as any indifference - in creating a destiny that is worthy of him - while he has the possibility of reaching it can't be amended and future generation won't forgive him for that.

Standard Humanism in his own place has tried to find a practical solution towards salvation and passage through the first and second levels and stages of human life and reaching the *suitable level of human life;* the thought of Standard Human has reached practical and strong solutions which can create great wonders in human life.

By understanding *Standard Human World* we will soon realize how small and dated our current universe is and as a result we will all join forces as soon as possible to change it to a human world which is worthy of mankind.

Standard Human thought becomes legal through the vote and confirmation of the people of this world and ultimately it will move towards formation of Worldwide Standard Human Society which controls and manages all the affairs of human world - while maintaining the sovereignty and independence of all the countries in the world; The thought of Standard Human presents a philosophy which by accepting its principles by the majority of the people of the world, fundamental amendments to human world will commence and the progressed and blessed life of mankind in the third millennium will be formed.

Standard Humanism will leash in the savage nature hidden or dominant over the spirit and nature of part of human beings (The Satanic 10%) and create the peaceful life of mankind in the third millennium.

Five - 3D - Principles of Standard Humanism

The thought of Standard Human as the first fundamental step and mutation towards amendment of human world, and eradicating the thousands year old effects of dominance of Satanic ignorance and oppression and for guiding human wisdom and heart and spirit towards human unity - which is the only tool in the hands of mankind and his only salvation from the Satanic 10% - presents guidelines to mankind; We have clearly understood that the tool in the hands of the Satanic 10% is creating *schism and enmity* among mankind, through whatever means that might bring him closer to his ominous goal! And we have realized that to fight this ominous satanic policy the only fighting way for mankind is *human unity!* Human unity is something superior to the mere meaning of unity! If we want to establish unity among mankind to conquer over the domination of Satanic 10%, it has to be a very special unity! Billions of people living on this earth have thousands of religions, culture, languages and beliefs, how can we establish a unity among them which will be able to unite them in a way that can solve their thousands year old problems!!! So when we speak of unity it is not a mere figure of speech, as this will be just naivety; *what we are talking about is human unity, not tribal, racial, cultural, regional or political unity* ...; Human unity includes all human beings, as a result it has to offer principles and solutions which include all human beings and attracts the consent of all humans with their colorful array of varieties!!! The principles of human unity should have such legitimacy, logic and great human backing to be able to attract human opinion and make him ready to accept it; at the same time mankind has to evaluate his own stance too! If some of these principles are not to his liking, he has to bear in mind that the rule of unity against great satanic forces - which has ripped him away from the possibility of having a life worthy of his status in the course of history - is much more important, which as a result it might cause change of the world towards the well-being of the oppressed people in this world.

The five principles of Standard Humanism are as follows:

1/ Belief in God. Whether a real and heartfelt one (Like what the followers of different spiritual and divine religions and beliefs believe in it) or as a symbolic and conventional one! As the absolute and ruling truth of the world and the only common point among mankind where the true or even symbolic belief in God can create a healthy and humanistic atmosphere, it is considered as the first point of human unity against the negative Satanic forces and energies!
(This means that there is energy and a truth ruling our world which is the origin of all that is right …). (Please refer to the pages: 288 & 291/ Worldview of S. Humanism and Reality & Truth).

2/ Believing in a religion and faith or credible humanistic school of thought. From any kind celestial, spiritual, social etc. which has positive and humane values!
(This means each man has the right to choose the path and method of his own life with total knowledge and wisdom …).

3/ Believing in law, morality, culture and common universal human rights. Which is derived from all the common points and teachings of all human beliefs and has been compiled based on them; such as veracity and honesty, the right to enjoy a life worthy of mankind, peace, equality and freedom and ....

(This means that in the universal culture of mankind the right of all should be considered ...).

4/ Voting in favor of establishing the Worldwide Standard Human Society. Made up of representatives from all the countries of the world to establish a group management for the world which includes all the political, cultural, scientific, economical and spiritual areas, while keeping the culture and sovereignty of all the countries in the world in a dynamic and animated manner ....

(This means that we need an international organization which supports the rights and belongings of us all so that we all have a life worthy of mankind ...).

5/ Taking care of personal hygiene and spiritual and mental tranquility. In our personal and social life ....

(This means we are wise species who need to live a life worthy of us ...).

All these principles are very simple, understandable and practical; there is no complicated or twisted fact in them! In spite of being simple and understandable they are very deep and true; *by accepting these five principles any positive man paves the way for human unity and overcoming and defeating the Satanic 10%!* The more people accept these principles the stronger and wider human unity becomes and the road towards human peace and salvation gets smoother; by acceptance and implementation of these five principles the road is paved for annihilation of oppression and darkness, and schism and enmity and the Satanic 10% is pulled into seclusion.

By accepting and implementing these principles, mankind of African and American and European and Asian origin etc. with any kind of nationality, race, culture, religion and human belief reach a unity and equity together! As they will be all placed under the umbrella of **one common human culture,** and as a result they will be all considered as human beings and equal to one another! By accepting these principles any type of racial, regional, religious and ideological discrimination will be eliminated, as following these principles will create an atmosphere where everyone is respected and the rights of all individuals are considered in an equal manner, and as a result the road to the penetration of Satanic 10% and schism will be blocked by this unity ....

These five principles are the basis for human unity and becoming a role model human being as a result! By accepting them while safe keeping our religion and race and culture and language, **at the same time** we will believe in principles which will guarantee our human and international unity (Through the culture it establishes and spreads in the world), annihilates the penetration of Satanic 10%, and as a result eradicates the supremacy and power seeking and schism spreading thoughts among us, and paves the way for establishing a peaceful human life; we have to add that acceptance and belief in this human unity for the 10% who live among us is very difficult and unbearable, and from the very first moment of announcement and spread of it, they will try to weaken and deteriorate and destroy it with a vary of ominous and Satanic, empty and rootless excuses; ... To weaken this thought they might say that it is not possible and fanciful; it is the result of a European and or Asian and or African thought ... or the result of a Christian or Muslim or Hindu or ... thought, and as a result, they will do their best to make it ineffective; ... a positive thought has its own positive values and it might have some shortcomings and problems, but biased efforts to make it ineffective is nothing but a *satanic and ignorant confrontation; mankind is forced to be in a continuous effort and to be thinking of correcting his universe, otherwise the negative forces of Satanic ignorance and oppression and selfishness will not allow peaceful human life to him.*

Poor administration of countries, and suffering and poverty of the people of the world, and the power-seeking and supremacy of the Satanic and negative 10% with the willpower and unity of worthy people should be diminished and eradicated; schism and enmity and supremacy should give way to friendship, brotherhood and equality and universal security; this is the right of mankind; we need the best world, this can't be achieved but with friendship and peace, and unity of all the people of the world, and in an equal and equivalent manner; ... *by accepting the five principles of Standard Humanism we won't be losing anything, but by cleansing our heart and soul from the bitter effects of schism making mentalities, we will reach human unity, cordiality and respect and as a result we will reach overall and universal peace and happiness and progress.*

Standard Humanism presents the most humanistic solution to solving human problems, in which the right, respect and equality of all human beings has been considered in it; to this date, mankind has not experienced any complete culture and thought, which has been common and acceptable, so that by accepting it he can reach his peace and universal unity! Each thought and culture in a traditional way insists on making the world accept its unilateral and limited principles; obviously under such circumstances no one will accept forgoing his thought and belief and accept the unilateral thought of someone else! ... **The only thought that can be accepted is one that considers the rights of everyone in a just and universal manner;** *the thought of Standard Human by creating a common universal culture, based on friendship and bilateral respect, will lead to human unity of mankind and guarantees his peace and salvation.*

Under the current circumstances of the world, each group only believes in himself and considers himself to be superior; *these groups and classes who all claim to have the best solution to the problems of human world, are taking the world towards division and schism each day by the disperse they sow in the world;* but the thought of Standard Human by establishing universal human culture and supervision of the world, will meet the ideals and goals and perspectives of all groups and beliefs in establishing a peaceful world, and at the same time it will give the chance to different thoughts and ideas to grow and self-correct themselves devoid of dilemmas of correcting the world, they will try to grow and correct themselves internally!

In fact, **the world making goals of all human thoughts and beliefs and philosophies which seek human peace and materialistic and spiritual progress of mankind will be visualized - in a more comprehensive and superior way - through the complete and dynamic system and method of Worldwide Standard Human Society!** And the concerns of all universal thoughts of human society will be eradicated this way.

Standard Humanism is a thought which is beyond religion and politics and culture which has a cleansing and purifying and guiding role for human life with the goal of a complete life which is worthy of mankind; a worthy life which will meet the right of all mankind with its universal management (Worldwide Standard Human Society)! A worthy life in which the domination of negative forces, oppression, crime, killings, addiction and ... has reached minimum in it and will be eliminated in it, and a luminous human life with greater and much higher perspectives than the second level of human life will be created in it and become real in it; this is all because it relies on positive forces; because all the wisdom of the world, riches of the world, management and policy of the world, and religion and beliefs of the world have a share in building it! Mankind will reach great progress through his unity and cooperation; much greater and magnificent than what he has achieved now!

Mankind (Christian, Muslim, Hindu, Buddhist, Shinto, Taoist, Sikh, follower of Confucianism, Zoroastrian, follower of Jainism, Jew, Communist, Secular, ...) by accepting the thought of Standard Human and its five principles - as the second layer of their social identity and personality -, will see greater ideals in front of themselves; by accepting the thought of Standard Human and believing in its five principles and applying them, human world will start changing and a great renovation which the Worldwide Standard Human Society - which is the fourth level and world of human world - will form as an extension to this change; Standard Humanism and the Worldwide Standard Human Society will manage the human world in a new manner where there will be no trace of incompetent governments, oppression, power seeking, poverty, corruption, assassination, insecurity and … in human societies, and as a result un-developed countries will reach the growth they are worthy of, and social, cultural, political, religion, economical and scientific poverty will become minimal and will be eliminated and wiped away from the face of the earth.

(Standard Humanism advocates a **"Two Layers Identity"** for every human being, *First:* by equipping all with five principles of it in order to eliminate the rules of ignorance, oppression etc. from their life and, *Second:* by insisting anyone to live according to his/her belief and culture - at its best form - in a safe world by the support and the administration of *Worldwide Standard Human Society*).

The world is being ruled and is under the control of the Satanic and ignorant 10%, so as a result positive people (From any religion and belief and race and nationality) should unite and get coordinated with each other through a unifying thought which considers the thoughts of all in order to defeat the satanic group and destroy them; defeating the Satanic 10% is equal to a life that is worthy of mankind.

The thought of Standard Human is the first common universal thought and philosophy of mankind which compiles the positive universal culture; ….

The management of Standard Human will control human shortcomings and turn his human management into a universal and pervasive one.

1/ Belief in God – <u>God = equivalent to energy, and sovereignty and absolute truth of the world, and rule of integrity and truthfulness</u> (Either by belief coming from heart or by symbolic and arbitrary one). *Please also consider p. 281 God ....*

God (here) **is synonymous with peace and justice,** which flourishes through all the colorful and various human beliefs in order to guide the human race in the direction of the life they deserve together with its full happiness based on the cultural, social, political and geographical capacity and ability; consequently, all the justice seeking and peacemaking beliefs of the mankind is stemmed from God and truth of the world and therefore it is all inclusive for the people under its shelter; though the path for their further growth and eminence may be open!

A great part and percentage of the religious, philosophical and scientific sects and beliefs in the world believe and trust in God and the creator and maker of the world, the force dominating the world, the source of all goodness and all positive energy, etc. in fact by using revelation, spiritual and immaterial beliefs or by scientific and logical proof human beings reached the conclusion and belief that his creation and the creation of the world around him is done by a special, conscious, dominating and governing force in the world and by specific harmony and purpose which is not in vain, accidental and without purpose ....

By having a vast vision and a wide point of view in the existence we comprehend that from the beginning there was a God and creator who dominated the infinite world and created the existence with his willpower and decision and decided to form this beautiful and harmonious world; If we go to the roots of the formation of the world and go back we reach a point where it is proven that the first element of existence was formed from nothingness and there was volition and a certain will before its formation and creation which created it, since nothing will result from nothingness! unless there will be a will, volition, decision and purpose which is what we refer to as creator and maker of the world and we take into consideration and worship, since we know Him (God) didn't create this amazing and beautiful world without having any purpose and just by accident, and has an omnipresence to watch the human behavior and faults; Therefore we pay attention to Him in order to get inspiration from the goodness God shines upon us and reform our deeds and behavior so that we could be worthy human beings; Belief in God has the least benefit and advantage of assuring us that there is a great, positive and just power dominating the world that we can get inspiration and energy from its goodness in order to perform our human deeds.

Belief in God transcends the human identity from the limited earthly level to the depth of existence; belief in God, regardless of which religion or faith made us believe in Him, results in a global unity among all the humankind! There exists, amongst a Christian believer, a Muslim believer, a Hindu believer, a Buddhist believer, or other human beings believing in any other belief who have faith in God (Existence of a higher power) a certain joint delicate and humane feeling and they feel a certain friendship with respect to each other, this feeling is an indication of the miracle of belief in God as a vehicle and factor in the direction of creating human unity with others!

(People who are under the impression of impurities and schism and tension-filled vibe of the world today feel this invisible friendship less than others …).

Belief in God (Positive energy dominating the world) *is the greatest shield of human beings;* belief in God is the greatest human shield available to 70 percent of positive people! Belief in God as the first principle of Standard Humanism results in the human unity among all the humankind with any religion or faith (Material or spiritual)! This belief, whether it would be a real one coming from the heart or a symbolic and arbitrary one! Will take all the good and positive men under its cover and unite them against the 10 percent satanic ones ….

Among the people of the world, there is a great percentage that believes God in their heart and worships Him; yet, there is a percentage who believe Him and its existence but does not worship it in accordance with a religion or faith and only believe that there is a God, whether effective and having an influence on human life or without any effect and concern about the daily affairs of human life; there is yet another group who basically does not believe in the existence of God at all! but are among the good and positive one of the humankind and are against the 10% satanic ones; Here, this question comes to mind that how the Standard Humanism can convince this group to believe in God and basically what is to be considered as the definition of the belief in God in this discussion based on the Standard Humanism?! The answer is, based on what was said before, belief in God (God as in the scientific and philosophical definition not the everyday traditional one! In traditional sense people assume God is a person and constantly ask Him money …), as the first principle of Standard Humanism in the path of humankind unity against the Satanic 10%, whether as a real belief coming from the heart or just a symbolic one in order to create **a unifying factor** among the humankind, is considered to be crucial! Human beings require the unity among its kind; without the human unity - which can unite them regardless of any religion, faith, nationality and race - it cannot resist against and be victorious against the 10 percent satanic ones who are equipped with all the negative energy and all the satanic and anti-human techniques and tricks!

The group which does not believe in God if considered as the positive human beings, shall believe that with this symbolic belief, they are actually announcing their readiness to participate in *the fight of good against evil* and play their role for the purpose of unity of all the 70 percent of the positive kind! Their least cooperation in this path and accompanying their *world-mates* can result in liberating the world from the negative dominance of ignorance and satanic cruelty and prepare the grounds for human growth as much as possible; *for them, this is merely a symbolic belief - synonymous with truthfulness and integrity law - which can officially put them in the category of Standard Human World;* This does not conclude in the obligation and commitment such as having a religious belief or performing a religious ritual; it is in fact an excuse to accept one principle of all the unifying and humanistic aspects of Standard Humanism! A human being who believes in the unity against the enemy called ignorance and satanic hegemonies should play its role and performs its duty for the purpose of global peacemaking and justice by accepting this fact which will result in the benefit of all the humankind; ... *belief in God unifies the positive side of the world against ignorant and cruel evils*.

Therefore, based on the thought and philosophy of Standard Humanism, human identity will develop into **a complete twofold identity:**

In *the first fold,* it will believe in the Standard Humanism in order to reach the human unity and peace and by this belief, it will reach unity and understanding with other human beings from any race, color and faith (Which the ultimate philosophy and ideology is unifying humankind and does not seek nothing more); in *the second fold,* since the Standard Humanism goes beyond religion and is universal, it will keep its personal religion and faith (If they have a real belief in God, they will continue their heartfelt and spiritual worship and if they seek to unfold the scientific and logical secret of their creation and the existing world, they are free to continue their scientific and philosophical efforts) ....

The Standard Human believes in the wholeness of human personality, and therefore by creating the thought and philosophy of Standard Humanism enters the human personality into a humanistic and twofold world; in *the first fold*, he sees the depth of philosophy and the infinite ideology of him in the humanistic unity with the purpose of reaching peace and tranquility of humankind and controlling the Satanic 10 percent and cutting their access to humankind possessions and by making such effort a humanistic life will be possible for him; in *the second fold,* considering the philosophy and deep belief in respecting the opinion of others and human thoughts, he is left free to utilize all his scientific and logical efforts and deep spiritual and heartfelt sincerity for the purpose of fulfilling religious tasks and specific school of thought belonging to him.

Standard Humanism respects all the credible humanistic beliefs and preserves the right of everyone for having a certain lifestyle and philosophy; *Standard Humanism concerns all the humankind and not a specific group having a certain religion or faith.*

The name of God (In this context, as the law of truthfulness and integrity which is present in all the material and immaterial belief systems) on the top of Standard Humanism and Worldwide Standard Human Society is a *logo* that covers the positive people's world and unite them together; ….

In the Standard Humanism philosophy, the concept of God (The truth of the world of existence) is considerable from two points of view:

1/ From the social point of view - regarding the dominant and absolute truth of the universe and the rule of truthfulness and integrity which is revealed <u>through all the peace and justice seeking humanistic religions and beliefs</u> (Religious, social or political = material or immaterial) and through passing through the path of reason, heart and soul in different places and times to guide the humankind to a more rightful lifestyle (Having **various** titles! and based on their capacity) directly or indirectly ….

2/ From the personal point of view - friend, creator and energy provider which <u>elevates the spiritual state of him</u> through celestial connection (By all means of worship, meditation, yoga, etc. and by the teachings of various religions); therefore, pure connection with Him increases the spiritual capacity of mankind in opposition with the difficulties and hardships of life and - *by comprehending the truth in a better way* - will ultimately result in the human beings having a more wholesome life in this world and a better one in the future ones (Whether in this world or others) ....

2/ Believing in a religion and faith or credible humanistic school of thought

Believing in a religion and faith or a credible peace and justice seeking school of thought or philosophy (Including: Abrahamic, Iranian, Hindu, Chinese, Indigenous, Political, Social, Cultural, etc.) - which has positive and humanistic values - the second principle of Standard Humanism is in establishing human unity and as the result creating a worthy world away from the Satanic 10 percent domination, which will lead to decreasing and eliminating the impact of illiteracy and hegemonies on man's life by creating a friendly and respectful atmosphere and increasing the level of consciousness of people - that happens as the natural response to of sincere study - in order to find the supreme belief in an individual.

Based on the thought of the Standard Human being all the credible, peace and justice seeking religions (Material or immaterial) have a root in the truth of the universe! through passing along mind, heart or soul and since they all follow the purpose of avoiding illiteracy and cruelty and establishing justice and peace, they all - holding any name and philosophy -

are credible in their own realm, therefore it is necessary for a worthy and exceptional human being that as a proof of his human understanding and wisdom **and also** along the path of establishing justice and peace in his society, to have faith in one of the credible religions or school of thoughts and make his life purposeful and dynamic by believing in such matter.

Having faith in a humanistic belief gives human beings identity and social credibility while without having such faith and purposeful principles, human beings will be aimless and clueless from the spiritual and psychological perspectives ...!

Without having faith and belief in his identity, human beings will go in the direction of nihilism and worldly intentions and his life become senseless, rootless, feeble and worthless ....

Having faith and belief in a religion with purpose - from any religious, political or social type - will further complete the individual and social personality of man ....

In facing with the daily issues of life, man would get tangled up in different moral and social challenges and without having a credible and proper identity and thought framework he cannot find a solution to his problems and, therefore, will face various spiritual issues and dilemmas; human soul (Together with his heart and mind) requires a proper identity and belief (Having faith in any worthy humanistic belief) and cannot be left alone to rely on his own mind in everyday life issues ....

The history of human beings is the biggest proof of the importance of having a religion and faith and further proves that human beings in all the historical eras - from primitive to advanced societies - all accepted the need for a belief in the form of a religious, political, philosophical or any school of thought which gives harmony to the personality of human beings, and this is part of the culture and civilization of man.

Without having a belief, humankind will be lost and without any identity! Having a belief creates an agreeable psychological and heartfelt peace and assurance which the human soul requires; more important is that a modern role model respectful human being requires to accept a credible humanistic belief (According to his own understanding and recognition) in order to reach an *understanding of mutual respect* with others in the developed world of today, otherwise, he cannot experience this mutual feeling in his world and with his entourage and therefore cannot reach the inner peace and tranquility ....

An individual, who does not believe in any belief from all the hundreds of different and varied beliefs, practically cannot reach the intuition that he needs and has to respect other's beliefs! He, who believes in a belief and his belief stems from consciousness and recognition, finds it necessary and crucial to respect other beliefs in order to create mutual respect; therefore, accepting a belief - based on study, recognition and awareness - creates an atmosphere of mutual respect between human beings! And therefore strengthens the friendliness and peace amongst human beings ....

Having faith in a credible humanistic belief simplifies the conditions for creating and accepting *the common culture of mankind* based on the supreme law and ultimate truth which is a part of all the humanistic beliefs and ideas ....

Having a humanistic belief is quite necessary since it will raise the awareness of man regarding the laws governing societies and changes a regular human being into a conscious, social and cultural one which can play an effective role in his individual destiny and that of his society and the world ....

Having belief leads mankind to participate the destiny of his world and makes him a true perfect man ....

Having faith creates a certain feeling of equality, brotherhood and friendship among the ones who share the same thought and assures him that he lives in a society in which others by believing in a belief are considered friend, brother and equal; in such condition, where a humanistic atmosphere is dominant, an individual would be ready to help, cooperate and devote himself in case a complication occurs to his brother and reach a certain deep satisfaction as the result that comes with an immaterial happiness which would not have been possible in an atmosphere lacking friendship and unity and he wouldn't be able to experience such immaterial depth, sweetness and high spirit ....

And finally, having a humanistic belief is the right of every person and will cause the social atmosphere to get warmer and friendlier so that life can be more peaceful and tranquil.

The personal and social advantages and benefits of having faith in a belief are very deep and uncountable, that is why the Standard Humanism emphasizes on establishing a world which is complete, dynamic and worthy world in which so that the human beings make an effort to choose a belief among all the existing and accredited ones in order to preserve their personal, social and universal soundness and observe its rules and practice it correctly and honestly.

The advantages of having a humanistic belief and religion are very deep and uncountable, but the emphasis of Standard Humanism is more on the part which:

1/ Will increase the level of awareness and literacy of human beings regarding other religions and faiths - as the result of performing sincere studies to find the supreme belief based on his spirit and needs.

2/ Will make him understand that others are free to choose their own belief based on their capacities, abilities and preference and practice it, so he respects all the beliefs.

3/ Sincere study on humanistic beliefs in the quest for finding the supreme belief, will make mankind aware of the historical impurities imposed on religions and beliefs, and will persuade him to choose the purest and more truthful one, so that he could increase his growth and level of awareness and that of his society which will result in growth and purity.

4/ *Performing studies correctly and the urge to find the belief and religious truth, will weaken and decrease the domination of satanic illiterates on humanistic beliefs and the mind of their followers.*

5/ The top advantage is that studying and finding the suitable belief will elevate the personality of an individual from a regular man to a worthy human being.

Regarding faith and belief in a credible thought, it is crucial to observe the following points:

1/ A fine, civilized, conscious and wise human being shall choose his religion and faith through performing studies and doing researches according to his understanding, comprehension and capacities and capabilities - of reason, heart and soul - with utmost consciousness.

Random, heretical and family choices ... do not have enough credibility! An individual who can find his best-suited belief based on study and research in humanistic beliefs - according to his recognition - does not deserve to limit himself to a belief based on traditions which is not in harmony with his spiritual, mental and heartfelt abilities and merely creates a traditional attachment in him resulting in weakening and limiting his *humanistic growth!*

In a dynamic humanistic world, correct choice of the best belief based on personal capacity and capability will result in that the individual primarily practicing his belief teachings having proper recognition and consciousness and secondly he can go on living having humanistic sanity and a more dynamic humanistic identity as the result of his wise and conscious choice and his true belief; The main purpose here is for man to have a true study and recognition about his faith and other beliefs; The least advantage of such study is that he realizes that there are other human beings living with faith in other beliefs which are respectful and credible for them ....

2/ *Since a human being believed in his belief by performing studies and recognition, he will consider the equal right for believers of other credible and respectful beliefs;* because as he expects others to respect his choice, he, in turn, respect others in this regard.

This logic and analysis is one of the first steps in eliminating the illiterate domination of the Satanic 10 percent on the mind of some people who believe that their belief is the best one and do not respect other human beings which result in the continuation of religious tensions among people in the world.

3/ The domination of the Satanic10 percent is so strong which creates an absurd mindset in some of the followers of humanistic beliefs that they should not respect or credit the followers of other beliefs coming from different races and nations; however, if they were born in such societies themselves! They would have seen their current belief strange and would not accept it! Since this group, coming from any race or nation, believe in their heretical belief and are prejudiced without any study or research, believe only their own belief and consider it the best one while considering the rest and other religions and beliefs unjust, illiterate and non-credible!

4/ **The superior belief is the one which is practiced by its followers in the most ideal, purest and most peaceful form,** and should not be a tool in the hand of the Satanic 10 percent by which they would spread hostility, tension, racism and hegemonies in the world!

5/ The humanistic beliefs are the rules and regulations of the human world and each one is formed based on the specific cultural, social, temporal and local conditions and situations which exist in a specific region of the world, therefore, its ideal and dynamic form will appear only in that part of the world; Thus, it is impossible to imagine that one day all the beliefs of the world would dominate the whole world! Instead, it can be imagined that each belief would be flourished in its geographical area (Considering its capacity and how universal it is) in its best, most ideal and most peaceful form and as the aggregation of humanistic, peaceful, positive and supreme qualities of them an international rule would be devised which would be acceptable by all the beliefs and human nations in order to manage and guide the world by its use; and that would be nothing but the ultimate truth and ultimate humanistic rule governing the world which is internalized in heart and soul of mankind by his creator and all the right-minded people would confirm this using their logic and try to practice it ….

Belief identity and having a humanistic ideology is what gives mankind a personality discipline which would turn him from a regular human being to a perfect one.

3/ Believing in law, morality, culture and common universal human rights

A fine, worthy and Standard Human being knows that all the recognized and credible human beliefs are stemmed from truth and are transmitted from creator, energy and ultimate truth of the world, because he believed in his belief upon study and recognition; therefore, he finds the supreme rule to be ***humanistic rule*** which is the rule set worth in accordance with the essence and nature of the human being; that is, the rule which orders truthfulness, peace and justice and consequently that rule is the humanistic rule which can be recognized through mind, heart and soul of mankind; human beings, believe in this rule and practice it through - direct or indirect - connection of his soul with the universal supreme truth and through his mind and heart; all the human beings are able to recognize and confirm this supreme rule! This is the rule which was discovered and practiced by all religions, faiths and philosophies (Whether material or immaterial; or religious, political, etc.) all the time in the history ….

The human universe has only one ultimate rule which is like a fixed subject depicted by different painters and, therefore, has endless appearances; They all have the same form, with the same subject but are different in appearance because they were depicted by different people in different times, look different on the surface; *They all order and guide men to humanity, justice, truthfulness, honesty and physical and spiritual sanity;* Consequently, a fine human being would respect all the humanistic beliefs and chooses between all the one which is more in harmony with his culture and spirit and let it guide him in the path of growth and material and immaterial improvement; He extracts and practices the mutual universal rule which is the truthfulness rule from the mutual points of all the religions and beliefs.

Primarily, **the harmony of human life** will result from this supreme rule and ultimate truth! The harmony of man's life and the law of managing the human life are established on the human unity and peace and results from material and immaterial dynamic improvement of the human society justly and for everyone; this harmony which is based on the Standard Humanism thinking is only possible through universal management of *Worldwide Standard Human Society;* the result of this humane and universal management of Standard Humanism is codifying the **charter of morality and belief** and that of **the human rights!**

This lawful dynamic stemming makes the sanity of the human world and completes observation of the human rights possible and takes the needs of all the people into consideration and tries to fulfill them; Therefore, it gives the universal peace an ultimate and consistent stability; A kind of peace which will result in the great growth of human beings and will last forever.

Some of these common laws of human life in the moral, cultural and legal respects - which stem from the Standard Humanism point of view - are:

1- The right of having the worthy human life and its material and immaterial gifts.
2- The freedom of choice and opinion and belief identity (Having religion and belief).
3- The right for benefiting from legitimate individual and social freedom.
4- Observing and strengthening unity and solidarity, and the kind of peace worthy of human beings.
5- Worthy human life together with honesty, wisdom and thought.
6- Politeness, respect and observing social character of society.
7- Avoiding hostility and animosity using religion and policy.
8- Generosity, charity and assisting others.
9- Avoiding cruelty, illiteracy and ignorance.
10- Observing justice and equity.
11- Acquiring knowledge.

….

Truth (What is correct …) is a constant and flowing concept which is present everywhere, in all the places and times; Truth through thought and logic, and reason, heart and soul of mankind in all the eras of the human life acts as light of his guidance so that it to guides man to find the way of his life! Truth passes through the soul of pure, sane and truth-seeking human beings and finds its legitimacy upon heartfelt and logical confirmation; truth is very dynamic, flowing, alive and fluid; all the good human being would benefit from its understanding; however, the level of their comprehension of the truth is not the same and depends on the sanity of oneself, knowledge, good thinking, logic and their capacity and spiritual capabilities! (In this regard and to reach the truth there are different criteria in different schools of thought such as: instinct, revelation, tradition, habit, intuition, mutual understanding, logical connection, observation and experiment, etc.). *Please also consider pages 286, 288 & 291 = Truth ....*

Belief in the common universal law which was depicted through reason and heart and soul of human beings throughout the history means that in the universal life the right of all the beliefs and religions shall be considered as equal; This conclusion and world-view results in establishing the Worldwide Standard Human Society and its management which considers the right of everyone, and as it continues and based on this universal law which votes in favor of truthfulness and honesty, justice and observation of the right of all the beliefs and all the human beings, it is the time for codifying *moral and faith charter of the global society* and then after *global human rights;* Countries and cultures are free in constituting their laws and their moral and behavioral culture in their own countries as long as it would not have any negative international impact; ... Regarding the *global political morality,* it shall be mentioned that at the time being and in the situation and reality of the first level of human life, the global moral is *Machiavellistic* in most parts of the world! Although, there is a tendency towards mutual understanding through establishing international laws and consistency and commitment (In some countries), the current moral and culture of the world is stained and is under the control of the Satanic 10 percent and it can only be eradicated through establishing the Worldwide Standard Human Society; in the Worldwide Standard Human Society the policy would lead to equilibrium and would get concentrated on the management, growth and all-inclusive development of the world as the result of humanistic and comprehensive management of the world and haltering the Satanic 10 percent; Therefore, the political moral of the world would reach its clear meaning and can be accessible.

In order to better understand the common moral and culture of the world and the effect that believing in it can have on consolidating peace and unity of the mankind, we bring an example here:

There are various colors around us; colors are present everywhere and are the outer and apparent layer and the main and illustrated part of everything; one of the most delicate and beautiful parts of our life are flowers; when we look at flowers, in the first level, their color attracts our attention and then their shape and form would enter our mind.

Colors, beyond the material cover of the world and the things around us, have penetrated in our spirit and taste as well, since we consider our favorite color in our choices as important as colors have direct connection with our spirit and by choosing our favorite color we reach a more complete satisfaction and peace in our choice.

Colors have different varieties; considering their specifics of light or dark, purity of the color and their color inclusion (Yellow, red, blue ...) the colors in the world around us are plenty ....

Now let us consider dividing the three main colors (Based on the interest in the color) into some groups: the group which prefers the yellow color on one side, the red group on another side and yet the blue group on another side; in such situation, do you think we can ask the yellow group to quit liking the yellow color and join the red group?! Or the admirers of blue invite the other two groups to their group and claim that the blue color is the more complete one and the best?! It is for sure that none of the above groups would quit their choice and belief to join other groups! ....

Consider that these three groups are willing to perform a social act all together; it is quite obvious that each group consider itself more competent and better in performing the act and believe that it can reach the best decisions by relying on its supreme beliefs and get completely successful! The yellow group would say we can prove we are the best and most capable by all our beliefs and all our ideologies and all our scientists; the red group which is a fair group considers the statement of the yellow group but would give a negative answer at last! We, by using all our scientists and all our beliefs would prove that we are more just and shall be prioritized; the blue group would think about the opinion of the first two groups deeply and with honesty, but since like the other two, can only see itself and its possessions would reach the conclusion that it is the ultimate truth! ....

What is the solution?

By doing a more detailed study we will realize that the base and root of all colors is the white color or in fact the light; we only need to put a prism in the direct sunlight, we can see that colorful rays of light would come out of it so it is revealed that the origin and root of colors is the light, apparently the truth is revealed by this discovery:

None of the three colors or any other color is considered the main color, but the ultimate and supreme truth is white and light! ....

When you would say *yellow,* I would say *blue* and someone else would say *red,* we are three separate beings but if I would say a common and humanistic rule for all the religions and beliefs and you would say a common and humanistic rule for all the religions and beliefs and the third person would say the same thing ..., our relation would be a perfect and humanistic one; which is in accordance to our position and dignity and this is the truth of unity and belief in one international rule which is practiced among all the human beings by preserving all their colorful beliefs which lead mankind to complete mutual understanding, friendship, peace, bliss and prosperity.

The members of one team feel more friendship and closeness with each other and feel more proximity with one another in happiness and sadness but the members of two different groups, no matter how fine they are with each other would consider each other different and apart and rival; the group of positive human beings having the clear humanistic rules such as truthfulness, justice, generosity; avoiding ignorance, cruelty etc. is the only worthy group which can be confirmed by majority of the people of the world, and by getting a member of it, one can get what is worthy of human beings through the Worldwide Standard Human Society.

When the common rule of truthfulness and honesty (Among all ideologies) is executed and peace and justice would be established, God will be present in the social level.

4/ Voting in favor of establishing the Worldwide Standard Human Society
(The Universal Society of Standard Human)

Each worthy human being votes in favor of establishing the Worldwide Standard Human Society with the goal of managing and guiding the developed world universally (Through Standard Humanism website, or the Facebook group and page of the Standard Humanism: www.facebook.com/StandardHumanism) because he believes that the organization of the best of the world in a universal association is the most suitable and peaceful way of preserving his world; the Worldwide Standard Human Society manages and guides the world affairs in a specific way, using a universal system and a comprehensive global management in all the religious, political, cultural, scientific and economic aspects and their subsets such as world security, industries, tourism, healthcare, sport and all the subsets related to the main five aspects in a modern and basic way!

The Worldwide Standard Human Society is the superior and organizational part of the universal management of the human world and each country is independent in its own affairs and handles its own civil affairs by getting universal cooperation, assistance, guidance and orientation based on their needs; countries have weaknesses in managing their own affairs but they can reach a faster growth simultaneous with preserving their independence through benefiting from universal assistance and cooperation; in fact, *The new universal system based on the Standard Humanism recommended method, is a universally democratic and federal one.*

The Worldwide Standard Human Society, by using mutual reasoning and prospects of mankind would manage and guide the world; this universal society is the pinnacle of the human unity with the purpose of creating a peaceful and developed life which would not come across any obstacles in the path of its positive and dynamic movement! The organization and management system of the Worldwide Standard Human Society is so big, developed and vast that would lead the global society to growth and development, stronger than any other engine in all the material and immaterial aspects! The Standard Humanism will wipe out the world off the penetrating Satanic and ignorant 10 percent by the use of its very powerful reformist tools and would prepare the grounds for the all-inclusive advancement of mankind in a way that it would amaze man of him and his advancement.

The Worldwide Standard Human Society is the result of the willpower of the positive forces of the humanistic world; The forces which regain its destiny from the 10 percent selfish and power seekers through different religions, beliefs, policies and cultures and would move toward the pinnacle of humanism, a move without any halt with the ultimate amazement and astonishment ....

Human beings, in the current background of its life, have done valuable efforts in the direction of globalism; voting in favor of establishing the Worldwide Standard Human Society can be the next big step; *(The Worldwide Standard Human Society's management and system will be forwarded with the full details in the fourth step and level of the human life).*

5/ Taking care of personal hygiene and spiritual and mental tranquility; In our personal and social life ...

The biggest social problem of the human world is the issue of observing the personal, collective, social and universal sanitation! Without sanitation mankind is not healthy; without sanitation man would be paralyzed and immovable, its great financial resources will go to waste, he will suffer and his life would be aimless! physical illnesses will consume him and the possibility to work, live and comfort will be dragged away from him; meanwhile, the spiritual and mental sicknesses will make him a dangerous and lonesome being; therefore, observing physical and spiritual sanitation is the biggest issue of human beings; in order to make him healthy and cheerful and this cannot be realized unless the world will be safe, healthy, and wealthy and only by having vast universal management and control and through thorough material and immaterial and advanced Standard Humanism system!

A fine human being is a clean and sane one; a fine human being is a wise and respectful one; just as the Standard Humanism depicts it and creates the necessary grounds and conditions for being a fine human being for all mankind in an equal way!

Personal, collective, family, physical, mental, food, public, social and professional ... sanitation is among the most important sanitation discussions in the world and observing it makes the human life sane and immune from sickness, suffering, poverty and misery ....

Forming and existence of inhuman and evil groups in the societies is a proof of the spiritual and mental imbalance in life.

Result of discussion

These five fundamentals are designed to form an identity which is called ***humanity, a standard and worthy world;*** in establishing the universal and global basics it is crucial to choose and design the priorities! We should get out of our physical and earthly self and see ourselves in an ultra-human way; the universal humanity fundamentals cannot be viewed from the limited earthly point of view! How can we aim and consider the universal humanity with a limited and unilateral viewpoint! How can an Asian establish a just set of rules, preserving the right of the Asian, European, African and American, and for someone else in another part of the world without getting out of the Asian culture and pattern of thought! An American, African or any other human being can only consider justice when he would get out of his pattern and consider the subject from the viewpoint of a human! How can, a Christian, Muslim or some other believer would establish some basics by which his right and that of others would be observed ultimately and equally! Therefore, in designing the fundamentals of the human society we should be ultimately human and even ultra-human! We should equip ourselves with the wisdom, logic and knowledge of the whole history of humanity and study, consider and establish the human truth and right - as a human - in an unprejudiced and honest way!

By having this logic and from an honest and un-prejudiced view at identity, personality and rights of human beings and as the first factor and reason and excuse in finding a mutual motivation to unite mankind, there exists the *belief in God!* A balanced and logical human being, without considering their real or unreal belief in the creator of the universe can approve that he is created on this earth! That means his life and his creation had a beginning and he is a creation and therefore had a creator; the same creator we call nature or a God or multiple Gods or the energy who organized the world! ... Whatever we call it, is the proof of the truth that **there is an intelligence governing our world** which mankind confirms its existence; whether through his logic and wisdom or supernatural revelations or any other humanistic logic ...; anyway, there exists a superior being which mankind believes in it since the day he started thinking about his existence on this earth and will continue believing in; This superior and higher truth in the life of man as his first common point which can be the best acceptable excuse of him in its way to unity has the utmost importance; believing in this superior and higher truth of man's life is the first human unity principle on this planet; believing in God and the superior truth of this world - from which all the harmony of the world and all the truth and righteous elements stem from - that positive energy gives a certain assurance and encouragement to mankind that makes him consider his creation and life meaningful and purposeful and consider a kind of identity for his being that goes beyond material form and is valuable; *believing in God and creator and the force that formed the existence, whether in the deep and real sense or in the arbitrary and symbolic sense, is the urgent need of the dynamic human life; Without having such a belief, human life would become small and limited;* Therefore, the Standard Humanism used the belief in God to reach the first principle of human unity and the first factor that can shelter him and the rest of the world with the united and common identity ....

When we talk about mankind and humanism, law and peace, and the truthfulness and integrity, the name of the nourisher of the world = dominating energy and truth and the law of truthfulness and integrity shall be put first; the name of the nourisher and creator of the world shall be put first in the human world and a great credibility would be given to the world of existence as the result; *(God is not a person, It (He) is a vast-wise-energy; ...).*

To continue, since the Standard Human is a symbol of an intelligent and superior creature being, has the personality and credibility to choose any of the credible human religion, belief and school of thoughts (Material or immaterial) having a distinguished humanistic value through his soul, wisdom and heart and choice, in the realm of his capabilities in order to consider it as the law of man making and personal and social identity making to form and complete his humanistic personality by its use; therefore, the Standard Humanism as the second principle of three-dimensional principles of human unity respects human beings in such a way that enables them to choose their own belief; *a human being who accepts a belief by using knowledge and study, respects other beliefs too;* but the one who believes in a belief only by tradition, without sufficient studies and by prejudice - whether it's a humanistic belief and an ideal one or not - finds himself superior in interaction with others in the world and consequently in order to satisfy his need for seeking power and superiority, creates tension in the global society and put humanistic peace in danger; these kinds of people, no matter in which society or environment they were born, find themselves superior and superior to others!

The second principle of Standard Humanism has a considerable effect in creating peace, security and insuring the global peace and it fortifies the respect and unity among human beings through observing the mutual respect regarding their thought.

Such a human being who, by believing in God and the ultimate truth of the world and in the continuation through study and honest choice of belief accepts one for himself, reach a higher level of wisdom and that is through study of belief systems he realizes the fact that all the humanistic beliefs whether material or immaterial are rooted in justice and truthfulness and so he finds common grounds in them; therefore, such a worthy human being in his universal interactions comes to the conclusion that the common law of the human society shall be organized as association of humanistic common grounds of all the beliefs and through special emphasis on respecting thoughts of others; *this worthy human being, in the discussion of universal law, culture and morality does not force his cultural opinion and belief because he believes in mutual respect,* and as the result considers the common specifications of the beliefs and mutual respect to the personality of others, the grounds for his universal morality, culture and law; This principle which is the third principle of the Standard Humanism elevates the solidity, arrangement and identity of human beings and gives him a kind of intuition to maintain such a worthy world and keep it from the danger of collapse and influence of ignorant and negative forces who want to spread hostility!

This is where the Standard Humanism presents its fourth principle and guarantees that peace and sane humanistic life up to reaching the unseen and unimaginable stages for the contemporary human being (Regarding reaching the pinnacle of extraordinary material or immaterial advancement) is organized by it; the fourth principle is the decision to constitute the Worldwide Standard Human Society! The Worldwide Standard Human Society is able to reach mankind to the level he deserves to in all aspects of his human life and enters man into the third millennium of his life! Such a human being has one stage left to complete in the path of being a Standard Human being and that is the fifth stage; The fifth stage is of utmost importance and has a value equal to that of the first four ones; the fifth principle is observing sanity, observing physical and spiritual sanity …; a Standard Human being values his personal and social sanity; the human world shall have the utmost sanity and a Standard Human is a sane being whether physically, personally, socially or mentally and spiritually; spiritual peace and sanity has a value equal to that of physical and corporal one; a worthy human being is a respectful and sane one and that is the person who can understands the truth ….

The third-millennium human being, considering all this knowledge and science, and material and immaterial development, is not a primitive and conventional being anymore and shall elevate himself and make himself worthy of *the status of Standard Human* through equipping himself with humanistic and superior principles.

The five principles of Standard Humanism create an identity and personality in every one of the human beings and by accepting the principles make all equal, whether African, American, European or Asian in any corner of the world with any color or race, language, religion and nationality - by maintaining their origin and belongings; since they all believe in the principles which make all equal, the same level of wisdom and respect each other; a kind humanistic respect, the one that make all equal.

Standard Humanism and the administration of the Worldwide Standard Human Society make all the mankind equal regarding the right of benefiting from an affluent life without suffering and poverty! Worldwide Standard Human Society organization answers the needs for human life such as proper housing, proper job, proper education, proper hygiene, proper entertainment and sports etc. by its universal management, and by benefiting from wealth and wisdom of the world in the service of man ....

Step and the fourth level
Worldwide Standard Human Society

Step and the fourth level,
Worldwide Standard Human Society!

Standard Humanism is a new school of thought based on respecting the beliefs, identity and existence of one another; and of course majority of human beings respect it; though there is only a small portion that don't respect this and as a result they have darkened human life! Only a small group of selfish, power-seeking and ignorant people follow them which have tarnished the bright face of life and human world through their deeds ....

Standard humanism is a new school of thought based on respecting the beliefs of others with the goal of international life based on peace and international human unity; the second part of this sentence verifies that this respect seeks a bigger goal and that calls for conditions to become real! Merely claiming that we respect the beliefs of others is not enough and it is very primitive and immature and basic! Establishing these conditions can become possible only through *one powerful universal body.*

A large percentage of human beings have always res-pected the beliefs of one another; but the main problems and schisms and frictions in beliefs have always been there, and have never even subsided ….

This respect should change form from its simple and raw form and seek a goal! So that based on that goal, a route is defined, principles are outlined, and conditions are met so that goal is met in an official and international way!

The goal is for mankind to reach international peace and unity and as a result all the existing and previous struggles and selfishness come to an end! The goal is to end the penetration of the selfish, oppressive and power-seeking minority, while the majority of the world is under penetration of the minority! The minority should come under control of the majority and they should be leashed and led by them; The goal is to reach the peace which is worthy of mankind and international human unity with true and practical respect towards each other's beliefs and understand and experience the happiness of a life worthy of human beings.

When the ideological problems and challenges are controlled and eradicated, the road is paved for a complete human life in all aspects; the inner frictions among religions and the inner frictions among politics, and the inner friction between politics and religions can all be solved with the thought and philosophy and principles of Standard Humanism! This is the goal of Standard Human and Standard Humanism.

Standard Humanism is a strong purifying and clarifying system for cleansing human life from the pollution of selfishness, power seeking, oppression and ignorance; Standard Humanism strongly believes that we need the best world as we are the best human beings worthy of best human life, so we have to cooperate to reach this worthy life.

Standard Humanism is a thought which goes beyond religions and politics, as it respects the rights of all humans, cultures and beliefs through the overall system of Universal Society of Standard Human and thinks of the best and the most complete method to form a world for mankind on this Earth.

Since Standard Humanism is a strong advocate of humanity and justice, and human peace and happiness to the benefit of all the human world, and sees himself responsible for establishing universal peace and humanity, as a result he believes that establishing justice and humanity should only be carried out through a universal, humane, and peace seeking powerful organization - who considers the benefit of all the people of the world with all their beliefs and cultures and tastes; ….

Standard Humanism forms the first humanistic, common, moral and official human law and culture <u>in international life</u> whose positive effects will be seen until the total eradication of poverty and illiteracy and ignorance and universal oppression and will overhaul and renovate all aspects of human life from religion, politics, culture, science, economy etc.

The old and current method of world correction by religious, political, philosophical and other beliefs and thoughts have a traditional and weak and incompetent system, (As these beliefs and religions and politics are under the control and or penetration of the Satanic 10%! ...) and are not compatible with today's conditions of human world and human knowledge and human expectations from a suitable human life! But the Universal System of Standard Human is a complete and modern system, which is corrective and international and considers the rights of all human beings in meeting a noble humane life that considers all aspects, and is complete and has variety.

If man can overcome his current position in the world and conquer the Satanic 10% and ultimately lure the 20% indifferent towards itself, there can be the hope that he can reach the goals and dreams of the second stage and level of his life; but now that he can have control over his situation why shouldn't he implement bigger goals and dreams! The perspectives of the dream world of the second stage and level of human life are great as they are the utopia of billions and billions of people on the Earth from day one to this date! But if man can design a device to visualize his dreams, why shouldn't he put his ideal as his goal and seek it! Man has this power to gain the best materialistic and spiritualistic goals that can be imagined in life through unity and programming; we need the best world, as we are the best people worthy of having a suitable life worthy of mankind.

What is derived from wisdom and sentiments are the five superior facts of human life which Standard Humanism has set as the pillars of its universal management; this realistic way of thought leads to the fact that we pay equal importance to the rights of all human beings with all their different personality wise tendencies which they have towards these human good and benevolence and as a result **Universal peace and justice** is established through a legal world organization which supports and defends these rights.

The five top human life facts

Whatever man has in his service, from religion and belief, and politics and management and world order to science and knowledge and culture, and economy and business and trade … are all the facts of human life! (I.e. they are affairs that have shown and proven their righteousness and finality and have been accepted as final and definite affairs) and we can't take a part and delete another part from human life and claim that human life is complete and perfect! Without any of these and even imbalance in equality, transposition, and importance and equality among them human life won't be complete! It can be said that by ignoring them or paying less attention to their role and importance in establishing *a complete human life* mankind will be facing numerous dilemmas, which will cause imbalance in his life and cause a variety of problems and struggles in his life!

There are five main and principle facts in human life and each of them include several subgroups, such as maintaining world peace and security which is one of the subgroups of the unit of politics, and or tourism which is one of the subgroups of the group of culture, and or hygiene which is one of the subgroups of the group of science (Based on the management of Worldwide Standard Human Society).

These top five human life facts are: 1/ Religion and belief and rituals and human beliefs, 2/ Universal politics and management and order, 3/ Culture and art and rituals and customs and all the beauties of human life, 4/ Human science and knowledge, 5/ Universal human economy and work and trade.

These five facts complete one another and a correct and complete human life is only possible through the accumulation of these five facts and through the simultaneous cooperation and unity of them in a unified human group.

Naturally if any of these five facts deviate from their origin and original and ideal form they will become disgusting and painful and a catastrophe! But thinking of eliminating or ignoring each of them with the presumption of them becoming tarnished with Satanic weaknesses and darkness (The power seeking and penetration of the Satanic 10% in them) is wrong and a clumsy act.

(The better man distinguished the truths ruling his life, the better life he can form for himself).

These top five facts ... each make up a major part of human life which find their identity next to each other and in cooperation and balance with one another; imagine a painter who wants to draw the landscape of human life and wants to delete each of these facts and ignore them! This is an impossible task, because:

1/ **Religion and belief,** are the sky of the landscape of human life, how can we imagine a complete human life without a sky!

2/ **Politics and management,** are the order of the universe and the order of human life, how can we imagine human life without order and management and politics!

3/ **Culture and art,** are the beauty and joy, and pattern and color of human life, how can we imagine human life without pattern and color and design!

4/ **Science and knowledge,** are growth and knowledge, and science and progress of human life, how can we imagine human life without science and knowledge and progress!

5/ **Economy and trade,** are job and prosperity and welfare and comfort of human life, how can we imagine human life without the activity of a dynamic economic system to the welfare of mankind!

Hence, these five elements are the five top facts of human life; ignoring or paying less attention to each of them in human life is a clumsy act and has roots in schism and enmity and the penetration of the 10% Satanic in order to make human life painful! The Satanic 10% tries to dominate over these five top facts of human life and tarnish them with all types of enmity and schism and ignorant darkness, in order to darken human life and act in a way that he can't take advantage of the abundance of these true human blessings! ….

The 10% ignorant and prejudiced, selfish and arrogant and power seeking and anti-human are Satanic and by dominating over these human blessings they have inflicted pain over human beings as much as possible in the course of history and made his life hell; these five top human life facts have been tools in the hands of the Satanic 10% to sow seeds of discord and enmity among human beings and keep him in pain and darkness till eternity, as the Satanic 10% are the enemy of the 70% sage, as the Satan is the enemy of man, as badness is enemy of goodness, as lies are enemy of truth, as darkness is enemy of light; and this enmity lasts forever, and until mankind has not reached his human unity he will not be able to co-mmence a life worthy of himself on this Earth and reach the higher levels of his life and ascend!

The Satanic 10% (The ignorant, the selfish and the power-seeking) put their hands on religions and make them their own; they put their hands on political centers of power and make them their own; they put their hands on cultures and make them their own; they put their hands on science and knowledge and make them their own; they put their hand on the riches and economy and business of the world and make them their own; so that by making changes in them they eradicate their benefit and purity; through power and politics they increase their penetration and dominance over the world, by penetration over religion and beliefs they take them towards schism and weaken them in order to destroy human unity and weaken the great power of the 70% facing them; through superstitions and world worshipping customs and rituals which are all nihilistic they tarnish the nice picture of human life, they employ incompetent managers for the governments of developing countries to fight development of science and knowledge and by keeping nations illiterate, they keep the academic and social growth of nations slow and keep them exploited and finally by putting hand on the riches of the world they make him poor and hungry and needy and weak to inflict pain on him and as a result take revenge of mankind; because they are jealous of the 70% (Humans) and don't want and can't see their superiority! These five facts are the most important tools through which the power seeking ignorant dominant maneuver over them and by using them make human world a place to dominate and rule over!

(The Satanic 10% are ignorant and prejudiced people who want more than they have and by dominating over all that mankind has, lead to his pain and poverty and lag; development of science and knowledge and strong and multilateral human management are among the most important solutions for eradicating the dominance and governance of these ignorant and arrogant people).

Standard humanism is a thought which goes beyond religion, politics and culture and has the role of cleansing and purifying and guiding human life with the goal of the complete life which is worthy of mankind; ***the goal of Standard Human and Standard Humanism is cleansing the top five human life facts from impurities and improbity which have been inflicted by the Satanic 10% and as a result guiding human life towards whatever he is worthy of and forms his healthy life.***

Negative forms of the five facts:

1/ Religion and belief incline to: I am right and the others are wrong! 2/ Politics and management go to power-seeking! 3/ Culture and rituals go to superstition! 4/ Lack of Science and knowledge go to slavery! ... 5/ Economy and trade go to money and world worshiping! *(Standard Humanism & Worldwide Standard Human Society will protect and purify the 5 top facts of human life).*

The philosophy of Standard Human is the philosophy of overall wisdom and human unity! This way of thought by applying the best policy and international management, the best and most peaceful human religions and beliefs, the best and most beautiful cultures, and also having science and knowledge and bountiful and rich economy, can be more successful at making his human world.

Imagine a gardener who wants to design a garden in its most ideal form and nurture the most beautiful flowers in it, under these circumstances positive energy and honesty and his human motivation, his management and order and system, his resources, his knowledge on flower planting, and finally the beautiful design of the garden building and his greenhouse prove that he is stepping in the right path and he will build his flower garden and his world in the best possible way; all these proves that he has enough knowledge of his environment and can manage and lead the world that surrounds him ….

The Universal Society of Standard Human with the above mentioned positive attributes is the only organization which deserves to manage and as a result improve the life that is worthy of mankind; scientific, religious, political, economic & cultural permeations and their cleansing through this universal organization is the best path through which the countries in the world can find solutions to their improvement and growth and development.

The reason human world beliefs and thoughts insisted on unification of mankind was that by friendship and cooperation and unification in all aspects of life one can build human world; but the schism resulting from the penetration of the Satanic 10% among the group that was not unified in their beliefs has been a reason for this not ever happening; Standard Human philosophy gives us the chance to target the root of the problems and by getting equipped with the principles of Standard Humanism and by maintaining the sovereignty of nations and cultures and beliefs we all reach a human unity through which Human world can be guided towards its ideal form.

*The method Standard Human has for unifying is un-
like past traditional methods and is a new and modern one
which has been formed based on observing the right of all the
people in the world and not the right of just a group of people
in the world;* the universal management of Standard Human
through Universal Society of Standard Human is a universal and
fundamental management, which covers the whole world and all
the aspects of human life with its method of strong management
which is fundamental and humanistic and corrects and turns it
over ....

Organization, goals and tasks of the Worldwide Standard Human Society

Goals and Tasks of:
The Worldwide Standard Human Society

Worldwide Standard Human Society is a great human organization; **this organ is an absolute humane organization,** and is made up of the most prominent, the most educated and intellectual human beings with management and political capabilities and scientific, cultural, religious etc. it takes form; this type of organization will have a great human nature and personality and there will never be any trace of prejudice, ignorance, unawareness, selfishness and power seeking in it! These supreme in knowledge and being the best will well know what the problems and needs of mankind is, and in the road to reaching these goals and the outlooks of ideal human life, they will do what it takes and take all their world with it too; such superior human organization is truly familiar with the top five facts of human life and reaching them and their subgroup are the goals for all his plans in life and all his managements.

Worldwide Standard Human Society will have five super organizational organs whose main job will be reaching the following goals:

1/ Worthwhile management of human world and eradicating the dominance of Satanic 10%

2/ Maintaining universal peace and justice and security ...

3/ Establishing healthy, clean and transcendental circumstances for human life ...

4/ Establishing circumstances for cultural and social growth and development

5/ Establishing circumstances for scientific growth and development ...

6/ Establishing circumstances for economic growth and development ...

7/ Protecting natural and geographical circumstances of life on Earth (Protecting the Earth, and all the nature and creatures and plants on it) and providing circumstances for a life beyond Earth (Life and research for life in other planets in the solar system) ...

Ethical and faith charter of:
The Worldwide Standard Human Society

Human society needs understanding and a defined explanation of his individual and social moral characteristic; based on respect towards human identity and personality and human society, Standard Humanism has reached definitions which considers human respect in its correct form and supports it; based on this definition of human personality, the ethical and faith charter of the Worldwide Standard Human Society will be as follows:

1/ Personality and social stance of human beings in Worldwide Standard Human Society

2/ Spiritual and faith belief of human beings in Worldwide Standard Human Society

3/ Culture, moral and spiritual belief of Worldwide Standard Human Society

1/ Personality and social stance of human beings in Worldwide Standard Human Society

In Worldwide Standard Human Society people have an identity and human personality and all enjoy complete and equal human rights.

In a human society people have priorities in terms of grouping, attention and considering rights, which is as follows:

The first group and level of human beings: Children and offspring and infants, from birth up to the age of 14.

The second group and level of human beings: Girls and boys from the age of 14 to 24.

The third group and level of human beings: Grandfathers and grandmothers and the elderly, from the age of 60 up.

The fourth group and level of human beings: Mothers and fathers from the age of 24 to 60.

The fifth group and level of human beings: Women...

The sixth group and level of human beings: Men...

....

The human position of all people in Human Society is based on above priorities, it means that the most important attention from materialistic and spiritual and planning point of view in the route towards forming better humans and taking care of human rights is dedicated to children and youth and establishing a happy, healthy and successful life with an outlook towards the future of this group, which is the first priority, then, following that, Human Society will take care of the issues and Human affairs of the second group - the group of the youth (Boys and girls); the future outlook for this group is in direct relation with the future outlook for the world and its ever growing strength; in the third level we have grandfathers and grandmothers and the elderly, who call for special attention dire to their elderly status and establishing the culture of respecting the elders in human society; the next level is paying attention to the status and position of fathers and mothers; the position of parents is the first position in governance of the family and the second place in governance in human society (After the governance of the elite in the position of management of the society); hence, fathers and mothers are the most important group who form human beings, and have a special respect in the governance of humanity over human beings.

Paying attention to the position of women on the society is at the next level; the main role of women in being constructive and management of Human Society is receiving special attention, as they are a hardworking group and the healthiest one who are constructing the society and their existence in the realm of constructiveness gives health and social credit to the society; also their presence in social and management areas will reduce the penetration and control of the Satanic 10% for gaining power - and their ruling over the society which mainly rises from the power seeking nature of men; the last position and stance is the position and stance of men in the society; in this regard, men are placed at the last group who take the most responsibility from power and management point of view (We mean the healthy men) and all their effort (Shoulder to shoulder with women) is paying attention to supervision and management of Human Society, hence they are placed at the last group and the group who accepts the most responsibility.

When human respect is measured by the age and social stance of people in the society, the identity and stance of men will gain meaning in its ideal form; this means that laws that are written and the priorities in taking care of human rights are called for and they should be carried out based on the priority and order listed above, and the human rights of mankind should be organized based on above priorities; this would mean that oppression, supremacy and power seeking will never rule over the society and as a result we will never witness ignorance towards the rights of the oppressed and hurt level of the human society and human society - *with continuous concentration* over children's rights, and girls and boys, and the elderly, and mothers and fathers, and the noble and hardworking men and women in the society - they will find their spiritual and mental health and maintain it.

2/ Spiritual and faith belief of human beings in Worldwide Standard Human Society

In Worldwide Standard Human Society all human beings due to the fact of having the right of personality and noble human identity, are respected and great; hence everyone has the right to find a way towards his own salvation through supreme human and religious beliefs, and for sure reaching this belief has been gained with research and knowledge (Devoid of ignorance and blind following) and with the goal of finding the better and elite truth and in the rout towards total salvation; as a result each person will reach to a result based on his own research and ability and mental distinguish and will follow a belief in which he sees the salvation of this world and the world after in it, and with this distinctive characteristic he will complete his social and human personality, and will be respected by everyone.

Reaching a human belief based on mental and belief spirit and ability will have two positive aspects for mankind: First of all as he has reached his belief through healthy research and devoid of any prejudice, as a result he will respect others who have reached a belief through research within their own power, as they deem this respect necessary for themselves (As they have thread on the same path within their ability to find salvation in this world and the world after); Secondly different beliefs by outing the superior aspects of their religion and belief as their role model, will propagate a healthy relation and interaction in the society without wanting to impose their belief on others.

3/ Culture, moral and spiritual belief of Worldwide Standard Human Society

Since the culture of human society and their culture and belief makes it, human charter orders that spiritual and moral culture of Worldwide Society gathers the best of positive aspects and beliefs that exist in the Worldwide Society.

As a result, the rules of Worldwide Standard Human Society is a collection of all human rules that govern the Worldwide Human Society, and universal organizations and those in charge of human society support and defend the best of human aspects and the sane beliefs that exist in the world and the fundamental principles and human constitution will form this way, and universal organizations will be means for execution of human rules that will be to the benefit of Worldwide Human Society, and the personality and identity of each and every one of the people will be respected completely and the people all across the world will lead their path towards benevolence and human salvation with total freedom of thought and in line with the materialistic and spiritual development programs.

Hence, no negativism and penetration of prejudiced beliefs and inhuman morality will exist and human society will be immune to any harm; and in such a society there will be no struggle and political tension for power among groups, and there will be a system which will guarantee complete stability forever in the universal society, and by eradicating the supremacy of groups that look for chances from human life, rule of humanity with the management of universal organizations will be established and Worldwide Human Society will gain identity and meaning in the world, and mankind will reach what is worthy of his dignity in the third millennium, ….

Formation and organizational chart of:
The Worldwide Standard Human Society

Worldwide Standard Human Society is a strong and powerful and giant management organization, with the goal of control, guidance and management of human life in the five main parts of life, including: 1/ management and politics, 2/ religion and beliefs, 3/ culture and art, 4/ science and knowledge, 5/ economy and commerce; and also all the subgroups of it which include all the affairs of human life ….

After accepting the five principles of becoming a model human being and human unity and entering the third level of his life and as a result cleansing from all the divisive and ignorant impurities of the first level of his life, mankind will reach to a level of human identity and control which enables him to guide and control his world with all his human wisdom and power!

The management of Worldwide Standard Human Society is a fundamental and perspective one! Based on a fundamental management, the basic and fundamental affairs of life are paid attention to and by correcting them stage by stage the other affairs that follow it and are its subgroup are corrected and managed; a fundamental management, draws and defines foundations and organizations and different parts of human life based on a new philosophy and thought, a new worldview and new expectations!

The main brain of Worldwide Standard Human Society is its *General Assembly* made up of representatives from all the countries of the world; all the affirmations and or negations with the rules and decrees passed in the committees and five main parts of the worldwide society are discussed here and get their final vote here, and receive their final executive budgets; *the general assembly plays the role of an organ with a parliamentary system whose main nucleus is its board of directors;* the board of directors of the national assembly of Worldwide Standard Human Society is made up of represent-atives from world countries who are chosen periodically, who should have special attributes and every two years will give their place to the representatives of the next country in a rotary manner ....

The general assembly of Worldwide Standard Human Society has a vast scope of responsibilities, options and obligations and just like a parliament - but in a giant and universal one - will control all the affairs of human life and guide them; this assembly (In addition to being equipped to a complete administrative system made up of all the financial and employee and backup and transportation and ceremonial formalities etc.) in its organizational chart it has five sections and mega organizations: politics, religion & beliefs, culture, science and world economy; these five sections have 5 representative offices in the assembly building itself and five administrative and managerial mega organization which work as an individual but under the supervision and management and control of the general assembly; the five mega organizations of the Universal Society each have their own vast and expansive organizations, made up of (Financial and administrative and ceremonial etc. divisions) and committees which control and guide and observe the professional affairs which are each specialized to each committee; these committees are made up of the most professional and knowledgeable designers, talented people and the sage in the world which are experts in different areas of human life who have the continuous duty of the affairs of their own department and offer the best solutions ever ....

The main organizations of the Worldwide Society preferably and due to security reasons and because of the strong democracy ruling over the West will be in the country of ...! The Worldwide Standard Human Society will also have five main and regional representative offices in the five continents and main and strategic points in the world, so that it can observe and follow up the universal affairs with better access and in a faster manner, … it will also have a representative office in the form of a main embassy in each of the countries in the world to follow up, transfer and reflect and directly exchange all the affairs of the Worldwide Society with countries; ….

The general assembly of universal society at the same time is a legislative assembly, all the rules of materialistic and spiritual life, individual and social and international rules of life are studied through the specialized five committees of the five main parts of the universal society and eventually they will be reviewed in the universal assembly and voted by the representatives from the countries of the world and passed ….

In regards to the internal affairs of countries, the universal assembly and its main parts due to the request of countries and it will act individually, hence if the officials of a country wanted a legislation regarding any of the important issues of their country to be reviewed by the professionals in the specialized committees of the universal society, they can hand in their demand in the form of a request and take advantage of the special and specialized and individual universal programming in their internal affairs; some countries prefer to manage their internal affairs themselves and control them, as a result the amount of the help received and the nature of it regarding the internal affair of countries depends on the decision and request of each country.

The members of the five main part and the specialized committees also are made up of representatives and experts from all countries of the world, in this way it is apparent that the aspects of the five departments and organization of the Universal Society is a gigantic one! The administrative immensity of the five main parts is because of their vast scope of activity! Each of these five departments in regards of their affiliating subgroups will have the scale and formation of an administrative office! For example in the department of culture and art, world architecture (In all its aspects including specialized committees of design and architecture of all countries in the world) exists which constantly monitors the best and the noblest aspects of architecture of different regions and countries in the world and present executive plans so that the architectural and urban façade of the world are presented based on the architectural plan of **the modern human world!** In this cultural department, there is a similar process ongoing regarding the outfit of the people of the world, so that beautiful and authentic outfits for all cultures and countries are designed and sewed in factories in countries all across the world so that from now on people from each region of the world wear authentic and beautiful and new outfits which have been designed by the best designers of the world and find their identity and originality ....

This variety in architecture and outfit and food and world customs which will be executed by the cultural department of the world means dynamics and justice; it means justice because as human world will practically prove that all human beings are equal and the culture and personality of all human beings are equal and shall be respected; so the road for the penetration and cultural attack of part of the world against all of the world will be closed and the people of the world with the support and heartwarming of the Universal Society will find their beautiful culture and safe keep it! … The more variety the world has the more beautiful it becomes; the doomed and dry machine life and it being uni-cultural has made the world depressed and afflicted it with all types of mental and spiritual diseases.

In each of the main parts of the five parts of the Universal Society in addition to specialized committees, there are common committees too which act as counseling bodies with the main committee; for example in this department of culture and next to the various specialized committees in all subgroups of architecture, clothes, food, customs, tourism etc. which are all subgroups of the cultural department of the Universal Society, counseling teams and committees from other main departments (Politics, religion and beliefs, science and economics) are also present to oversee the execution of the cultural department and give the necessary and specialized advice, so as a result probable future redundancies are prevented! As we know all the plans executed in the five committees and departments of the universal society will be sent to the general assembly of the universal society and over there they will be attested and reviewed for the final draft by all countries, as a result if we ignore different and pro and con outlooks and not receiving enough votes, they will be returned, so it is better before presenting the final vote by the experts and professionals of other departments it is overviewed from other angles.

In addition to management and control and complete legislation in all aspects of human life and design and correction of life affairs in all the five main departments and its vast and numerous subgroups, the universal society has the responsibility of execution of all his legislations and plans all across the world! The Universal Society of Standard Human is equipped with the most powerful management system of the world, control over all the riches of the world - through membership of countries of the world and their financial contribution - and having experts and scientists and the sage of the world, with its universal credibility and authority, it is the only organization which can build human world and administrate and control it, hence mankind can be hopeful that with the help of the culture of Standard Human and leadership of Universal Society of Standard Human it will be able to eradicate the domination of the Satanic 10% and pass through the primitive first and second levels of his life and by reaching the third and fourth levels he will be able to overhaul his world in a complete manner.

Universal Society of Standard Human is also responsible for controlling the health of the world from infliction of any kind of corruption and weakness in all management affairs and it will have a very powerful international monitoring system which will carry out its monitoring and overseeing duties under the direct supervision of the general assembly of the Universal Society; ….

Ultimately we can simply state that the system that is ruling over the world today is very old and small and antique in all its departments; we are the best human beings and need the best and most powerful universal system to lead our world at the highest speed possible towards multilateral progress from materialistic and spiritual point of view; we don't want the world at its current state; **we want the best human world** in which human management and politics, illuminating religion and beliefs, beautiful and various cultures, a knowledge which pushes our world forward at the fastest speed, and an economy which will eradicate hunger from all the people of the world, and guarantee the job and business of human beings and flourish it, is present; we need the best of the world, as we are the best human beings.

The world of the Satanic 10% is a small world and tangled in a thousand year old, redundant vicious cycle which has not been effective, but the world of Standard Human of the progressive world of the third millennium has hope towards giant materialistic and spiritual leaps, which will visualize exiting from the current primitive and traditional life and entering the next elite world and worlds.

In the world of Standard Humanism all the beliefs, cultures, races, nations and human beings while keeping all their various and beautiful and colorful belongings will shine in their ideal and standard level.

If mankind doesn't understand the world of Standard Human and Standard Humanism, he will remain in the world of the Satanic 10% for another few centuries to come! ...

The Satanic 10% are a strong group, so before it is too late we need to save our world by accepting Standard Humanism.

Only a strong philosophy, a scientific system and a human unity can make the penetration of the Satanic 10% weak and obliterate it.

Universal Society of Standard Human

Universal Society of Standard Human will have five central representative offices in five continents of the world and a representative office (As a mother embassy) in each country which will take care of all the international affairs of all the countries – in each country – and through replacement with existing embassies they will be run in a more dynamic and intensive manner.

The Universal Society of Standard Human is a very strong and powerful and giant management organization, with the goal of controlling and leading and management of human life in five basic departments of life including: 1/ Management and politics, 2/ Religions and beliefs 3/ Culture and art 4/ Science and knowledge, 5/ Economy and commerce; and also all their subgroups which include all the affairs of human life ….

Five management departments of Universal Society of Standard Human

First department/ Management and Universal politics & order
A brief about the history management and politics of human world
The goals and duties of the management and politics department
Management and cleansing
  2+2=4
The proposed government system of Standard Human
Management and politics and its subgroups

Second department/ Thoughts and beliefs and religions
A brief about the history of religions and beliefs of human world
  A list of the religions and beliefs and thoughts of human world
The goals and duties of the department of religion and belief
Management and cleansing
Religions and beliefs and their subgroups

Third department/ Culture and art and the beauties of life
A brief about the history of culture and art and customs and rituals of
human world
The goals and duties of culture and art department
Management and cleansing
Culture and art and their subgroups

Fourth department/ Science and knowledge
A brief about the history of science and knowledge of human world
The goals and duties of science and knowledge department
Management and cleansing
Science and knowledge and their subgroups

Fifth department/ Economy and commerce and business
A brief about the history of economy and commerce of human world
  ….
The goals and duties of the department of economy and commerce
Management and cleansing
Economy and commerce and their subgroups

1st Dept. / Management and universal politics & order

Politics and applying political methods in handling human societies, was studied and discovered by ancient Greek philosophers for the first time in a methodical and concentrated manner (About 2500 years ago), the philosophers of ancient Greece in search of finding a better way and method for governing and handling human society, and on the route towards establishing a society based on manners and justice made a lot of efforts; ….

From the time man entered political discussions and political studies he has threaded a great route in the way of scientific growth and development; in the course of several centuries thought and contemplation and political philosophy in the vast area of human life has had a spectacular progress, and has gone forward in its path towards guidance of human beings for establishing a science which by making use of its fundamentals and rules can give his life a systematic and human order (With the goal of taking into consideration complete human rights in all aspects of his individual and collective life), today politics enjoys a vast scope, and as a pervasive science, it has taken human world under its control and administration.

A brief about the history of M. and Politics of human world

Mankind is the only creature who has a wise and intelligent relationship with his environment – whether his natural habitat and whether his social life! Mankind tries to recognize the environment and the different circumstances of his life and coordinate them based on the goals and his individual and social needs and organize them; this recognition and coordination and order which man follows in his life is the thing that has forced him to contemplate on his relation with himself and his being and the circumstances of his life! It was from this golden point of human life that he has started and followed the main route of his social life in a systematic and targeted manner; in this way mankind has gone through very primitive stages of his collective life and by passage of life he has passed a great process.

The world of politics has mainly started from *Greece* and the *West* and after passing through metaphysical thoughts and beliefs, they have commenced political thought in its rational manner; the circumstances of political life has been the main source of evolution of political thoughts and beliefs in their progressed and dynamic and targeted manner; the ancient Greece was made up of cities which were scattered in valleys and coastal cities and several islands; these cities were politically individual but at the same time they had common social and political institutions.

The metropolitans of ancient Greece were the hub for dynamic and active and vibrant social and political activities! Political struggles, social developments and the boom in business and commerce and ... had created a favorable environment for a vibrant social and political movement for them; the two metropolitans of *Sparta* and *Athens* were the biggest metropolitans of Greece; these two metropolitans had two different governmental and social systems: Sparta was an agricultural society and had an organized and conservative government, but Athens was a society with commercial and nautical and craftsmanship life; these two metropolitans each had a different model of different types of government and was an inspiration for different political thoughts and beliefs.

Anyway under such ripe political and social and active circumstances, great philosophers and sage lived and appeared which formed the world of politics in the main form we know today; here *Socrates* and *Plato* and *Aristotle* started the main period of world of politics with their thoughts and deliberations; Socrates by contrasting his thought with the incompetent democracy of Athens which cost his life because of his thought! Plato with his thoughts and theories such as: *justice*, through which he pursued total social coordination; *Ideal State* and *Philosopher King Government,* through which he wanted to present the best type of government; also for realizing the necessary conditions for training the Philosopher King he organized special educational programs by establishing his *Academy,* which by its thorough educational program and courses he could train the most ideal and powerful and philosopher kings and leaders, training such kings and leaders was one of the greatest preoccupations of Plato in regards to establishing an ideal government; also for training the best and the most knowledgeable kings Plato presented his limited Communism plan (Family Communism and ownership) which created conditions in the life of commanders and governors through which they had no preoccupation in regards to everyday issues and getting involved with family and or gathering money and property and ... - they would just think about governing over their society; although this part of Plato's program was more idealistic and not practical.

Next to Plato and in line with his theories and programs we have Aristotle who is one of the biggest philosophers of history; among the greatest and most valuable theories of his we can name his emphasis and indication towards the importance and position of law; from Aristotle's point of view in a good and ideal society law must have the main authority not an individual; Aristotle also names the terms for a good government and believes that a good government should be analyzed based on its real circumstances, and the best government is the one which can be achieved in real life; from Aristotle's point of view the right of private ownership has special importance in the society, as it is a good incentive and encouraging factor for people to pursue their vocation in the society in a more serious manner, and also because it creates a sense of satisfaction and freedom in people ...; In the discussion of different types of governments Aristotle points to the imbalance among governments and concludes that this imbalance is the reason that changes the governments; for example democracy tends towards the government of illiterate masses, or the government of the sage noblesse will lead to power seeking and dictatorship; one of the other reasons that governments fall apart is that they don't observe justice and equality in the rights of people which will cause the spirit of justice seeking among the masses and eventually will lead to revolution; in line with this Aristotle suggests coordination and balance among the opposition inside the government, so by maintaining the balance among them the probability of toppling of a government reduces; a combinatory government is the best model of a government; as in such a government stability among its pillars are best maintained; Aristotle divides governments into three main categories: 1/ *Monarchies*. 2/ *The government of Nobles*. 3/ *The government of the middle class* ….

Following this beginning era and flourish of the arena of politics, the history witnesses another stage which commences with the death of Aristotle; since the theories of Plato and Aristotle in regards of citizen's rights were not to the liking of the majority of people and in fact they neglected their rights, the people took notice of their rights and individual and social freedom and as a result it brought massive demonstrations which formed and established the school of thoughts after that period; among them we can point to the schools of *Epicureans* and *Cynics* …; The next and important stage of the history of politics starts with the *Roman Empire* and the philosophers such as *Polybius* and *Cicero;* the Roman Empire put an end to the social life of the metropolitans and established a magnificent empire which continued to live for centuries on, and in its struggle with the church in *Middle Europe* era it formed a great part of the history of the West and established it! Among the most important theories of Polybius, we can refer to the rotational theory of governments which he believed that each kind of government after some time will create a condition that through an evolutionary cycle they lead to their own decline and eventually end up back to the initial stage where they were formed! He also proposed the theory of *Combinatory governments,* in which he believed in accumulation and gathering of the best aspects of existing governments (*Monarchy, government of nobles and democracy*) in one single government! He considered the best model of this type of this government to be the government and the Roman Empire which in its three main parts (*Consulate, Senate* and *Assemblies*) they had applied the best characteristics of monarchies, governments of nobles and governments of democracy; after Polybius, Cicero was the first Roman philosopher and sage who paid special attention to the uniqueness and superiority of the laws of human world, he believed there is no such thing as different laws in different eras in human world, but there is one universal and un-changeable law in all eras which guides mankind; Cicero also believed in equality and freedom of all mankind in the eyes of law and supported it ….

After *Christianity* and in the Middle Ages of European history sages such as *Saint Augustine* appeared who had great impact on the formation of the powerful world of the *Popes* and the domination and pervasive penetration of kingdom and governance of the church; Saint Augustine by proposing theories such as *Christian city and government* and *Non-Christian city and government,* and emphasizing on issues such as justice and peace was able to turn the balance of power and government to the benefit of church and power of the Popes; with such an overall domination over power by Popes, which resulted in sovereignty of power seekers and oppressors and of course oppression and negligence of the rights of people, movements started from inside and outside of the churches towards limiting the power and dominance of the Popes and also fundamental reforms started in the management of churches; from inside of the churches by priests who deemed themselves responsible for reforms and limiting the God-like power of Popes and from outside by sages and thinkers such as *Dante* and

Marsilio and in the end philosophers such as *Martin Luther* and *John Calvin* and others who were against the government and the dominance of churches over the management of society in their own world; these efforts and actions for correcting the church and its power seeking though very important and vital, was not able to make the necessary impact on the world of the Europe in Middle Ages! Until another era of flourish started with the advent of the era of enlightenment and science which cleansed the dark epoch of dominance of the church with its light and eradicated it; in between and when the church was at the peak of its power the 800-year-old Roman Empire toppled and gave place to the closed system of *Feudalism!* Lack of a powerful government which could handle the world of those days following the toppling of the Roman Empire was the basis for forming of Feudalism; though the Feudalism era is recalled as the dark era of human history, but the experiences gained in that era established valuable achievements in the way of formation and enforcement of social relations of humans and brought about new experiences in this arena which was followed by many valuable changes in the formation of modern urbanization!

Feudalism was based on contracts that called for a solidarity through which the society would find its social identity; its basis and foundation was working on agreement between *owners of properties* and *farmers;* owners of properties in return for the overall support and the land which they put at the disposal of the farmers for farming and beneficial exploitation, would make use of the aid of their human force at the time of need (As military forces)! Anyway, urbanization and scientific and cultural growth and development led to *Renaissance* in Europe which brought about the atmosphere of modern world which led to the eradication of Feudalism from the history of human life.

Renaissance also witnessed a new era in the arena of politics which started with the advent of a genius such as *Machiavelli!* Machiavelli was the product of Renaissance and the child of his own time! He who suffered from the toppling of the Roman Empire and lack of universal and powerful government - which could bring a suitable social and political unity and overcome the social and political unrest - which was governing over *Italy* at that time, offered valuable thoughts and theories whose application is unique to the conditions governing his own time! Although his thoughts which were expressed bravely and honestly were massively taken advantage of by politicians and governors (Whether at his own time or in the future)! ... He believed that in critical times only a powerful man could govern order and discipline and social solidarity, a governor is allowed to use any ethical or unethical means to reach his political goals (= a stable State)! With the advent of Machiavelli and expression of his thoughts the era of modern political thought commenced ....

We are now going to get to know new thinkers who have had a great role in the route to formation of today's modern world - with their theories and thoughts; among them we can name theorist *Thomas Hobbs* the British theorist; he was the founder of the moral and political philosophy of Britain; his theories are about human nature and his life, and social contract, his most famous discussions are about politics and his political thoughts; … *John Locke* is another British sage who emphasized on natural human rights such as the right to live, freedom, the right to ownership and also on *individualism* and observance of individual human rights in the society … *Montesquieu* offered the important theory of separation and monitoring of three powers on one another, … *Jean-Jacques Rousseau* presented the very important theory of *General Will* and offered it as the basis and foundation for formation of the power of the society, and defender of freedom, equality and brotherhood … *Jeremy Bentham* was another British thinker and philosopher who presented the *theory of utilitarianism* which emphasized on satisfaction of the people in the society and avoidance on any act which might dissatisfy them; Bentham also had valuable theories and plans for establishing changes in the form and structures of prisons and more importantly creating circum-stances for education and working and hobbies for prisoners, through which they could reach a feeling of satisfaction and being beneficial; this clear-sighted theory of Bentham was the origin and reason for great and positive changes in the traditional and dark methods of jail administration ….

The next person who was the founder of great changes in next centuries of human life with his thoughts was *G.W.F Hegel;* Hegel's political philosophy was the platform for circumstances which led to the toppling of *Napoleon!* The theory of *wanting and dream* has been presented and discussed as the final element in politics; also in line with the importance of the theories of Hegel we have to mention that the basis of Marx's Socialism which is a materialistic dialectic has been based on the fundamental basis of Hegel's principles; the political theories of Hegel cover all the fundamental elements of racism, nationalism, …!

As we go on we have another British philosopher, *J.S. Mill* with his theories on *freedom of thought* and individual thought, which according to him this freedom of thought and idea leads to growth and development of individual personality which in return would lead to the growth of the society; Mill even emphasizes that in the conflict between the thought of the individual and society, it is the thought of the individual which must carry out the final judgment, unless the society is able to persuade him in a correct manner ….

In the following and completing era of the political world of the West, we witness appearance of *Karl Marks;* Marks expresses the claim that *production* is the basis of all the activities of mankind, and with this claim he took the cycle of politics towards jobs and production and ultimately the issue of exploitation of the world by the Western capitalism and World exploitation system, and presented a world which led to the *Communist Revolution* of the Former Soviet Union and led to huge changes in human world - which despite all the hardships and perils which dragged human life to the verge of annihilation - guided the world towards rapid progresses in all fields of politics, economics, science, social, … through the competition of its cold war (Between the Eastern block and the Western block); The political, economic, scientific and other com-petitions between the *USA* and the former *Soviet Union,* had great lessons and achievements for humanity, and paved the way for democracy and world peace! Today man knows that peaceful life with business and commerce is better than political and ideological struggles.

In the course of the past 25 centuries and since human beings have become political to this day they have been through a lot of ups and down; the political history of mankind has been witness to several realities; today's political life of mankind is the result of all the experiences and the outcome of the knowledge and thought of philosophers who have made an impact on our world with their thoughts and theories and made it grow; The life of mankind today is the result of wisdom and thought of philosophers and also human support and resistance who have tolerated a lot of bitterness to reach their human rights in order to correct their destiny and change their life in a humane manner and in the route towards benevolence and public welfare, and eradicate the dominance of ignorance and power seeking of oppressors and put an end to it; the political history of mankind is the history of all his efforts for reaching justice; the same thing which was first proposed by Plato in a philosophic manner, this justice is the thing that brings all the good and trueness with it, justice gives identity to human life, justice brings about peace and makes mankind satisfied with his life; but after 25 centuries and tolerating all these ups and downs is justice apparent in today's world?! Maybe in a small area of the world and for some of the people justice is visible and feasible, but surely for all the people in the world and in all the parts and areas of the world justice is not ascertained and visible!

Several more centuries shall pass so that justice is established for human beings all across the world?! Mankind has experienced great mutations in the past centuries of his life, and has the ability to pave the way for next bigger mutations in his life too!

In a short survey of the history of the politics of human world (The West) we realized that the history of human politics has had a slow but positive growth towards establishment of a society based on wisdom, logic and knowledge; mankind in the course of his history has gained valuable and hard experiences in order to realize that his ultimate way is the one which is to the right of all human beings - in enjoying a fair life along with peace and universal security - this must be paid attention to and this right must be met; although this reality has been quite clear from the beginning of human history but reaching a universal system and culture which paves the way for humans in the way to reach this goal has been real hard due to the ignorant penetrations! In this turbulent route wisdom and logic and politics, thought and politics and philosophy of the East has had a weaker appearance, the reason is that generally east has been more in a spiritual peace rather than universal adventure!

Anyway mankind today stands at a position that we can expect the hope of jumping towards a better situation from him and be hopeful towards it; today's technology of the world, and the general knowledge and information of today's mankind and universal efforts in the way towards international understanding and the universal partnership of countries, strongly created this hope that we are able to move towards understanding and choosing the path and a more correct and more complete method of living - which is the right of all human beings.

In the world of Standard Human the role of the East due to having deep spiritual and moral characteristics is more active from its current pale position, and it will be considered a good complement for cooperation with the powerful management and technological power of the West; to this date and in the course of the history of his life mankind has carried out many big efforts in different sectors of the world and has gained numerous materialistic and spiritual achievements for mankind, but there is only one great and main job left which he has not yet been able to fulfill it! And that is complete materialistic and spiritual cooperation, a multilateral and complete cooperation and not just a uni-lateral economic and or political and or cultural one!

The stages of human life growth & evolution:

1. Primitive: primitive and traditional; slavery; feudalism.
2. Renaissance ....
3. Capitalism and economic growth.
4. Welfare state and Modernism.
5. Standard Humanism! The perfect life of 3rd Millennium.

The goals & duties of the Management and Political dept.

The Universal Society of Standard Human has been established for reaching the goal of establishing peace and justice, and multilateral universal materialistic and spiritual growth and development which is the ultimate goal of human beings, and the goals and duties of management and politic department of it is as follows:

1/ Maintaining peace, security, law and universal justice.

2/ Reinforcement and stabilization of political borders of the countries of the world.

3/ Effort in reinforcing the political and friendly relations among nations.

4/ Sourcing suitable managing methods for the countries in the world.

5/ Helping weak countries in the world to amend their management and political affairs.

6/ Carrying out international governmental and management educational courses.

7/ Reinforcing and equipping the physical borders of the countries of the world in order to control all types of smugglings and terrorist penetrations ....

8/ Protecting the Earth and its Nature.

9/ ....

Management and Cleansing

The main subject of discussion of Standard Humanism is cleansing! Cleansing and stopping the penetration of the Satanic 10% from all that human beings have! In this line Standard Humanism apart from presenting the culture of international individual, social and humane morality through designing its five human making principles (The principles of Standard Humanism), through management of the Universal Society of Standard Human he has also founded a system so that through its strong and dynamic management with the goal of ultimate cleansing of the thought and ignorant and selfish domination of power seekers - and or those who think they are here to correct the world and as a result with their deeds they take the world towards chaos - he can put an end to it all! This cleansing is carried out in a diverse manner, and very scientific and practical solutions results from it.

In this section of politics, the situation will be corrected in such a way that at first and after formation of the Universal Society of Standard Human with the partnership of all the countries of the world (and or the majority of the countries of the world) control of the security of human world is left to the politic department of Universal Society! The political department will be made up of representatives of all the countries of the world and control and the responsibility of maintaining the security of the world and also the responsibility of reaching the goals defined in its department.

In a human world maintaining security is one of the most important issues; it is only under the umbrella of security that human affairs will find their balanced and correct way; security gives peace and tranquility to mankind; security will be a reason that human affairs in all its departments (Politics, religion and belief, culture, science, economy and ultimately in performing all its subgroups) with all power - and without any concern and wasting human materialistic and spiritual energies - thread its natural way and reach its goals.

Maintaining security can't be reached unless through a responsible and illegible international organization, whose credibility and legitimization has not been established through power seeking or creating blocks and …; in the course of the history of his life - apart from some cases of exception - has been after a unipolar and or single-minded system for administration of his world; this motivation at times has been a sign that *the ruling power* has been the best and the most impartial system of its time and as a result by equipping his power he does his best to fight with the forces that create problems and are a threat to human peace, and has reached his goals too; and or *the ruling power* has been trying to conquer the world to the benefit of the politics and imposing his ideology and tried to control and have universal dominance; in neither of these cases human success has not been complete and pervasive and the result has been the opposing powers (Whether good or bad) at the first possible moment and with the goal of reaching their rights have started wars and conflicts, and put world security at danger and imposed the heavy load world wrecking materialistic and spiritual losses on mankind (In an unwanted and forced manner); the strange point is that in today's world too establishing this unilateral security is still an ongoing problem; as a result human peace and security has been put to danger and kept as a threat! This is the eternal and everlasting fate of mankind based on the political culture that is currently ruling his world; but based on the enlightening, uniting, notifying and warning principles of Standard Humanism, and in line with its human management, this primitive situation will change and be amended.

The role and security importance of Universal Society in the world, and the role it has in helping the countries in the world, and in a humane and overall manner, is way beyond mere establishment of peace and security! Peace and security along with reforms and a powerful and overall universal control, will be a reason that all the ideologies that claim of establishing peace and justice, after witnessing this correct and humane international change, will see their unilateral ideological and thought facing that very little and weak, and as a result the Satanic thought will see his position making through which he tried to establish his ideology in the world, and by controlling the world take power of it, sees all his efforts futile, and hence peace and tranquility will govern over all the thoughts that claim governing over the world!

Under current circumstances of the world, it is natural and obvious that each group and belief and politics (Either honestly or with the goal of universal dominance) would claim that he can have the best solution for universal peace and security! But what can be gained from the sum up of the best of the world on the way towards meeting the needs of the entire world, would be beyond and more legitimate and more acceptable than what **one thought** might claim! *One thought* can't bring peace and justice for all the people in the world, but a **Universal Society** based on meeting the rights of all mankind can.

Since Standard Human has a logical and realistic personality and identity as a result in drawing a management system each of its main departments (Five parts: politics, religion and belief, culture, science, economy) will think realistically and with logic; hence in the organization of each department - which is made up of representatives from all the countries in the world - will appoint a management and brain and central core which is made up of the best of each de-partment! For example, the central management core of the political department is made up of countries that in practice have the most powerful and the best dynamic and successful politics of the world (Having an eye towards the strategic position of countries and also paying attention to the management dispersion of the world); hence, the 10 best countries from political, military and strategic and regional power point of view among the countries of the world is selected! As an example these countries are: USA and Russia, China, India, Brazil, Australia and three countries from the European Union and one country from the African continent …! Also 10 other countries which will be chosen periodically from all the member countries – and without any prejudice – which on the whole 20 chosen countries of the world will be responsible for management and policy making and maintaining universal peace and security; The necessary budget for this department - on the way for maintaining universal peace and security - will be provided by all the member countries.

With such a safe and pervasive system, world security will be maintained in a complete manner and mankind will think of better scopes and goals; power seeking countries who like to keep countries in a state of chaos so that by selling their weapons they can reach astronomical benefits, from now on will spend their talent on more humanistic goals and benefits which have better results; so that insistence on creating tensions and keeping mankind in pain; also stupid and primitive thoughts of ignorant groups who think that by terrorist acts and killing innocent people they can take control of the world will be eradicated and deleted from their minds and they too will reach peace, and be active in human activities and works which is worthy of them and up to their dignity and status.

The strong management system of the management and political department of the Universal Society of Standard Human which will simultaneously be in an official and close connection with the four other departments of the Universal Society will have the world in their absolute control, *and will close any way of penetration that can be thought of for the Satanic 10% forever,* and mankind can start his real life after thousands of year of experimenting!!!

The management system of the political and management system, on the way towards cleansing the management and politics of the world has special corrective measures in his agenda including cleansing the political and governmental systems of the countries of the world; on this way first the management and political department of the world will study and reinforce the existing borders of the countries of the world …; after defining the comprehensive and approved map of countries of the world where the political and geographical borders of countries have been signed again by all the countries (To resolve the border disputes and understanding and solving once for all the problem of borders that has existed between countries of the world), the political management of human world will correct the political and management and governmental structure of the countries! ….

We need to repeat again that Universal Society is nothing but an organization made up of all the countries in the world, and it is obvious that in its decision makings all the countries of the world will participate, and it is natural that the final decision maker in the internal affairs of countries or anything which has got something to do with the internal affairs of them will call for the affirmation of the country in question as the condition for the final universal decision and confirmation, and of course each country will well realize that is the dynamic environment of the Universal Society where everything has a humane route with peace and understanding, without doubt its decisions will be based on general wisdom; anyway among the corrective duties of the political department of the world which will bring about positive universal consequences is that suitable political systems of the world based on the historical and cultural and geographical and tribal and other characteristics of them will be evaluated and the best political system which can salvage a country from its management shortcomings and internal political tensions will be presented to that country; since the political department of the Universal Society is made up of the most knowledgeable and the best politicians and political philosophers of the world, as a result the political solutions that are given by this department will be the biggest political help to the countries of the world so that by choosing the suitable system and picking logical solutions for solving the political problems of their countries, they can free their countries from the existing political dead ends and guide them towards a more stable development; I have to remind you in the fourth world of his life and after realizing the fact that he has to set free from the domination of the Satanic 10%, will no longer be the mankind who with his current morals wants to pass his life and affairs, as a result when a proposal and plan comes from the Universal Society to a country, the countries will confront that proposal and plan with **logic and morality of Standard Human,** and not in an ignorant and selfish and power-seeking manner! As a result, countries on the route towards reaching faster growth will welcome any constructive proposal.

Since the dynamic and humane world of Standard Human is a totally different world from the ignorant world which is dominated by the Satanic 10%, as a result the nature and shape and goals of the politics in it is very different; in the world of Standard Human there is no place for ignorant and power seeking competition and the management system is totally different; **in the Universal Society of Standard Human from one direction the whole world is managed, and from other the countries under universal supervision will grow in their internal affairs, and as a result, the whole world will walk on the road towards complete and overall humane growth simultaneously and in the best possible manner, towards a peaceful and complete humane life, to the benefit of mankind** (70+20 percent …)**!**

To understand the current political and management situation of the countries of the world, and also the dilemmas and the great and numerous obstacles that retarded countries create on the road of universal materialistic and spiritual growth, and also the wonderful corrective impact which overall management of Universal Society of Standard Human can have on the growth and development of Universal Society, I draw your attention to the following example:

2+2=4

Imagine a classroom in which some students are sitting and the teacher wants to teach them for the first time that two plus two is four; at that time and first instance that the teacher presents the question and gives the answer the more intelligent students of the class understand the question and its answer and once the question is repeated they answer the teacher without hesitation and are praised; some other students aren't as intelligent, but after some contemplation will give the answer; some other students will need some guidance to remember the answer and give it; but to our surprise we realize there are some lazy and playful students that can't give the right answer and basically don't want to study and they are only after creating mischief and playing and laziness! And as a result they are always behind from all of their classmates and are always repeating the same class; … In the arena of politics and governance of countries, the top students are countries such as Japan and some others such as South Korea and or Malaysia and … and or some are slow but finally will find their way and reach growth and development such as …; but there are dimwitted leaders and politicians too who need help to find their way; and of course and unfortunately there are some evil and dangerous students too who need to be dismissed and expelled! ….

This example shows the current state and the governmental and political power of countries of the world which some find the solutions very fast and find the way to their development, and some are slow, and some ignorant and power seekers who have kept their country in poverty, and their poor and oppressed nation, deprived and under-privileged and under-developed!

Weak countries are the unsolved dilemma of human world! With their weak policy and management they add fire to their local competition and internal tensions; with the weakness in the political and management control of theirs, they make the security of their country an unachievable dream; by not having a correct humane ideological understanding and as a result not realizing the issue of international understanding, they become a dilemma on the path towards international peace and tranquility; weak countries have greater dilemmas from management point of view also in their internal affairs, including that as they have political and management shortcomings they have economic shortcomings too; as a result, they will have cultural problems too, and also scientific and ideological and many other problems ... and ultimately they will be a dilemma in road for the *multilateral progress of mankind!* These weak countries (Either from management and political point of view or from the issue of understanding humanity and justice) will keep mankind retarded.

When the universal management of Standard Human starts ruling, firstly poor countries will enjoy human aid as much as possible in all aspects of human life - which is the duty and one of the goals of the Universal Society and the human right of the countries of the world; secondly, the domination of ignorant and power seeking people will come to an end because of the wisdom and awareness of the people in those countries, and as a result they will never come to power; and even if they come to power *the universal unity of mankind* and *the management of Universal Society* will topple and reject them very soon! The root of lag of the countries in the world is that power in these countries is in the hands of incompetent and power seeking politicians and leaders and they only think of maintaining their dominance and governance, naturally such people will not be competent managers, hence we witness their lag and the pain of their nation!

This way, it is clearly proven that how Standard Humanism and Management of The Universal Society of Standard Human can solve problems and be saving; in the first place when the thought and morality of Standard Human becomes Universal and mankind is equipped with the five humane principles of it he will be free from the selfishness and power seeking and laziness and with honest effort he will engage in his political and governmental affairs, in the second place he will get prepared to accept any proposal and plan and positive humane way and method which can speed up his growth; hence the importance of the political department of the Universal Society and the immense impact it can have on maintaining the security of the world and also management of the countries will become evident clearly.

It is worth mentioning that the methods of aiding different departments of the Universal Society is done in various and different forms and types: In some instances the proposals are merely theoretical; in some instances they come with financial aid; in some instances they come with human aid and actual presence in place; anyway in management of the Universal Society the science of world, proficiency of the world, riches of the world, politics of the world, will be at the service of the whole world, and it will not be the case that a country or a nation stays at the peak of riches and success and his neighbor will be a poor nation and under governance of a group of lazy and or ignorant and or oppressive group! ....

Among other valuable benefits of Universal Society of Standard Human is that it guarantees the stability and constancy of development of countries! Under the current circumstances of the world there is this possibility and threat that a country is moving towards its development, it goes through a political upheaval and all that it has gained - due to any incident which can easily take away its security - lose it all and impose new pain and poverty over its nation, so that they are forced to tolerate new hardships because of a group who have taken away power from the previous rival! This is while in Standard Human system the best route for materialistic and spiritual growth and development of countries through extensive universal studies has been defined, and the clear path for multi-dimensional growth of countries has been defined and planned, and there is no need that a party or group put the stability of a country into danger on the pretext of presenting a better method or program! In this way the time and energy, peace and stability, and growth and progress of the world won't be put at peril because of a destructive whim or power-seeking of *a small ignorant group,* and or a group of honest but illiterate people and the nations of the world will witness their multi-dimensional growth with a precise speed and attention.

The body of human society has grown and has been equipped with universal monitoring system, as a result it is the duty of humane society to be sensitive towards the old and ancient parts of it and tries to renovate it, as a result in the

management and political department, the human world should
come to the help of the poor countries with a strong and modern
and overall method and system from management point of view
and renew their system and help them to step in the route of
correct and healthy human progress; Today's human world
should cleanse itself from ancient management thoughts as soon
as possible, and this is the duty of a universal organization made
up of representatives from countries of all across the world.

*Healthy and powerful renovation of Universal Society
of Standard Human will be different from a unilateral single
powered method which is currently governing the world,
which has been trying to – and may to do so in the future too –
correct the world with his own method by war and massacre.*

The current unilateral actions on the way towards
establishing political stability in the world even though necessary and praiseworthy, but as they are mostly following one
directional goals, and also they are not carried out by a legal
organization which is accepted by the whole world and believed
by it, as a result it has created a lot of tensions and opposition in
the world ….

The management and political department of the Universal Society would be a legal international body which will
gain legality through votes of the people of the world and the
votes of all the countries in the world, such an organization with
universal eligibility will have a much correct operation than
those of powerful countries of the world, who come to the arena
to tear apart a fox and or a wolf and or a sheep! And as a result
they kill an innocent or a guilty party and afflict their world with

war and tension and insecurity; although this is the only current and existing method in the world but the correct and humane method of it will be possible only through universal management and through Universal Society and the management and political department of it.

Since the thought of Standard Human is based on respecting the thoughts and beliefs of the world it can have enough legitimacy and overall and universal management.

The management and political department of the Universal Society also have the immense and heavy duty of protecting the earth! Based on the thought of Standard Human the Earth and nature and plains and sea and deserts and sky should welcome billions of men who are supposed to commence their new life in the third millennium on it, as a result the Earth and the wonderful Nature of it should be protected in the best possible way and by all the world through the most powerful legal and legitimate human organization; protecting the Earth and its nature calls for serious and pervasive measures in this field; among the most important corrective and security and defensive measures is protecting it from any chemical and atomic pollution! This is human duty and commitment in line with the measures for eradicating tensions from the society which will bring peace and security to the world with more guarantee; when tension making ideological and political power seeking which causes tensions becomes minimal with the corrective measures of the system & thought of Standard Humanism, other measures such as the necessity to protect the Earth, as a totally safe place would be a reason that arms and atomic games of the Satanic 10% also becomes minimal, and by control and leashing it in by the universal management and political department, we will witness its eradication and finally its total wiping from the surface of earth! ….

What was said was a brief about the fundamental management method of Standard Humanism in competent guidance of human world; this was only a part of it and a brief of what man can and should do about his world; these immense reforms start from individual reforms and after believing that we deserve a dynamic human life it leads to Universal Society of Standard Human!

In the course of the past thousands of years, both the Satan of ignorance and unawareness and power seeking and the selfish and power seekers have become tired of mankind! How much longer do they want to kill one another and trample on one another's rights and rule over the world and be oppressors and create wars? They are tired and await the day that the knowledgeable man pulls up his socks and finally start their right and humane life on this Earth, so that they too rest a while and attend to themselves and maybe become reformed! ….

The proposed political system of Standard Human

Standard Humanism defines an ideal human governmental system as follows:

The type of Standard Human government from Standard Humanism point of view is a Liberal Democrat System in which the logical and human rights of all people and groups have been considered and kept through the constitution; ….

In the democracy system of Standard Humanism the main pillar and the main management is in the hands of a public parliament and the house manager is the same as the president of the country and the leader of the country! … The representatives of the parliament *every four years* will introduce 10 of the most educated and the most competent of their elected representatives to people and during a free referendum and with popular power of vote the most righteous man will be elected as the President (Management of the country through the parliament); … People will choose among the selected the man who has the superior personality, management and scientific characteristics and as a result by getting inspired by his elite character with a sense of freshness and more hope towards the growth and development of their country they will continue their life; *In the proposed system of Standard Humanism the leader of the country is the representative and directly in charge of the nation and he is not the absolute governor of the country!* (The president will carry out the executive duties with the help of his deputies …).

In the government of humanity over mankind the society does not witnesses party rivalry in order to gain power and impose the points of view of particular party, as a result the parliament is an organization which is far superior than a party; the members of such a parliament, as a result, have representatives who act beyond politics who are among retired university professors of the country who are the most elite and the most knowledgeable members of their human society who are elected through voting and free elections, and only based on their merits, their educational, scientific and vocational records; such members will be the best, most knowledgeable and healthiest people of their society who better than any other individual and group will have the scientific capability and management understanding and correct human legislation; as a result the criteria for selection in such a government will only be based on the axis of competence, merit, humanity and execution of law.

The main pillar of the government is public parliament; which - based on the basis of five main departments: Management and politics; religion and beliefs, culture and art ...; science and knowledge, and economy and commerce; which are the main communication channels (Through mother embassies) with the five main departments of the Universal Society in each country - has five main duties, including 1/ Legislation. 2/ Planning and execution of overall development of the country, and monitoring the execution of the approved programs of development. 3/ Central Bank and General Treasury. 4/ Maintaining National Security. 5/ International Affairs.

(The key role of the five pivotal departments is very important here as even before foundation of the Universal Society of Standard Human countries of the world thread on the route towards growth and overall development much faster and sooner than expected through cleansing the five superior fact in their country; *the political system of Standard Humanism is the salvation for underdeveloped countries and a cause for growth for progressed countries*).

In Standard Humanism system the constructive department is the duty of a *quasi-government* (With the leadership of a prime minister) whose only duty is executing the legislations and development programs which are presented by the planning department of the parliament, as a result this department is only an executive arm; this quasi-government is an organization like a government which with the help of private sector manages and executes all the programs for development of the country in all areas of social life including religious, economic, cultural, educational and nurturing, hygiene and … affairs; *This executive department manages the executive affairs of the country under the supervision of the main departments of the parliament and carries them out!* The international affairs of countries are carried out through the representative offices of the Universal Society (Mother Embassies); ….

Eradicating political and party rivalry from the country and the legislator parliament and also differentiating authority and the responsibility for planning from the government and lightening it will lead to the cleansing of the government from control and domination of the power centers and the energies of the country are concentrated for positive activity and healthy planning to the benefit of the country and the nation; ... *Party rivalry in the world of Satanic 10% is only done because each group and party and school of thought claims to have the best solution for growth and development of countries! But in a world that the best and the most correct solutions are presented by wisdom and collective wisdom and knowledge, a party is a traditional and historical discussion.*

In the proposed system of Standard Humanism the **Supreme Court** has the responsibility of judicial control and is the direct body responsible and patron of executing law in the country; ... The supreme court executes the law and is its patron and is in charge of controlling the legal health of the society from any breach of law and governmental and social corruption; in this regard the police works under the supreme court; ... In addition to that in Human Society *General Inspection Office* and the *Mass Media* act as the eyes and ears and the conscience of the country and with full legal authority and complete in-dependence interacts with popular parliament and the Supreme Court carries out its legal and social and humane activities; Also as a legal and legitimate guarantee in line with applying the laws of the country by the government and its organizations, the people have legal and official right to refer their views and complaints directly against any organization and government body in the Supreme Court and if it is not addressed (In a proper time span) they have the right to declare their complaints directly to the management and political department of the Universal Society and the International Human Rights Court and follow it up in an general and effective manner ....

The armed forces, the army and the air force and the navy of the countries are in common and direct relation and cooperation and pact with the management and political department of the universal society, in addition to cooperation in controlling the borders and preventing the hostile and or terrorist penetration they will have complete preparation so that as helping forces in emergency cases and under management and cooperation and supervision of the management and political universal department they can come to any kind of aid; armed forces work under the National Security division ....

Emphasis on difference and diversity on party-beliefs on democracy which is among the most important guarantees of governments for prevention of falling into the pit of dictatorship and tyranny, in Standard Humanism is carried out through its modern system of government and with the centrality of the five main department: politics, belief and thoughts; culture; science and economy – made up of representatives of all famous and logical schools of thoughts of the society! Hence the issue of checking and balance on its regulatory form through presence and collective cooperation of all the departments of the elite and informed parties of the society is guaranteed, and the management system of the society with deleting the ancient form of current *party-power-seeking* – which after going through a historical period of *conquest of power* from dominance and control of kings and religions and beliefs it falls in the hands of parties – in a more complete and coordinated manner (With the monitoring of Public Opinion, Mass Media and Supreme Court) *The Government of Humanity over mankind* has been prevented from any downfall and stability of government and growth and progress of the society is guaranteed.

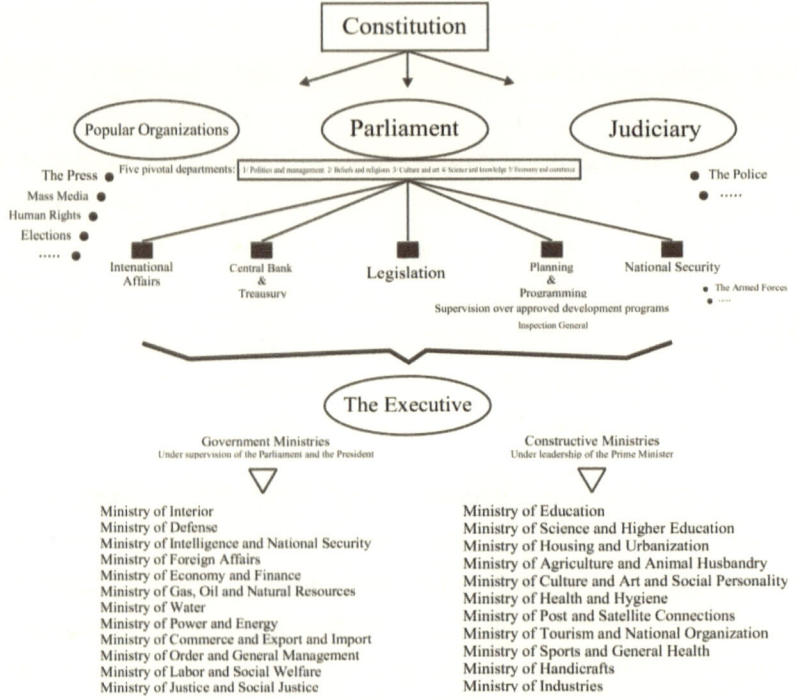

All the above ministries will have affiliating organizations and foundations which will complement them.

In the above system the goal is to have a precise order with a clock like coordination among different departments of the government so that the affairs of the country can go on in the best possible manner.

In Standard Humanism there is no such thing as government over people as it is customary, what we have, is a management system made up of four main parts which work with the support of the constitution.

The internal management and government system of countries ... is formed in coordination with political, ideological, cultural, scientific and economical needs of each country, and with counseling and planning and coordination with the management and political department of the Universal Society, as a result it will be a miniaturized model of management which has taken patterns from the system of the Universal Society of Standard Human in addition to maintaining the special conditions of its own system from government and political and social combination.

Since the thought and idea of Standard Humanism emphasizes on a humane system, and basically sees the fundamentals of creation of problems in the essence of thought and power-seeking of the Satanic 10%, as a result by cutting down the hands of the negative forces, it creates a healthy and powerful management humane system which is based on international understanding and coordination, hence in such a system and under the supervision and coordination of such a management the affairs of human society will carry on in a smooth and coordinated manner.

Standard Humanism has melted away the concentration of power & tendency towards parties & following persons, and stabilizes and reinforces the government of humane constitution in the hands of mankind.

Management and politics and its subgroups

The subgroups of management and politics department of Universal Society has a special span; since the goals of the management and politics department is vast and pervasive, as a result its subgroups will include all the management and politics of the world!

The subgroups of the management and politics of Universal Society are as follows:

1/ The Council for protection of Universal peace and security.
2/ The Council for friendship and unity and international cooperation.
3/ The management and government research Council.
4/ The Council for political reform aid and cooperation.
5/ The Council for amendment and reviewing political borders of countries of the world.
6/ The Council for reinforcement and equipping the physical borders of the countries of the world.
7/ The Council for studying Mother Nature and protecting the Earth from environmental dangers in parts such as the Earth, sea and the sky ….
8/ The Council for cleansing and protecting the Earth from the possibility of chemical and nuclear and other pollutions and dangers.
9/ The Council for unexpected and natural events such as floods, earthquakes, volcanoes etc.
10/ The court for overseeing the implementation of law in the countries of the world.
11/ The specialized committee for finding and preventing the penetration of the ignorant and the selfish and the power seekers to the field of politics and management of the world.
12/ ….

These committees and councils will have legislative and administrative duties and they will be directly in charge of carrying out the duties defined for them, and actively and legally they will start and carry out their job under the supervision of the management and political department of the Universal Society of Standard Human, which is made up of representatives from all the countries of the world.

The Universal Society will be made up of representatives from all the countries in the world and all of them are involved in the management and execution and policy making and legislations of it; as a result the understanding and cooperation and collaboration will be at its height, there will be no obstacle in front of the Universal Management, Universal Society and on the route to executing the universal commitments and duties!

Fundamental and perspective management, and pyramid and step by step order of the management of Universal Society of Standard Human will delete any parallel organization and foundation which imposes additional costs from the management construction of the world and establishes a kind of organizational harmony, this will be what we will call **the government of humanity over human,** which will be managed by the wisdom and knowledge and science of the world and to the benefit of the world, and will guide all the world in a harmonious and coordinated manner towards progress and development; such a system will demolish the heavy and depleted management structure of the countries of the world and replace it with a system which is beyond this world and coordinated and influential, which will not only renovate the internal management and government structures of the countries of the world, it will unite the countries of the world and with a universal supervision and control - will push forward the countries of the world as units that complete one another - and on the route towards universal coordinated development.

The amendments and measures which will be taken by a great management and universal organization, and the wonders and the positive and overall impacts it can leave on human life is conceivable and acceptable by all people; especially that such measures by Universal Society of Standard Human, will be carried out simultaneously and coordinated in a pervasive manner and in all departments and life affairs of mankind! Hence, I will cut short additional explanations and hammering on the benefits of it; it suffices to add this that for example in regards to unexpected events and the aids the countries of the world and the Universal Society can give, if the management of Universal Society is ruling over the world, sending materialistic and food aids and sending human aid etc. will be carried out at such incidents at one instance and with a single management, and the afflicted country will not await sporadically scattered aid from different parts of the world as charity and in a weak manner, there will be no need to declare to the world that we are in a critical condition and need aid; ... but under such circumstances and under the management of Universal Society of Standard Human the management and political department and the department and the subgroup of unexpected incidents, will hold an emergency meeting, and with having all the riches of the world and the facilities of the world can rush to their help from the very first hours, and at the earliest possible time they will prioritize what has to be done in the best possible manner; this is while today, though months have passed from the earthquake in Haiti (September 12, 2012) the earthquake victims are still waiting for aid from people from across the world, and the flood-ridden Pakistanis are waiting for aid from flood, ... And there is this concern that due to corruption ... the helps from the people of the world would not reach to the hands of deprived people in a correct and appropriate manner! ... A part of the world went under water and was washed away in front of the other part of the world, but rescuing aid was sporadic and weak!

The Universal Society of Standard Human has this power and management responsibility to manage and control the whole world with the support of the whole world, the Universal Society of Standard Human is a government beyond normal governments and is a legal and legitimate and powerful humane mega-organization, which is equipped with the wisdom and riches and management of the world and as a result will do the right thing in the best possible manner.

The thought of Standard Human and the government and management of the Universal Society of Standard Human is the powerful and modern government of humanity over mankind, whose greatest goal is safe keeping the life of people and establishing suitable conditions for materialistic and spiritual life for all the people in the world, in an equal manner.

2nd Dept. / Thoughts and beliefs and religions

Thoughts and beliefs and Religions create a collection which is made up of tens and hundreds of divine and non-divine beliefs, and different political and philosophical and ideological thoughts! All these have appeared to guide mankind towards a better life! All of these have formed and created and appeared to lead and guide mankind on the route towards a better life and in their own method, and save him from his problems! Part of them emphasize on spirituality and supernatural thoughts to reform mankind and the society, and some by emphasizing on the spiritual principles and rules and based on introspection and self-making, and some from the angle of a social outlook and based on a scientific principle try to seek for the happiness of mankind! … Religions and beliefs and thoughts of mankind are the spiritual and scientific and social result of his for reaching eternal and permanent peace and happiness!

Human religions and beliefs are as man reforming and society reforming, as they are an important getaway for the penetration of the Satanic 10% - who wants to control the human world to his own benefit - and this the best evidence we are witnessing that in the course of history humane and elite beliefs have appeared, but after some time has elapsed from their appearance schism and enmity has started among their followers and fans which has led to the fragmentation of that - initial pure and unique - thought by the hands of vicious lions each of which wanted a bigger share to have more power and dominance over the world of the human beings! And to introduce themselves as the most righteous ones to all the people! ….

Human religions and beliefs (Religious, political, cultural ...) contain the outlook and ideology of mankind towards the response to queries such as the truth of the world, the goal and the reason for the evolution of mankind in this world, and what is the best manner and method of human life in this world, and on the whole, it involves the philosophy of coming into existence of mankind and his goal in this world ...; all the religions and religious and political beliefs from the day of their evolution to this day have been looking for an answer to above questions and are still seeking, each in their limited time and place have tried to discover the infinite truth of the world and develop and extend their point of view to the whole world!

All the religions and beliefs and religious, political, humane etc. groups follow two major and complementary goals: one part is propagating the spiritual and social teachings and beliefs which will lead to the reform of the individuals and the society and in various belief systems and cultures it is made up of different forms of prayers and individual and group behavior, and another part is the honest effort for convincing others to also conceive the superior truth that they have understood, in order to attract more followers to get to their goal which according to them is the only way to salvation of mankind; the first part is totally personal and selective, in a way that individuals and groups can choose the superior religion and belief and thought which they have deemed appropriate and chosen they can reach their ideal life, but in the second part history has never been able to prove that any superior religion or belief can in practice convince all mankind and bring them all united under one umbrella of beliefs, this has never been visualized in human society and man in the course of the history of his life has always been involved in the fight for excellence and struggles for beliefs and politics, as reaching superior and common belief and thought has always been along with imposing of thoughts and prejudice, and followers of no group have ever been ready and will be ready to let go of their belief and accept the beliefs of another group without any conditions.

The issue of superior belief and distinguishing the superior belief, the superior way of life for mankind has been the main and eternal issue of talk for mankind from the first day of his evolution to this day! Men have created tens and hundreds of religions and beliefs to prove the other group that they conceive the truth better, in order to grab the government of the world through this type of logic and administer it in their own method! ….

A brief about the history of R. and B. of human world

Evidence and proof of existence of religious beliefs goes back to hundreds of thousands years ago, i.e. the middle and ending era of Stone Age, archeologists believe that the core of the first religious belief and thought started from the time that people 300 thousand years ago would bury their dead based on their customs and thought; the history of evolution of religions and beliefs is not clearly evident for mankind; but what is acceptable and accredited is that belief and faith has always been there with mankind, belief and faith in a correct way saved his life from mistakes and obliquities so that by considering the superior principles of the received belief or the one he has invented he can create a better life for himself.

The oldest credited and known human religions and beliefs are known as Faith of Abraham which has roots in belief in God and the creator of universe, also some which are not included in the Faith of Abraham like Indian and Oriental, Iranian, tribal and ethnic and ... which in different ways have supernatural roots and deep spiritual beliefs to the superior and senior truth, here other peace-seeking and justice centered beliefs have formed in contemporary era which are not considered in the mentioned groups ....

The most famous and oldest human religions and beliefs are as follows:

1/ Faith of Abraham - around 1800 to 2000 BC

2/ Hindu religion - around 1500 BC

3/ Judaism - around 1250 BC

4/ Zoroastrianism - around 660 BC (1740 BC ...)

5/ Shinto - around 660 BC

6/ Taoism - around 604 BC

7/ Jainism - around 599 BC

8/ Buddhism - around 860 BC

9/ Confucius Rituals - around 551 BC

10/ Christianity - 30 AC

11/ Islam Religion - 622 AC

12/ Sikhism - 1496 AC

& ....

In the contemporary centuries and era of human life religious and non-religious rituals and thoughts, with different and various natures were formed whose complete list and history and philosophy and thought can be found by referring to the following sources.

Religions and beliefs, and pure and healthy human thoughts will do their best so that in each time span and location and special cultural circumstances which rule over that special time, and with the present language of that era guide them and show them the best way towards salvation and happiness in this world and the world after based on the circumstances and capacities they have; ....

The list of Religions, Beliefs & Thoughts of Human World

Due to existence of complete information and data about all the known human religions and beliefs which have been present through Wikipedia website and or other research or information websites and through the internet, there is no need to give a list and complete description of them in this book, I invite those readers who are interested in more research to search through below addresses:

1/ http://en.wikipedia.org/wiki/Religion
2/ http://en.wikipedia.org/wiki/List_of_religions
3/ http://en.wikipedia.org/wiki/Major_religious_groups
4/ http://en.wikipedia.org/wiki/List_of_belief_systems
5/ http://en.wikipedia.org/wiki/List_of_people_by_belief
6/ http://en.wikipedia.org/wiki/Religions_of_the_world
7/ http://en.wikipedia.org/wiki/List_of_new_religious_movements

8/ http://en.wikipedia.org/wiki/List_of_religious_organizations
9/ http://en.wikipedia.org/wiki/List_of_religious_populations
10/ http://en.wikipedia.org/wiki/List_of_political_ideologies
11/ http://en.wikipedia.org/wiki/Category:Religion_by_country
12/ http://www.xenos.org/classes/papers/5wldview.htm
13/ http://en.wikipedia.org/wiki/philosophy_of_religion
14/ http://en.wikipedia.org/wiki/Religious_humanism
15/ http://en.wikipedia.org/wiki/Humanism
16/ http://www.religionfacts.com
....

Searching through above addresses truly shows the extent of human's thoughts and his efforts to find the superior way for his life based on the mentality and science and culture of the nations in the world, and it clarifies the fact that mankind from thousands of years before to this date has been looking for a more suitable way for his growth and elevation! Of course there has been a group who has found his path and another group who are still looking for a path and idea which is coordinating with their mentality and spiritual capabilities.

What was mentioned above is only a short brief about human achievements in regards to human religions and beliefs in the course of his life history, mentioning this brief is important only in the way that in a simple glance we realize that what a global understanding mankind has had from religious and ritual concepts, and how well, whether negative or positive, he has taken advantage of religions and beliefs in his life! Man today, after a simple glance towards the history of the life of his ancestors will realize that although they had a great spiritual and mental understanding of their religion and beliefs, but they have never been able to use their achievements in a correct and peaceful manner which helps reform the society in spiritual and ethereal fields, take their world towards social and global friendship and towards understanding and comradeship and transcendental human life, but still and even now they are living in stress and struggles! (By "mankind" here we mean the whole body of humanity with all its religion and religious culture and not only part of human world, without a doubt always and in the course of history parts of the world has been witness to a dynamic religious life with a high human and celestial conception).

Paying attention to this fact is very important, that in the course of human history many big and small crimes have been committed by ignorant followers of religions and beliefs, and in return what expenses have been made to reduce the mutual tensions, all of these are the good and bad achievements of the world of religion and belief of mankind, which have inflicted a lot of materialistic and spiritual expenses on mankind! Tensions over beliefs of mankind will cause him to spend his materialistic and spiritual capital in a big way for compensation of losses incurred due to these tensions; whenever in any corner of the world we witness tensions over beliefs a lot of thought and time and costs are spent in other parts of the world to find suitable solutions to solve those tensions, these finding solutions means a waste of time and human expenses, in a way which could have been avoided in the first place by mutual understanding and even not formed, in addition to that, these tensions over belief will create chaos in the calm world of human life in other parts of the world and make it fervent and upset it.

This discussion becomes important only due to one point, so that we know that man in the course of his religious and social history has not shown a victorious and successful role from him! And his positive achievements in this regard has been mere and weak in a way that after thousands of years from his spiritual and celestial and social life he has not gained a fundamental growth in the way towards establishing peace and mutual understanding and human respect through religion and belief; ….

Imagine a water dam which keeps a volume of water since the time it starts working, and after some time it proves that it has a positive and abundant background and saving, when people stand at the other side of the dam and by opening the gates of the dam want to evaluate its capacity and make use of it, without doubt at a suitable position by opening the gates they will witness the life-giving eruption of a big volume of its savings, but the question is by opening the historical dam of human religions and beliefs will mankind get surprised by the positive things he has gained? Or he will witness the dirt and pollution of tension and supremacy and power seeking in the midst of the clean and limpid water of his religion and belief! ….

The goals and duties of the dept. of Religion and Beliefs

The Universal Society of Standard Human has been established with the goal of establishing peace and justice and overall materialistic and spiritual growth and development which is the ultimate dream of mankind, and the goals and duties of the department of religions and beliefs is as follows:

1/ Cleansing human beliefs from historical pollutions that have been inflicted on them.

2/ Presenting the most correct and purest way of all human religions and beliefs and thoughts and all those that are legitimate in human world.

3/ Formation of organizations in which human religions and beliefs are taught in public level in all countries of the world so that the literacy level of the people in the world is raised and religious and belief peaceful human coexistence and understanding is formed.

4/ Making suitable circumstances for social and spiritual human growth.

5/ ….

Management and Cleansing

The main subject of discussion of Standard Humanism school of thought is cleansing; cleansing and stopping the penetration of the Satanic 10% to all that mankind has! Along with this line Standard Humanism in addition to presenting the culture for individual and international, social and human morals through design of its five principles of human reforming (The principles of Standard Humanism), it has an overall effort to cleanse the impurities which cause schism and have polluted human religions and beliefs through Universal Society of Standard Human and as a result pave the way for more cooperation and friendship among human beings through religions and human beliefs, ….

With an extraterrestrial outlook we realize that there is an infinite world which holds the Earth within itself and on this Earth creatures live among which the smartest and the most superior and the ones that have the most impact on defining their destiny are called human beings, here tens and hundreds of religions and laws and beliefs have appeared and created to present the correct and superior way of life to him and save him from bewilderment and confusion and take him to the stage which he is worthy of, and show him the absolute truth and the superior way for spending his life!

The absolute truth is fixed and single but under different circumstances in different times and in different cultures, it is manifested in a different shape and color! The truth is the same but each religion and belief tries to show that its take from the truth is the most correct one, and of course each religion is the best for the people it has under its umbrella and the culture it is ruling, but necessarily it is not the best choice for all the human beings, as a result we can't expect that a single belief although very good and one of the best to be accepted by all unless some accept it willingly, this trend has been a normal practice always in the course of the history.

Religions and beliefs are the second vast arena for the Satanic 10% to roam around (…), which enables them to control and put under leash the centers of thought and philosophy of religion and belief and extend their domination to the merest issues of internal affairs of human life and take control of human life so that they can spread enmity and schism among them in whatever way they want and make their life dark and dim.

All human religions and beliefs from any kind, be it supreme or from this earth in its original and preliminary form are correct and noble and right and the best guide for mankind in the area of culture and the area they were evolved; they were the necessity of their time, and appeared in a correct way with philosophical and historical roots; human religions and beliefs from any kind, celestial and humane are the spirit of human world, and should be deeply respected by human beings; the impurities that the Satanic 10% have inflicted upon human religions and beliefs have been cause for this respect to be ignored by mankind in some instances and in some historical eras by some human beings, and the worst part is that the impurities inflicted upon human religions and beliefs in the course of history have been cause for some that out of goodwill but in wrong give other definitions from one single belief! This has made things much more complicated *and has been cause for a pure religion to turn into several impure religions!* Some of them have been formed due to the penetration of the Satanic 10% to tarnish the vision of the pure and clean religion, and some other have been formed through the honesty of people and deviated who in their mind wanted to present a more correct form, but have created another thing! These sided or simpleton masterpieces eventually has been cause to the fact that first of all some clean hearted and logical and sane people have doubted religion and beliefs as an effective means for materialistic and spiritual constructive measures in life and generally make them refrain from pure humane religions and beliefs and thoughts and abhor them!

Since Standard Humanism has established its principles in a noble and deep and realistic and humane way and with the goal of finding the absolute truth of human life, as a result by finding the roots of the problems it comes to the conclusion that by referring to the base of the human religions and beliefs and thoughts one should survey and present the beliefs in their pure and primitive form; the specialized committees in the religion and belief department of Universal Society are made up of representatives of all the human religions and beliefs and also representatives from all the countries of the world who have the duty of continuously going through and cleansing all human beliefs, and it is the main and legitimate universal organization and it safe keeps the correctness and health of human beliefs from the penetration of the Satanic 10%; *Religion and beliefs belong to all human beings and not only to the group who believe in it!* As a result it should get rid of the penetration and domination of the Satanic 10% and be presented by representatives of all nations of the world in its pure form and be protected by human world, so it doesn't become a tool for tormenting and oppressing people, and keeping them short sighted and illiterate, ... *Cleansing religions and beliefs in their pure and primitive form will lead to the eradication and removal of Satanic leeches which have stuck to them each of which have changed the vision of religions and beliefs in their own way, and introduce it in a prejudiced and ignorant manner;* these leeches set violence and prejudice and superiority-seeking as their culture in world relations.

Human beliefs have an immense importance; beliefs are the sky of the life of human beings, so these skies should be cleaned from any darkness of ignorance, prejudice, violence and ineptitude, and this can't be achieved unless through a great universal and truth-seeking human organization which through its strong control and preservation takes away the demon of ignorance and darkness from human religions and beliefs.

Taking human religions and beliefs out of the dominance and control and penetration of the Satanic 10% and new leadership of it by representatives from all human beliefs in a legitimate and international organization will pave the way for cleansing and purifying them.

Each group who introduces itself as the follower of a clean and pure religion and thought, necessarily can't prove its legitimacy through claims, there may be a group that is among the Satanic 10%, and by taking over part of that religion and belief want to impose their Satanic and schismatically imposed opinions to others, and as a result create chaos and insecurity; *control and preserving human belief and religion in Universal Society by the cleanest and most credited known followers of them is the only legitimate and legal religious and faith-based guarantee, and whatever is out of this circle is Satanic penetration and struggles to take control and dominate over beliefs.*

Cleansing beliefs and correcting them will create a colorful and beautiful collection which will illuminate the eyes of all people and believers in spiritual and social human religions and beliefs, and will lead to the spiritual, mental, moral health of human world; Strong and pervasive management and protection of Universal Society of Standard Human is the strongest guarantee of belief which will cut the control and penetration of the Satanic 10% for ever and will be cause that their ignorant followers and their stupid thoughts will be eradicated from human life gradually and only the light and brightness of religion and beliefs will remain and safe kept.

Religions and beliefs and their subgroups

The subgroups of the department of religion and beliefs of Universal Society have a special vastness; since the goals of the department of religion and beliefs is vast and comprehensive, its subgroups contains all the religions and beliefs of the world!

The subgroups of the department of religion and beliefs of Universal Society are:

1/ The committee for research, finding the root and cleansing the religions and beliefs and human rituals.

2/ The individual committee for compiling the correct and original form of human beliefs.

3/ The committee for approximating and unifying religions and beliefs.

4/ The committee for compiling the common points of religions and beliefs.

5/ The committee for finding the truth of Human World.

6/ The committee for setting up the educational and propaganda policy of religions and beliefs.

7/ The committee for studying religious and social behavior of mankind.

8/ The committee for control and monitoring and protecting religions and beliefs.

9/ The committee for distinguishing between beliefs and thoughts and philosophies of new beliefs.

10/ The specialty committee for recognition and prevention of penetration of the ignorant and the selfish and the power seekers to the arena of religions and beliefs.

11/ ….

3rd Dept. / Culture and Art and the Beauties of Life

Each human individual or society, and each nation and culture has his own special personality and nobility, and he can only understand his true value and reach his overall limit of progress and development, that he has grown through knowing his self and finding his self-based on his nature and talents and capabilities, and reach the nobility so that he can shine like a gem among other societies and cultures and shed his light, this is a sure fact that this growth will be a reason for us to witness different societies with their unique beauties next to one another, and instead of blindly imitating each other, we will be reason for growth and elevation of each other next to one another.

For sure cultural purification and purifying each culture will lead to overall and progressive growth and progress in him; the effects that will occur in the mind and soul of human beings are nothing but becoming alive; the succulence and freshness which is obtained due to paying attention to original values of human life by the people in the world will be so deep that they will leave great mental and spiritual, and physical and meta-physical effects in all aspects of human life.

Human Society should be original and beautiful and clean in the best possible way; beautiful in culture and customs and rituals, and architecture and clothes, and appearance and the nature of everything; Human Society in Africa, Europe, Asia, America, Oceania and any other part of the world should and strongly must be beautiful and clean and happy; human beings should be happy; a humane joy, not a satanic and fake one! And not sad and depressed.

In a world where good and humane and positive thinking children and girls and boys and women and men live, the world must be at their service and clean and colorful and happy; *it is the ominous satanic world which is dirty and polluted and dark; the world of human beings should be happy and bright so that the light of it can eradicate the darkness of ignorance and superstition and delete it;* this is the innate, natural, legal and celestial right of all human beings to enjoy life in the cleanest, most beautiful and purest and the happiest world.

A brief about the history of culture and art and customs and rituals of human world

Human world is formed by culture and art, and customs and rituals and takes identity and meaning; culture and customs and rituals are the same as his behavior and different forms of his life which build the beauty and design and color of it; mankind in each spot of the Earth and under the influence of different circumstances and geographical and environmental circum-stances, has reached an abundance of varieties in methods of life, customs and rituals, architecture and clothing, the type of food, language and race and nationality; it is this beautiful variety which is the result of his spread in different parts of the Earth, that has created many beauties which even astonishes and makes mankind happy!

Culture and art, and human customs and rituals, have had an important role in the formation and enrichment of his civilization; in general, civilization is a social order, from which *Human Culture* is formed; and only in a healthy and calm humane background human talent flourishes and beautiful human cultures are created.

The culture of human society and his civilization from the beginning of the history of his creation has had a close and inseparable relation and growth with one another, and what can be distinguished today is fundamentally - made up of all he has gained in his life in the field of politics, government and economy and science and religion - mixed and mingled with it; in studying the history of civilization and formation of the culture of mankind we can refer to the civilization of Indus, Sumer, Egypt, Babylon, Assyrian, Persia, India, China, Japan, Greece and Rome and the beautiful civilizations and cultures of Africa and Latin America and ... On the whole all the cultures and various and rich aspects of history of mankind, which one after another have presented different forms of colorful and different behavior and principles and rules and customs and rituals of human beings, ...

Human culture is the most beautiful achievement of his life which mingles his life with joy, leisure, fun and variety ....

The goals and duties of Culture and Art department

The Universal Society of Standard Human has been founded to reach the goal of establishing peace and justice and multilateral universal materialistic and spiritual growth and development which is the ultimate wish of mankind, and the goals and duties of the culture and art and customs and ritual department are as follows:

1/ Supporting the foundation of family as a natural organization which is a social entity which makes up humans.

2/ Studying and finding the origin of the culture and customs and rituals of nations and countries of the world.

3/ Cleansing the culture and customs and rituals of human beings from the superstitions which have entered it.

4/ Supporting and presenting the most beautiful aspects which exist in the culture and customs and rituals of the society, architecture, clothes, food, ceremonies and ....

5/ Designing new human and universal urbanization, having in mind human spirit and subtlety; and **avoiding design of ugly spaces which are tight and deserted and lead to stealth and or growth of the spirit of the Satanic 10%.**

6/ Designing new human and universal urbanization based on the correct dispersion of population among cities and villages.

7/ Designing new human and universal urbanization based on correct geographical situations and conditions.

8/ Design and environmental beautification of the world with the goal of living in a world which is beautiful and clean and pure.

9/ Paying attention to spare time and creating the infrastructure for movies and leisure time and healthy pastimes.

10/ Defending various languages and dialects of human beings.

11/ Development of universal tourism; (Hotel hospitality and ...).

12/ Management and supporting sports of the world.

13/ Controlling World population.

14/ ....

Management and Cleansing

The main discussion of Standard Humanism is cleansing! Cleansing and stopping the penetration of the Satanic 10% from all that mankind has! In line with this Standard Humanism presents an international moral individual, social and humanistic culture and at the same time, through design of its five constructive human principles (The principles of Standard Humanism), has an extensive effort to cleanse the impurities which have entered the human culture and art and customs and rituals through Worldwide Standard Human Society, and as a result pave the way for more cooperation of mankind through human culture and art and customs and rituals.

Standard Humanism has deep belief in keeping human nobility and values in all departments and aspects of his life; bear in mind the difference between an artificial flower and a beautiful and fragrant and natural flower; everyone can feel this difference quite well and distinguish it; an artificial flower lacks the splendid and exhilarating natural beauties, but a natural flower from any kind and form and color and type is gracious and beautiful and brings joy; the life of human beings at present is boring with non-dynamic cultural goals and artificial! As a result mankind should be salvaged from this artificial life and commence his natural human life; by a natural life we don't mean that all people should go to the heart of Mother Nature and leave their urban life! But we mean he has to form his life in a suitable and beautiful way and by considering all the prerequisites of a complete human life.

In a complete human life everything is placed in its correct, beautiful and beneficial position and without congestion and any complications; man should reach its origins and by recognizing his roots and knowing his culture he should set the foundation for rules and regulations, and build a beautiful and clean society based on complete needs of his human life; such a beautiful human life will be visualized in a world where population is controlled; dispersion of population and building of cities and villages, and wide and safe roads and highways, should be done with international study and expertise; the architecture of different countries and cities and villages should be executed and designed based on the new map and the superior universal engineering; in each region and country and village in the world a factory is established which produces clothes of that region so that in addition to providing suitable job, the authentic and beautiful outfit of each region is produced and supplied in that region; the feeding of the people of the world is controlled by a universal great organization, and hunger is eradicated in all regions of the world; the superstitious and ignorant ceremonies and rituals and customs in some parts of the world will be removed, and through an extensive study carried out by the culture department of Universal Society, suitable customs and rituals and ceremonies and religious and non-religious services will be designed to substitute and as a result the national identity of different countries of the world and tools to create joy and variety in their life through creating entertainment with their cultural rituals is provided ....

Hence, succulence and effervescence which is gained by people of the world because of paying attention to noble values of human life will be so deep which will have great spiritual and mental and moral effects in all aspects of human life, and this is *Human originality,* and reaching the human nature which is lost and has been attacked by cultural ignorance and inaptitude and superstition and superiority, ...

The culture and art and customs and rituals dep-
artment of Universal Society of Standard Human protect the
noble human cultures, who follow their flourish in their own
limitations; based on the thought of Standard Human each
nation and country should and it is called for them to appreciate
their architecture and clothing and customs and rituals and
culture in a noble and animated and modern way, and they
should defend implementation of their culture against any
cultural attack of the Satanic 10%! The Satanic 10% weakens
other cultures through cultural propaganda by all marketing and
destructive methods, and try to develop their culture and way of
life; hence, nations should be alert and by wearing beautiful
clothes with original and at the same time modern designs by
the designers of their country and their culture, and also with
their wonderful architecture, and their food and national and
ethnic customs and rituals, they will give priority to their own
culture and defend their originality; the culture of each nation -
provided it is supported by a universal organization which
supports all cultures - it suits that very nation; cultural alienation
will have no result but mental and spiritual crush for the
defeated nation; cultural alienation and mental and personality
defeat which is resulted by it, will make the spirit of man
depressed and tired and uncertain, and as a result the joy of
human life is lost.

The culture department of Universal Society will defend
the culture of nations in an equal and original way, in a way that
their self-confidence and pride in using their beautiful local
culture among people in each part of the world will reach its
peak, and each nation with a personality which is supported by
the thought of Standard Human - in addition to keeping its

cultural identity - will appreciate other cultures and respect them just like his own culture and see the value of human world in the variety of its culture.

The spirit of human being is the origin of all that is good and right and have roots in the order and infinite beauty of the world, this is why any disorder and impurity makes him uneasy, hence cultural correction is among the great human needs in the third millennium which is carried out by Universal Society made up of representatives from all cultures and countries in the world for the purpose of *reviving human life* on Earth.

Culture and art and its subgroups

The subgroups of the department of culture and art and custom and rituals of the Universal Society has a special span; since the goals of the department of culture and customs and rituals is vast and pervasive, as a result its subgroups will include all the culture and art and customs and rituals of the world!

The subgroups of the department of culture and art and custom and rituals of the Universal Society are as follows:

1/ The committee for supporting the organization of family as the most important secure human organization.

2/ The committees for supporting the execution of customs and rituals of the nations of the world.

3/ The design committees in charge of presenting the best original and modern architectural and urbanization displays of the world, with the goal of maintaining the architecture of different regions of the world based on their originality, and also mingling them with the best aspects of architecture and fortified and modern international structures.

4/ The committee to supervise the architecture and urban-ization of the world, to control and take into consideration the fundamentals of design and aesthetics of architecture in different areas of the world, and protecting the architecture from penetration of alien architecture.

5/ The committee for design and presenting the most beautiful original and at the same time modern displays of cover and outfits of the people of the world, with the goal of maintaining the original and beautiful and various cover of different areas and regions of the world, and encouraging people to wear national customs by different nations.

6/ The committee to supervise the outfits and cover of the people of the world, and prevention of cultural alienation towards national cover and cover culture problems.

7/ The committee for design and study of the roads and highways of the world based on the new position of universal urban design.

8/ The study committee for the nutrition of the different people of the world and enriching the nutrition of poor nations.

9/ The committee for establishing the infrastructure for leisure time and spare time.

10/ The committee for local languages and accents.

11/ The committee for controlling the world population.

12/ Tourism.

13/ The committee for universal sports.

14/ The specialized committee for recognizing and prevention the penetration of the ignorant and the selfish and the power seekers to the arena of culture and art and customs and rituals of the world.

15/ ….

4th Dept. / Science and knowledge

To combat ignorance and prejudice and misdirection, and to oppose and overcome the penetration of the Satanic 10% in human life, Science learning and gaining knowledge should be placed at the head of all human affairs; this must be done continually in order to absolutely prevent the penetration of ignorance and misdirection; having faith and belief in the five principles of Standard Humanism and control and pervasive and powerful management of Worldwide Standard Human Society reaches its peak only with the consciousness and the scientific knowledge of the world's population, and thus guarantees the peace and felicity of the human world for good; this effort, is a continuous struggle and a moment of pride and ignorance can open the way to penetration of Satanic 10% and endanger the human peace and happiness.

A brief about the history of S. & Knowledge of human world

Science and knowledge, are the result of human efforts in order to find answers and solutions that he faces in his life; science is a set of theories, opinions and practical and experimental activities which are trying to discover the secret of the natural world; science and knowledge are developed and used by researchers and scientists - with an emphasis on observation, experience and description of the world - with the help of scientific methods and techniques; the range of researches, studies and scientific findings of human are vast and include numerous subjects and branches; among which, we can point to biology, astronomy, botany, chemistry, paleontology, geology, physics, mathematics, trigonometry, anthropology, economics, algebra, calculus, geography, geometry, statistics, linguistics, logic, nutrition, political science, sociology, psychology, agriculture, computer science, pharmacology and …; these sciences go under the main categories of natural sciences, mathematics, social sciences, technical and medical sciences; ….

In prehistoric times, science and knowledge was passed from generation to generation in an oral tradition; then the discovery and development of writing system enabled the man to store and conserve the scientific findings from getting lost and destroyed; scientific history of mankind has witnessed an extensive growth and progress; these scientific findings began from ancient Sumer in Mesopotamia 3500 years ago with detailed records; then the amplitude of growth and development of the scientific findings of man reached from Mesopotamia to Egypt, Greece, India and China; … The scientific development and growth of man has traveled from ancient period to Islamic scientific growth period then to central European scientific period; since then and during the next centuries, science entered it's efflorescence period and traversed the growth path rapidly; human scientific findings over the last two centuries have changed his life miraculously.

Truth is discovered by the means of *philosophy;* … the world of Reality thru *science;* … and *knowledge* encompasses both ….
*- and the third path is the intuition (Thru Heart) ….

The goals and duties of Science and Knowledge department

Worldwide Standard Human Society has been established in order to achieve the goal of providing peace and justice, and comprehensive universal materialistic and spiritual growth and development of the world which is the ultimate desire of mankind, and the goals and duties of the science and knowledge department of it are as follows:

1/ Public education and eradication of illiteracy, ignorance, prejudice and villainy in all scientific and social fields ....

2/ Maintaining and controlling the worldwide physical and mental health.

3/ Supporting the establishment of educational institutions at all the levels from elementary to higher academic levels.

4/ Establishment of international organizations and research centers.

5/ Financial and moral support of scientists, researchers, geniuses and inventors in all fields of science and research.

6/ ....

Management and Cleansing

The main subject of discussion of Standard Humanism is cleansing! Cleansing and cutting the influence of the Satanic 10% of all that human beings have in possession! In this regard Standard Humanism in addition to providing individual moral culture, social and international human culture, takes comprehensive efforts through designing its five human making principles (The principles of Standard Humanism), to clean impurities entered the science and human knowledge, and thus provides a better collaboration and interaction between mankind through human science and knowledge.

From general point of view, science growth throughout the history and especially in the last two centuries has been fast and pervasive; but the growth of human life's standards in regard to his society and standards of living, social welfare and basic literacy has remained of very poor quality! The subject of scientific researches is a fundamental issue, which requires the continuous human pursuit so that he could access more findings, but this point shouldn't be forgotten that these findings relate to humanity and must be used and understood by all human beings in order to synchronize the level of human knowledge with the World; if in the poor parts of the World, part of the science and scientific behavior stays useless, due to low basic literacy, it can't be claimed that human beings have a good level of knowledge; basic science must be upgraded simultaneously and coordinately with the technical science growth in all its aspects and subcategories so the scientific understanding of human gets to a higher level in general and evenly; the World's population remaining illiterate in Third world countries and especially in poor parts of the world, slows down the scientific growth of humans just imagine if only in medicine and health section, we could increase the general literacy and people of the world would take care of their physical health and hygiene due to correct education; it is easy to understand that this way the heavy responsibility of further care and therapies will become lighter and in addition to financial cost savings, opportunities to improve human's knowledge and science would increase as well, and thus human's time and financial resources would not be spending constantly on global public health issues; in this regard and as a first urgent solution, simple and systematic educational courses should be designed to teach simple and scientific subjects step by step and in short terms to people in deprived areas, so they gain gradually general awareness and get the necessary education in various personal, social and hygienic issues; this urgent method will raise the level of literacy and general knowledge of people in deprived areas in no time and with lower costs in a more practical way without getting them involved with time-consuming classic educational systems, and will improve in general the level of awareness and literacy of the man; elevating the level of world's public education regarding personal health and sanitary issues and social communications, and knowledge and public awareness leads humankind one step forward to a better understanding of human as well ….

Simple lessons along with the quick and urgent in-formative methods in deprived areas contribute to a quicker learning process and with the support of the science and knowledge department of the World Society of the Standard Human facilitates its way to reach an appropriate and adequate global level; this short term training courses should include all the educational topics with the subject of literacy, health, religious awareness and healthy and anti-superstitious belief, peaceful human culture and ethics, general information, geo-graphy and history and … (At the top of its concerns); increasing public awareness is a guarantee to stop human exploitation and colonialism.

Human scientific growth hasn't been equal and identical to the theoretical and global growth of science; knowledge and the science department of the Universal Society of Standard Human will fill this gap with its radical and comprehensive management, and will raise the human knowledge to its adequate level with elevating the public education level as well as the technical education in parallel, ….

As the public parliament of the world's countries, according to the proposed governmental system of Standard Human, are composed of deputies elected among university professors, and these groups have a great influence on the proposal and approval legislation of their respective countries, the development of higher education and modern academic systems is extremely important ....

Science and knowledge and their subgroups

The science and knowledge department of the world society have a very rich subgroups; since the goals and subjective of the science and knowledge department are extensive and comprehensive, so its subgroups deal with all the global knowledge and scientific issues!

Subgroups of the science and knowledge department are as follows:

1/ Committee to support international scientific and social literacy and poverty alleviation.
2/ Educational and informative committee to defend human social rights.
3/ Global Health Committee that seeks to maintain physical and mental health.
4/ Higher Education Committee.
5/ Committee to promote and support complementary skills.
6/ Committee to protect scientists and inventors and geniuses.
7/ Specialized committee to identify and avoid the influence of ignorant and egoists and power seekers on science and knowledge domains.
8/ ....

5th Dept. / Economy, commerce and business

One of the greatest efforts of human in life - along with his efforts to establish a just government during the history, and discovering the truth and understanding the World, as well as finding the best way and manner of spiritual and social life - has been his efforts to creating jobs and promoting his livelihoods; having a job, making a profit, earning a living and looking for a life without poverty and insolvency have been always the greatest concern of the man during history, and of course like other important things in his life he has endured difficulties in the path to reach them, and he has been exposed to exploitation and oppression extensively.

History has witnessed the constant efforts of man to achieve the minimum subsistence to survive his life, to the extent that to escape poverty and access food he has launched many wars! To seize the belongings of others and save himself from hunger and poverty; man - even in the current era and with abundant facilities and resources and wealth and food products - has never been able to get rid of hunger and poverty!

A brief about the history of E. & Commerce of human world

The world of business and livelihood and ultimately the world of economy and commerce has witnessed lots of up and downs; Social class differences, hunger and poverty, oppression and exploitation, illiteracy and social and cultural backwardness have always been the source of all the human miseries; man has never been able to overcome his poverty, because he didn't possess the necessary knowledge and the sufficient science and management, or he has been caught by greed and avarice that has taken from him the opportunity to establish the justice in his economic life.

Man through the acquisition of knowledge in economy, production and distribution has tried to reach a fair system so he could overcome the problems of unemployment and poverty with the help of better management of resources and his productive assets; ....

Economics is a science that according to the shortage of goods and means of production and the unlimited needs of human, deals with the optimal product allocation; the fundamental question of the economic science is gaining the maximum satisfaction and desires of humans; this knowledge is divided into two main branches: *Microeconomics* and *Macro-economics;* Adam Smith is known generally as the pioneer of modern economics; nowadays, this science has been taken away from the other human sciences because of using the mathematical models; for example: the Game theories which are expanding with a topological approach ...; or in the macro-economics fields where the differential equations and the optimization of functions and the utility of integral with differential equations constraints known as the *Hamiltonian* equations are common ....

Microeconomics

Microeconomics studies the economic behavior of individuals and economic markets and analyzes the methods of distribution of products and the costs between them; microeconomics considers the individuals as workers and capital producer as well as the final consumers; and it looks the same way to the economic enterprises as the capital and labor consumers, and the products manufacturers; micro-economics seeks to identify the effect of rational behavior in humans; according to the limited resources (For example workforce, capital, land, management ability and …) peoples and economic markets are willing to take the most out of the existing resources; functions of supply, demand, production, costs, markets, general equilibrium and welfare economics take part in this field of economics.

Macroeconomics
Macroeconomics deals with the study of economic issues of a country on a nationwide scale; international economy is in charge of studying global economics; subjects like economic stability, foreign trade balance, economic growth, employment, inflation, government expenditures and revenues, economic recession, financial crisis, unemployment, poverty and deve-lopment economics are examined in this field of economics.

Unlike microeconomics, macroeconomics is not con-cerned with individual's behavior, yet it is shaped by the sum of the individual behaviors; *Keynes,* the father of Modern Economics, has presented a clear example of the same behavior in the area of micro - and macro - levels, which is known as the paradox of thrift; if people save their money individually, they will have more financial strength in subsequent years and will be able to make use of their accumulated capital, but if all the individuals increase their savings simultaneously and save most of their incomes, the whole economy falls, and this will also reduce the production rate, as a result the future income of individuals will drop; hence increasing the savings can be useful for individuals, however it could have different effects on the society as a whole than on the individual's life.

Another example: if a company replaces one or more members of its staff with the new machinery, it will turn undoubtedly out to its advantage, but if all the companies act the same at once, the rate of unemployment evaluate and the national income will reduce, so it leads to a lower demand for company's productions and their profits will drop; so the demand for company's productions will fall and their profits will drop; that's why the effects at the macro level can be opposed to those at the micro level; ….

The Branches of economics
Economics can be best divided into following branches:

Media economics, Political economics, International economics, Welfare economics, Industrial economics, Agricultural economics, Public economics, Natural resource economics, Environmental economics, Energy economics, Development economics, Urban economics, Regional economics, Microeconomic, Macroeconomics, Public sector economics, Managerial economics, The Economics of exhaustible resources, Transport economics, Theoretical economics, The Economics of renewable resources, Mathematical economics, Engineering economics, Sports economics, Health economics, Education economics, Business economics, population economics, Jungle Economics, ….

Schools of economic thoughts
Schools of economic thoughts are classified as below:

Scholasticism (Ethics-oriented economics), Mercantilism (Trade oriented economics), Physiocracy (Economics based on Nature's originality), Classical political economy, Institutionalism, Historical school of economics,

Socialism economics, Neoclassical economics (Marginalism), Keynesianism, Neoliberalism economics, Neo-Keynesian economics, Chicago school of economics (Monetarism or money supply oriented economics), New classical macroeconomics, New Keynesian economics, Structuralism economics, Austrian school of economics, Reaganomics (Supply-side economics), Real business cycle theory of economics, Economic theories of ancient Greek philosophers, ...

Economic systems

Economic systems are classified as follows:

Slavery's economic system, Feudalism, Capitalism, Imperialism, Socialism, and ....

The goals and duties of the E. and Commerce department

Worldwide Standard Human Society has been established in order to achieve the goal of providing peace and justice, and comprehensive universal materialistic and spiritual growth and development of a world which is the ultimate desire of mankind, and the goals and duties of its economy and commerce department are as follows:

1/ Establishing cooperation between economic sectors and international trade.
2/ Studying and balancing the global production among the world's countries.
3/ Strengthening and expanding of industry and international industrial cooperation.
4/ Supporting and producing strategic products and their distribution in the world.
5/ Providing job opportunities and international job security.

6/ Supporting the weak parts of the world and contributing to the improvement of social justice, and having the minimum needs of human life.

7/ Controlling and eradicating the global poverty.

8/ Promoting and development of agriculture on a worldwide scale.

9/ Development of industry and technology.

10/ Providing energy and development of clean energies.

11/ ….

Management and Cleansing

The main subject of discussion of Standard Humanism is cleansing! Cleansing and cutting the influence of the Satanic 10% of all that human beings have in possession! In this regard Standard Humanism in addition to providing individual moral culture, social and international human culture, takes comprehensive efforts through designing its five human making principles (The principles of Standard Humanism) to clean impurities entered in the economy and commerce of human world, and thus provides a better collaboration and interaction between mankind through the economy and commerce of the human world.

Economic cooperation among developing countries of the world, fair system of production and distribution, establishing security and creating employment opportunities and money making and income, etc. have largely faded the problem of poverty and unemployment in human societies of the actual modern world; but do the people of the world benefit from the economic justice and do they have the right to enjoy the human world's resources in a proper way? Have the poverty and unemployment been eradicated in the world's richest countries? Have International commerce and cooperation been able to cover poor countries, and allow them to enjoy a safe living - without worrying about unemployment and hunger? ....

Since when man should witness poverty and un-employment, therefore its ominous consequences like robbery, murder, addiction and using drugs, the growth of drug and arms trafficking (In various forms) and the strangest one the terrorism?! It may seem strange but possibly the terrorism and half of the reason of the formation of terrorist groups in its various forms are due to unemployment! Unemployment in deprived areas of the world encourage the negative and bad mentality, and consequently leads to the creation and formation of all kinds of offenses and crimes, and formation of smuggling gangs, and ultimately to the formation of terrorism and terrorist groups, and as a result of this the human world would be faced with a variety of risks and dangers and their tragic, bitter and sad consequences.

Global tyranny and oppression and authoritarianism and wealth amassing - combined with the exploitation of poor countries - and thus the occurrence of injustice in human life make some countries poor and this leads to the unemployment of their competent and skilled forces! This unemployment drag the mind of a suffering and oppressed human to thousands of illegal and inhuman works, one of a which is smuggling (In its various forms), and another is the formation of reformative thoughts among suffering groups; these groups which are composed of talented and unemployed people appear in a way that make their surrounding unsafe, and gradually with penetrating to the other areas - through ideological influence - transform to a threat and danger that target the humanity;

On the one hand they endanger global peace and (International) stability, and on the other hand they claim global modification in their own style! Certainly their ideology and their thoughts are not universal, because it comes from revenge and imagined superiority; nevertheless they form a claiming group that by creating insecurity drag the world toward chaos and anarchy.

In a healthy and normal world, such a reformative thought and claiming groups would never be born; if the world goes routinely and accurately and the management shows a high capacity in the World, then some bored and unemployed people would not think about the reformation of the World! And therefore like other people or other thinkers would be engaged in their own work; in a stress-free and unperturbed situation, and in a safe condition of existence of a healthy human life, these people would never think about the ideas above their intellectual capacities; if the administrators of the human societies couldn't dispense/serve the least human justice in all sections of the human life and in the global society, it is natural that every small or big group would claim to be able to modify and reform the human world with its ideology! And the worse is that in a world plagued by poor management, the time and thought of all the human beings would be involved with reforming and development of the world; and eventually it would be headed toward widespread stress and tension; ….

Fair distribution of wealth, job creation and job security, social justice and … will prevail the peace and tranquility in the World, and aside from preventing the formation of the groups who claim the global reform, this will even calm the religions and all the global reasonable thoughts! In a society where an inclusive and humanitarian law that protects everyone's right govern, in fact a large part of the ideological tensions and superiority dominance and claims and arguments and theories will fade and the man reaches a calm state, and can begin to experience the best life! ....

Imagine a group of scientists and specialists and normal and honorable men that have been kept from working and captivated by a problem, their working efficiency will fall as long as they are involved with that problem, but once the problem is solved, they begin to focus on their life and their work, and would be able to achieve enormous progress with concentration and tranquility; man throughout the history has always been involved with many problems that has taken away from him the opportunity to live a human life; so with solving his problems by comprehensive thinking and humanitarian management he would be able to reach real peace and satisfaction, and engage in a healthy human life, together with greater attention and efforts to achieve financial and spiritual horizons.

A good management, healthy beliefs away from divisiveness and superiority, beautiful cultures, science and knowledge, and dynamic economy and commerce will supply the human world with total prosperity that man deserves.

Economy and commerce and their subgroups

The economy and international commerce department have very rich subgroups; since the goals and subjective of economy and commerce department are numerous, so its subgroups embrace all the economy and the global commerce issues!

Subgroups of the economy & international commerce department are as follows:

1/ Committee to study the economic and commerce and the world's trade cooperation.

2/ Committee to determine and recognize the global allocation and production capacity.

3/ Committee to provide job and international job placement.

4/ Global wealth fund and financial support of the Earth's renovation.

5/ International fund of maintenance of global security.

6/ International fund of research and study of human life on Earth and other planets.

7/ International fund of disasters and poverty alleviation.

8/ Committee to support and provide financial resources for international road construction.

9/ Committee to support and provide the clean energies.

10/ Global Exchange.

11/ Specialized committee to identify and avoid the influence of the ignorant and egoists and power seekers in economy and commerce domains.

12/ ....

The goals and duties of the five Managerial Departments of the Universal Society and its subgroups are far more extensive than what was mentioned in this chapter briefly; therefore it is hoped that after the formation of the Universal Society of Standard Human and the global expert reviews, a comprehensive system of Universal Society of Standard Human would be developed and would start its global move toward creating a complete and a massive world of humanity.

The Final Conclusion

CHAPTER 3

Final conclusion

A brief on the globalization of mankind in the past 100 years

The first attempts of mankind for friendship and international comradeship among the countries of the world, which will result in establishment of legal international entities, preserving universal peace, development of commercial, economic, hygienic and other cooperation etc. started officially in 1919 with the establishment of *League of Nations* and entered its main and international stage; this universal movement was the first official international milestone towards understanding and unity of mankind, and it started from the time that mankind came to the necessity of formation of organizations for preserving universal security and peace in order to save himself from occurrence of international fatal wars; *the League of Nations* had valuable achievements for mankind, and the most important of them was that he was able to create this way of thought in the mind of the countries and the people of the world that in the way towards solving the big problems of mankind and securing world peace they have to stay united; in the second step and stage mankind established a more developed establishment (United Nations) to be able to reach greater and more extensive achievements in solving world problems and prevention of pervasive wars; *League of Nations* was the first official organization of human world and it is natural that along its valuable achievements it had some shortcomings too; hence *United Nations* was founded with a newer face and vaster dimensions after the dissolving of *League of Nations; United Nations* had a more complete universal coverage and reached very valuable achievements in the fields of maintaining world peace, development of friendly relations among nations, development of economic and commercial cooperation, support of human rights, development of world hygiene, development of artistic and educational cooperation, supporting the right of workers and working agencies, foundation of International Monetary Fund, and many more achievements and goals, in line for supporting human society and through its different committees.

League of Nations which was established in 1919 was dissolved in 1946 after 27 years of valuable activity and effort due to its shortcoming in control and reining in international problems; it was during this time that *United Nations* was founded officially in 1945 after World War II with a new image and vaster responsibilities and capabilities; though *United Nations* has a greater dimension and organization, it lacks the necessary organizational system and capabilities; as a result in the past decades there has been suggestions for correcting its organization from countries and international organizations and is being followed up.

With a correct understanding of the organization of international foundations, and after control and management of his world, through understanding and dialog and following human rights, mankind can enjoy the right of taking advantage of a peaceful life without war and stress and enter a humane world, which paves the way for international cooperation; this human understanding and achievement started from the time that mankind understood that under no circumstances he can take all human beings under his control, and idea and policy; the very same thing he has been after for centuries and under no circumstances and no way he couldn't achieve it, and he couldn't add anything but crime and tyranny to his records! Anyway he has the understanding of great human values and he has to reform and reinforce global management, and cut all ways of penetration of ignorant power seekers to human life forever and guarantee peace and tranquility along with great spiritual and physical progress, even though he is still very weak in this regard as:

A brief about the recent wars and power-seeking of history of mankind, with the goal of political, economical, religious, cultural and scientific supremacy ...

The history of mankind has been witness to numerous wars, power seeking, and domineering for the reason of control over the life of others, and as a result imposing their thoughts and ideas, and eventually governance over human world; below items are only a brief through introducing websites which talk about them in contemporary era:

1/ http://en.wikipedia.org/wiki/Category:Wars_by_type
2/ http://en.wikipedia.org/wiki/Religious_war
3/ http://en.wikipedia.org/wiki/Category:Religion_and_violence
4/ http://en.wikipedia.org/wiki/Category:Religion-based_wars
5/ http://en.wikipedia.org/wiki/List_of_wars
6/ http://en.wikipedia.org/wiki/List_of_invasions
7/ http://en.wikipedia.org/wiki/List_of_treaties
8/ http://en.wikipedia.org/wiki/List_of_wars_and_disasters_by_death_toll
9/ http://en.wikipedia.org/wiki/List_of_ongoing_conflicts
10/ http://en.wikipedia.org/wiki/List_of_wars_2003current:

The list of the wars which have happened since 2003

This is a list of wars launched from 2003 onwards

(Other wars can be found in the historical lists of wars and the list of wars extended by diplomatic irregularity.)

Start	Finish	Name of Conflict	Belligerents	
			Victorious party *(if applicable)*	Defeated party *(if applicable)*
2003	2009	War in Darfur		
2003	2003	2003 invasion of Iraq	United States United Kingdom Australia Poland KDP PUK INC	Iraq Syrian volunteers Arab volunteers Ansar al-Islam Foreign Volunteers
2003	2010	Iraq War		
2004	Ongoing	Baluchistan conflict		
2004	Ongoing	War in North-West Pakistan		
2004	Ongoing	Iran–Party for a Free Life in Kurdistan conflict		
2004	2004	2004 Haitian rebellion	United States United Nations Stabilization Mission in Haiti National Revolutionary Front for the Liberation of Haiti	Haiti
2004	2007	Central African Republic Bush War	Central African Republic Chad	UFDR rebels APRD rebels CPJP rebels FDPC rebels

				MLCJ rebels
			MINURCAT MICOPAX (CEEAC)	
2004	2004	Operation Rainbow	Israel	Hamas Islamic Jihad PRC
2004	2010	Sa'dah insurgency		
2004	2009	Conflict in the Niger Delta		
2004	Ongoing	South Thailand insurgency		
2004	2004	Operation Days of Penitence	Israel	Hamas
2004	2004	2004 French–Ivorian clashes	France	Côte d'Ivoire
2004	2009	Kivu conflict		
2005	Ongoing	Civil war in Chad (2005–present)		
2005	2008	Mount Elgon insurgency	Kenya	Sabaot Land Defense Force
2006	Ongoing	Mexican Drug War		
2006	2006	Operation Summer Rains	Israel	Hamas Fatah (Al-Aqsa Martyrs' Brigades & Tanzim) PRC Islamic Jihad Palestinian Army of Islam
2006	2006	2006 Lebanon War	Both sides claim victory	
2006	2006	Operation Astute	Australia New Zealand Malaysia Portugal East Timor (Government Troops) UNMIT soldiers	Renegade elements of the FDTL
2006	2009	War in Somalia (2006–2009)	**2006-2008 Invasion and Insurgency** Ethiopia Transitional Federal Government Punt land Galmudug pro-Ethiopian warlords United States United Kingdom AMISOM: • Uganda • Burundi	Islamic Courts Union

			• Kenya **After 2009 Ethiopian withdrawal** Alliance for the Re-liberation of Somalia al-Shabaab Ras Kamboni Brigades Jabhatul Islamiya Muaskar Anole Eritrea (alleged)	
2006	2009	Fatah–Hamas conflict	Hamas	Fatah
2007	Ongoing	Operation Enduring Freedom – Trans Sahara		
2007	2009	Tuareg Rebellion (2007–2009)		
2007	2007	2007 Lebanon conflict	Lebanon	Fatah al-Islam Jund al-Sham
2007	Ongoing	Civil war in Ingushetia		
2007	2008	2007–2008 Kenyan crisis	Kenya	
2008	2008	Operation Hot Winter	Israel	Hamas
2008	2008	2008 Mardakert skirmishes		
2008	2008	2008 invasion of Anjouan	Comoros African Union: • Sudan • Tanzania • Senegal • Libya France[1]	Anjouan
2008	2008	2008 conflict in Lebanon	Hezbollah Amal Movement Syrian Social Nationalist Party Free Patriotic Movement Lebanese Democratic Party	Future Movement Progressive Socialist Party
2008	Ongoing	Cambodian–Thai border stand-off		
2008	2008	Djiboutian–Eritrean border conflict	Djibouti	Eritrea
2008	2008	2008 South Ossetia war	Russia	Georgia

			South Ossetia Abkhazia	
2008	2009	Gaza War	Israel	Hamas Al-Qassam Brigades Al-Aqsa Martyrs' Brigades Abu Ali Mustapha Brigades Islamic Jihad Al-Quds Brigades PRC Other
2009	Ongoing	Sudanese nomadic conflicts		
2009	Ongoing	Insurgency in the North Caucasus		
2009	Ongoing	War in Somalia (2009–)		
2009	2009	2009 Nigerian sectarian violence	Nigeria	Boko Haram
2009	Ongoing	South Yemen insurgency (2009–present)		
2010	Ongoing	Yemeni al-Qaeda crackdown		
2010	2010	2010 Eritrea–Ethiopia border skirmish	Eritrea	Ethiopia
2010	2010	2010 South Darfur clash		
2010	2010	2010 South Kyrgyzstan riots	Kyrgyzstan	Kyrgyzstani **Kyrgyz** gangs • Pro-Bakiyev Kyrgyz Other pro- Bakiyev forces • Tajik contractors • Tajikistani Tajiks • Russian Tajiks • Other mercenaries Uzbekistani Kyrgyz • Sokh Uzbekistani Kyrgyz[1] • Sogment Uzbekistani Kyrgyz Islamic Movement of Uzbekistan (alleged) Kyrgyzstani **Uzbeks** • Pro-provisional government civilians Uzbekistani Uzbek civilians • Sokh Uzbekistani Uzbeks

				Uzbekistan (limited involve.)
2010	2010	2010 Kingston conflict	Jamaica	Shower Posse drug cartel
2010	2010	2010 Mardakert skirmish	Nagorno-Karabakh Armenia	Azerbaijan
2010	2010	2010 Israel–Lebanon border clash	Israel	Lebanon

References (From Wikipedia, the free encyclopedia . 03/09/2010):

1.   ^ AFP (2008-03-25). "African forces invade rebel Comoros island". *Relief Web*. http://reliefweb.int/rw/rwb.nsf/db900sid/MMAH-7D39UC?OpenDocument. Retrieved 2008-10-01.

Due to the small and big wars and conflicts of recent one and two centuries, tens and hundreds of millions of innocent people have been killed or become homeless and vagrant; the tyranny and crime like this which has been imposed on mankind is unbelievable and unconceivable; and this is exactly the thing which has occurred and has been inflicted due to the selfishness and power-seeking of the Satanic 10% for gaining power and dominance over the life of oppressed mankind! ….

A brief about the human actions and efforts of mankind, for eradicating tensions and establishing pervasive peace and tranquility, through foundation of international organizations and universal measures and …

Mankind in the course of his history and through his general peaceful religious and or political and cultural callings has tried to maintain his humane tranquility and growth in his life and establish it, but in the recent one or two centuries his efforts have become more pervasive; below this article - as a list and in the form of website addresses - we have listed recent efforts of mankind for establishing peace and international cooperation:

1/ http://en.wikipedia.org/wiki/League_of_Nations

2/ http://en.wikipedia.org/wiki/United_Nations

3/ http://en.wikipedia.org/wiki/World_Federalist_Movement

4/ http://en.wikipedia.org/wiki/United_Nations_Global_Compact

5/ http://en.wikipedia.org/wiki/Dialogue_Among_Civilizations

6/ http://en.wikipedia.org/wiki/Interfaith_dialog

7/ http://en.wikipedia.org/wiki/Institute_for_Interreligious_Dialogue

8/ http://en.wikipedia.org/wiki/Peace_movement

9/ http://en.wikipedia.org/wiki/Global_citizenship

10/ http://en.wikipedia.org/wiki/Parliament_of_the_World's_Religions

11/ http://en.wikipedia.org/wiki/Democratic_World_Federalists

12/ http://en.wikipedia.org/wiki/World_government

13/ http://en.wikipedia.org/wiki/World_Social_Forum

14/ http://en.wikipedia.org/wiki/Earth_Charter

15/ http://en.wikipedia.org/wiki/University_for_Peace

16/ http://en.wikipedia.org/wiki/Alter-globalization

17/ http://en.wikipedia.org/wiki/Global_governance

18/ http://en.wikipedia.org/wiki/World_Peace

19/ http://en.wikipedia.org/wiki/Global_Peace_Index

20/ http://en.wikipedia.org/wiki/1973_World_Congress_of_Peace_Forces

21/ http://worldparliament-gov.org

...

And in the field of Human Rights are:

http://en.wikipedia.org/wiki/Universal_Declaration_of_Human_Rights
- History of human rights
- Human Rights
- Humphrey Draft of the Universal Declaration of Human Rights
- Portal: Human rights
- Timeline of young people's rights in the United Kingdom
- Timeline of young people's rights in the United States
- Declaration of Human Duties and Responsibilities

Celebration of the 60th Anniversary of UDHR

- Maryland Law UDHR 60 Conference – 23–25 October 2008
- UDHR 60 Connecticut Conference – December 2008
- Know Your Rights 2008
- Youth Celebrate the 60th Anniversary of the UDHR CASHRA, the John Humphrey Centre and Taking IT Global join forces
- Interfaith Cooperation and the Protection of Human Rights and Dignity. Event celebrating the 60th anniversary of the UN-UDHR

Non-binding agreements

- Cairo Declaration on Human Rights in Islam, 1990
- Vienna Declaration and Program of Action, 1993
- United Nations Millennium Declaration, 2000
- Declaration on the Rights of Indigenous Peoples, 2007

National human rights law

- Golden Bull, Hungary, 1222
- English Bill of Rights and Scottish Claim of Right, 1689
- Virginia Declaration of Rights, June 1776
- United States Bill of Rights, completed in 1789, approved in 1791
- Declaration of the Rights of Man and of the Citizen, France 1789
- Canadian Charter of Rights and Freedoms, 1982

International human rights law

- European Convention on Human Rights, 1950
- Convention Relating to the Status of Refugees, 1954
- Convention on the Elimination of All Forms of Racial Discrimination, 1969
- International Covenant on Civil and Political Rights, 1976
- International Covenant on Economic, Social and Cultural Rights, 1976
- Convention on the Elimination of All Forms of Discrimination Against Women, 1981
- Indigenous and Tribal Peoples Convention, 1989
- Convention on the Rights of the Child, 1990
- Charter of Fundamental Rights of the European Union, 2000

Rights of peoples
- African Charter on Human and Peoples' Rights
- African Commission on Human and Peoples' Rights
- African Court on Human and Peoples' Rights
- Declaration of the Rights of the Negro Peoples of the World
- Declaration of Rights of Peoples of Russia
- Declaration on the Rights of Indigenous Peoples
- Judges of the African Court on Human and Peoples' Rights
- Universal Declaration of the Rights of Peoples
- Universal Declaration on the Rights of Peoples

Rights of future generations
- Foundation for the Rights of Future Generations

Linguistic rights
    Universal Declaration of Linguistic Rights

In the course of time the more the wars and conflicts have become, the more the efforts of mankind has become to solve them; but it seems these efforts and measures will never end! ....

The necessity of formation of:
Universal Society of Standard Human

Standard Humanism is a new thought based on respecting the beliefs of one another; with the goal of international life based on international human peace and unity; Standard Humanism deeply believes that we are the best human beings and are worthy of spending the best complete human life; hence in order to reach a world which is worthy of our human life, first of all, we must respect one another in the most complete manner which is possible and respect the right of one another; from the viewpoint of Standard Humanism all the positive things that human world has gained are the facts which have been created by the Creator of the world which should be respected! A model and worthy human being that knows his right and his limit, and in a human world respects them, as a result respects the right and limit of others in an equal way and respects the human rights of all human beings in enjoying a life which is worthy of mankind and deems it legal and acceptable .

From the viewpoint of Standard Humanism all that the positive things that human world has, is the truth and legal, and enjoying them is the right of everyone, as a result he believes in the formation of Universal Society of Standard Human to achieve all that human gains to the benefit of all human beings; because it is only through a pervasive human society (Which is the right of all the people of the world) which this becomes possible.

Based on the thought of Standard Human:

1/ Management and politics of the world is a truth, hence all the people of the world should take advantage of a humane government and management devoid of penetration of the Satanic 10%; a government which will build the best and the most successful human society with its guidance and control, and prepare the conditions for materialistic and spiritual regional and universal growth and development.

2/ Religions and beliefs, and human thoughts and beliefs are truth, hence all human beings should take advantage of the best and purest beliefs based on their assessment and need, and saturate their spiritual and celestial and social needs through it.

3/ Culture and art, and the customs and rituals of the world are the truth, and as a result they should be revived in the most beautiful, and noble and dynamic and the most modern manner possible and change the shape and color of the world beautiful; this is the right of world nations to use all their cultural knowledge and design their life in a beautiful manner and spend it.

4/ The science and knowledge of the world is the truth, hence all the people of the world should take advantage of the gifts of science and knowledge, and the light and growth it bestows to the life of human beings.

5/ The economics and commerce of the world is the truth, hence all the people of the world should take advantage of healthy work and commerce circumstances and economical activities, and get rid of hunger, poverty, toil and oppression and be saved from them.

Standard Human is a human who is just and truth-seeking in an absolute manner ....

These are all the main and preliminary rights and the necessary and essential rights of mankind; all human beings have the right to take advantage of these gifts in an equal manner and make use of a suitable human life; *the responsibility for creating practical framework for realizing these rights and supporting them is the direct responsibility of Universal Society of Standard Human* - which is made up of *representatives of all the countries of the world -,* which through coordination of government and internal management of the countries of the world will provide circumstances to make use of them; this is a reciprocal management and executive system which makes universal cooperation and coordination reach to its peak ….

In return of the guarantee and execution and making these apprising these rights, human beings, groups, nations and countries of the world have some duties in return too; to understand and distinguish what to be understood from reciprocal human rights against making use of these infinite beautiful materialistic and spiritual gifts, which is quite impossible and difficult for the Satanic 10%, but very simple and quite understandable for the 70% positive by understanding humane and moral principles; as follows:

Individual and social, and international and universal reciprocal rights of mankind versus saving measures taken by Universal Society of Standard Human

In Individual and Social Life: (Regarding people)

1- You believe in a belief; first of all if you have acquired it in a domestic way or inherited it, you should have an honest study to find the truth regarding the thoughts and beliefs and other rituals, so if you come to the conclusion that your belief is not the ideal belief for you and not the one you have been dreaming about! Eventually you change it and choose the more correct and more complete belief; secondly if you realize that your initial belief is a correct and acceptable one, you will implement the teachings of your belief with a better knowledge from now on; and this honest effort of yours at the same time will expand your outlook towards the world around you and you will realize that there are other human beings who live in this universe, which have legitimate and acceptable beliefs for themselves, and are living their lives through following these teachings and customs.

2- If your belief has another subgroup, which in the course of history, and in different forms has gone through changes, try to go to its roots and find the truth about it and study it and reach the origin and truth of your belief, so you can eradicate the impurities in the beliefs of your society which has fallen on your shoulder as much as you can and by following the correct and true principles of your belief and viewpoint help towards cleansing and health of your belief.

3- Your belief and your belief towards the culture and society and your understanding and need is the best and the most correct one for you, and the belief of another person depending on their knowledge and understanding is the best for them; as a result one should respect all beliefs and thoughts and shouldn't create chaos in the atmosphere of his life and society with prejudice and satanic and ignorant superiority.

4- Carry out the teachings of your belief in a correct and complete way as human beliefs and thoughts have a man forming and society forming role.

5- Take care of your personal and social hygiene and cleanliness.

6- Try to propagate humane morality and respect and decorum in all aspects of your life.

7- Respect the social rules of your society and universal society.

8- Carry out your job and vocation and social duty with honesty and in the best possible way.

9- Make use and preserve the nature and cleanliness and the greenness of your environment and the world.

10- With mental calmness, and deep honesty of your heart, and mental understanding and logic try to live your life and make a living.

11- Take care of the health of your body and soul through continuous exercise and movement.

12- Try to help other people in any part of the world in any possible manner, in case of need.

13- Donate from your property and wealth to make the poor and those in need happy and also bring joy to your soul and give alms; giving away your money is a suitable mental exercise against the penetration of the energy and the attribute of penny pinching which comes from the Satanic ignorance; As a result by giving away your money and also by forgiving those who have oppressed you unintentionally you will purify your soul and save it from the dominance of mercenary and violence.

14- Always seek for reaching for the best, healthiest and the most superior, bearing in mind equality and fairness and observing the rights of others.

15- Stand strong and stable against oppression and injustice and support justice and peace.

16- Treat the ignorant with humane and psychological methods - and not through stubbornness and harsh reactions.

17- Observe the personal sanctum of others and don't enter it without permission.

18- Prohibit immoral acts and indecent acts and support humane acts.

19- Observe justice and fairness in all aspects of your in-dividual and social life.

20- Never leave studying and seeking science and truth.

21- ....

In International and Universal Life:

(In regards to governments)

1- Your efforts and programming, on the way for international understanding and cooperation, should be in an acceptable manner for taking care of international regulations.

2- In cases where it is needed, with humanitarian aid they should help countries which need aid.

3- They should avoid aggressive and power-seeking thoughts which is exclusive to the Satanic 10%.

4- If you are in political and ideological and cultural and other tensions with other countries, consider understanding and dialog as the only means for solving your problem and don't look for tension and hostile frictions.

5- If a country is against the existing universal order, - whether due to approved or unapproved reasons - it should understand that any change is only legal and acceptable through a universal society and not through individual stubbornness and creating tensions and terrorist acts and ….

6- If a country has a thesis and theory and thought which can change and reform world order, it has to be legalized through universal organizations; history of mankind has been witness to one-sided measures of small and big powers for several times, which has led to nothing but defeat of that thought and creation of universal insecurity, as a result the only solution for re-forming the world is a solution which is legitimated by all the world and accepted universally; *the claims of justice seekers without presenting any solution that satisfies the whole world and takes into account the right of all human beings is nothing but an effort in line of power seeking of the thoughts of the person who has made the claims; ….*

7- Countries and thoughts which have the imagination and thoughts for universal reform should know that they first should reform themselves, but this type of claimants who mostly are among the Satanic 10% only think of power seeking and disrupting peace and tranquility of mankind.

8- Thoughts of a single party ruling over countries and es-pecially the varied world is a traditional and outdated belief, and even super powers, whether good or bad in the course of history have not been able to establish a universal government which is successful under the governance of a single party; such a government may be able to govern over a small area of the people of a country and unite them and force them to unite and imprison some of them and or remove the opposition one way or another, but it can never force the people of the world to obey it and or kill some of them and think that it is governing over the world! This type of belief belongs to the Satanic 10% who have tried to take control of the world in the past decades, but never succeeded and will never succeed.

9- The solution to world problems is only through universal unity and through international organizations.

10- The solution to world problems is only through wisdom and logic and understanding.

11- If oppression and anarchy rules over human world, the way to fight it, is unity of the countries that fight oppression through their own unity and reform, and as a result uniting other countries with themselves step by step, until positive forces gain power through political, cultural and economical relations and eventually they can have a positive impact on their world and move the human world towards justice; countries who are against universal oppression and try to be against the world through ignorant and stubborn methods will only attract universal hate and lack of international cooperation towards themselves.

12- A country which cannot overcome its problems is not eligible to have a legal and acceptable claim for solving the problems of the world.

13- It is favorable that leaders that have not been able to carry out their legal duties in the field of leading their country, should honestly apologize to the people of their country and quit their job.

14- There is only *one rational law* which can be the fundamental and basic base of international rules, a law which is the result of collective intellect of human world, and not only one country and or a thought and a special group which will meet the favorable and opposite right of all the nations and people of the world.

15- The present world, is not the a world which is worthy of the life of present human beings, and through order and a great and inclusive system it has to be reformed.

....

All these and many other issues seem very complicated and complex in the mind of the Satanic 10%, because these are the same people who are not able to solve simple equations such as 2+2=4; of course even if they know the answer, with the goal and intention of bringing chaos in the world and reaching their Satanic purposes they will endanger the security and world peace! ....

The government attributes of the Satanic 10%

1. Power seeking, avarice and superiority; 2. Weakness in management of the country, in political, ideological, cultural, scientific and economic departments; 3. Political weakness in correct international interactions; 4. Political self-immersion; 5. Inclination towards dictatorship and repression of the opposition; 6. Hiding the truth and lying; 7. Justification of one's deeds through envision and making one superior over others; 8. Threatening world security; 9. Annihilating world peace and tranquility; ....

The individual attributes of the Satanic 10%

1. Selfishness, being an egocentric and seeking superiority; 2. Violence in his behavior; 3. Prejudice and ignorance in his belief; 4. Being bad-tempered and ill-behaved towards those who are weaker than him; 5. Ignoring the rights of others; 6. Oppression and crime; 7. Moral corruption; 8. Being occupied in immoral and inhuman affairs; 9. Disrupting social comfort; 10. Running away from law; 11. Mercenary; 12. Worshiping persons; ....

Basically why Standard Humanism hates and loathes the Satanic 10% so much?! *(Please see page 293)*

The reason is:

1/ In the area of management and politics, they were either retarded and demolished the materialistic and spiritual resources of nations and countries with their mismanagement and keep their country underdeveloped, or they are sly and lying and power seeking and trick their people to implement what they want by coming into power and become dominant over the power and riches of nations and countries, and make life bitter for them and oppress them.

2/ In the area of religions and beliefs they are either prejudiced or seeking superiority and power seeking, and or businessman and an investor! They spread schism among the pure human religions and beliefs in order to create their own party and group within them and spread their superiority seeking; they spread the culture of worshiping persons so that by showing the fact that they are near to that superior person they can elevate their position and stance among people and establish their own set up for exploiting people; *the Satanic 10% are person-followers and worshipers, but Standard Humanism is absolutely law worshiper;* They have lost their stance in the face of the naivety of people who have considered them to be great human beings and they believe themselves to be superiors in this world; some of them who realize that their beliefs are rootless from the beginning will keep quiet in the face of their followers so that they don't lose their stance and job; ... Basically all human religions and beliefs emerge and find identity and are created from celestial revelations to prophets or truth seeking individuals, as a result in their original form they are complete and correct, but the followers of ignorance and power seeking will make its identity national and patriotic by polluting it and mingling it with superstition, and make shift customs and rituals, and confiscate and take possession of it to their own advantage; some of these beliefs may have the capacity to gradually walk the path of evolution, naturally this type of beliefs and their branches and subgroups are exceptions and deserve respect; ....

Religion is made by the Truth, and customs and rituals is made by people (By religion we mean all materialistic and spiritual human beliefs!) and here also we have some rituals which have <u>national and patriotic inclinations</u>, but beliefs which have <u>universal inclinations</u> if deviate from their original pure form and incline more towards national and patriotic form they can no longer implement their universal goal; as by the change and limiting a religion and dynamic and pervasive belief to the national rituals and customs of a country, it will resemble a bird imprisoned in a cage who loses his freedom and dynamism and gets limited and small; this is one of the most important goals and ominous attacks of the Satanic 10%, to spread schism among thoughts and beliefs and tear them apart and divide each part among one nation and keep them busy with this thought that they have got the share which has the better and more correct part in it and as a result you have conceived the truth better and you are the most superior!

Religion and belief has a pervasive human identity, and *customs and protocols have a national and patriotic identity;* *world truth* forms religion to bring us the gift of peace and justice and pave the way for human beings, (Religions and beliefs form in the route for seeking pure truth and better life) and customs and protocols form by *people!* So that the beautiful and colorful regional life on earth, and their national and patriotic life is formed by it; changing the pervasive and truth seeking truth religion and belief to national and patriotic rituals and customs are one of the tricks of ignorance and Satanic deception for deviating them and neutralizing them from *the main route of forming human beings and their forming the society!*

3/ The Satanic 10% annihilates cultures and civilizations, and through wars and or propaganda etc. they show themselves as the superior race, and try to show them as better people through fake razzle-dazzle of customs and rituals and cultures and govern it over human world, so that through political, ideological, cultural, scientific and economic superiority-seeking, they try to dominate over human world; on the other hand and also from within (From inside the culture of countries) the ignorant forces who have joined forces with Satan will present an archaic and old picture of the culture and customs and rituals of nations of the world by entering superstition in them so that the ways of cultural penetration of alien culture can be completely opened, ...

4/ Also in the area of science and knowledge the Satanic 10% call the mental science sidetracking, and by keeping the people and nations illiterate they spread their pervasive domination and exploitation, ...

5/ In the area of economy and commerce, by domineering over sources of riches, they keep human world poor and under their domination while it is at the peak of being rich, and it is kept under exploitation and domination, ...

Under any circumstance expansion and penetration of them is for the purpose of oppressing human beings in an extensive and pervasive manner, hence the only way to save human beings - and also keeping their authenticity - is a strong, dynamic and systematic human unity ....

Hence Standard Humanism which thinks only about humanity and honesty deeply abhors and hates the Satanic 10%.

Note: From Standard Humanism point of view *religion and belief* is a collection of truth-seeking principles and rules with the goal of establishing peace and social justice (Including philosophies and different materialistic and spiritual outlooks towards the world) which might have their own special culture deep within themselves; *culture, customs and rituals* engulf the shape and color and beauties of life; *culture and civilization* is made up of all that a nation has; ....

By Satan and the Satanic 10% in this book we mean the ignorant, selfish, prejudiced, avarice and power-seeking nature of a group of human beings who have made the life of human beings painful and dark with their ignorance and oppression and avarice.

The Satanic 10% the prejudiced and ignorant, selfish, and power-seeking and avarice people who dominate and control over all that the human beings own and create schism, pain, poverty, problems and lag for human beings; the expansion of science and knowledge and the strong and pervasive universal human management are among the most important solutions for eradicating the domination and control of this group of ignorant and avarice people.

Standard Humanism after cleansing human world through development of science and enlightenment, and humanism and justice, and also through strong management will protect the life of human beings from the penetration of ignorance and oppression and selfishness and power seeking of the Satanic 10% over human life.

Standard Humanism will leash in the vicious carnal nature which is concealed or dominant over the soul and nature of part of human beings (The Satanic 10%) and will form the peaceful life of the third millennium of humans.

The conclusion is considering all the measures taken and the valuable efforts of human universal society in the route for establishing peace and tranquility, and also growth and universal development in the past 100 years, his achievements based on the existing data is very weak and negligible, hence to eradicate the dominance of the Satanic 10% and establishment of permanent peace and justice formation of Universal Society of Standard Human and its human and pervasive management is inevitable and vital.

Human Life in Worldwide Standard Human Society
In the world and Universal Society of Standard Human:

1/ Collective knowledge, and collective belief, and collective management will be established and ruling.

2/ The management of Standard Human will control human weaknesses and will control all aspects of his life (Politics, religion, culture, economy and science) in the best possible way, and create a world which gives grandeur to human beings.

3/ By accepting the doctrine of Standard Humanism the traditional ignorance which spreads schism and is ruling over some of religious and ideological groups - Which has been a reason for a large group of clean hearted people to run away from healthy human beliefs and incline towards pseudo beliefs - will fade away, and by establishment of clear human laws they will get near to the true essence of human unity and peace.

4/ Standard Humanism will visualize the dream of peace and human unity which is the ideal for human religions and beliefs.

5/ With the thought and management of Standard Human, human life will freshen up and become renewed in a spectacular way; the authenticity of cultures will be preserved in a beautiful manner and architecture, attire and customs and rituals of them will reach their origin and dynamism, and they will shine brightly at their ideal and standard level.

6/ After understanding and Standard Humanism school of thought becoming pervasive and establishment of Universal Society of Standard Human, a lot of political and religious groups, and superstitious cultures and economic organizations which ransacked people were dissolved and vanished from the face of the earth and never had the chance to be present in the humane and animated human society - to impose pain and ransack people.

7/ The thought of standard human is the thought of moving towards positivity, without discussion and tension and involvement and ideological tension with other ideas.

8/ The thought of standard human is the first common universal thought of mankind which heralds a peaceful life along with respect towards others.

9/ The Satanic 10% is vicious and power seeking, selfish, superiority-seeking and cheeky and wanton, and the positive people are weak in face of them and under oppression; as a result the only way to overcome these oppressive and avarice ignorant people is human unity; otherwise oppression and pains will always spread its wings over human life; *human unity under the umbrella of universal law,* will control the Satanic 10% and will nullify its negative force and make it ineffective.

10/ Positive people under the shelter of law will fight with the Satanic 10% and by following the five humane principles of Standard Humanism and voting for establishment of Universal Society of Standard Human, will take control of their world.

11/ A model human being by accepting the five principles of Standard Humanism and practicing them will nullify the penetration of negative forces to human life and create a world devoid of selfishness and pride and avarice and greed and avidity and ignorance.

12/ Standard Humanism is a new humane experience, which will elevate humane level of thought and expectations one step further, and approximate it to the level of elite universal mentality and understanding and consideration.

13/ The Universal Society of Standard Human is a new universal management which will leave the control of the world in the hands of human beings.

14/ The management of the Universal Society of Standard Human is the management of honesty and wisdom and correctness.

15/ The management of the Universal Society of Standard Human, is the management and governance of humanity over human beings.

In the world and Universal Society of Standard Human:

The architecture of the world will get modernized and changed, and cities and villages and countries will be built again, in appropriate geographical locations where they are safe from flood and earthquake and storms and …; also the disperse of the population will be in a way that the population of cities will be based on need and proportionate with the capacity of the cities,
….

The architecture of cities and countries of the world will be designed and executed based on the geographical and climate situation, and based on their architectural culture, and with a combination of the best aspects of modern architecture, so that it can make human world new and modern once again; since *universal tourism* is one of the most important goals of

Standard Humanism, hence the world of human beings should have a lot of variety and should be beautiful and wonderful, and here architecture has the first word, ...

With the design and construction of a modern and beautiful world which has variety, wherever in the world we go to, we will see the variety in the architecture in cities, streets, buildings, shops, houses, parks, squares, monuments, churches, mosques, temples, restaurants, hotels, recreation centers, inns, roads and also the nature of the evergreen and beautiful world of ours and we will get joy from living with such variety in architecture in all parts of the world, and learn numerous lessons; also in our *human journey* to different parts of the world, we will get to know the people of the world and the numerous noble and beautiful cultures, the variety in customs and rituals, wonders, marvels, innovations and colorful cultural and artistic improvisations and all kinds of foods and delicacies and will taste from all of them, with the joy and tranquility that is our beautiful and worthy world because of the pervasive management of Universal Society of Standard Human all the poor and pained and needy people are saturated and rich! And there is no trace of privation and poverty in the world.

The world of Standard Human is the beautiful and noble world full of variety.

In the world and Universal Society of Standard Human:

1/ There is no trace of pain and hardship and poverty and oppression and adversity and misery there.

2/ World economy works for the benefit of the people of the world.

3/ There will be no poor country in the world to send humiliated people to the world so that they are forced to do humiliating jobs in other parts of the world and in rich countries, not because these jobs are humiliating in nature, but because you immigrate to a rich country because of the poverty in your country, you would be forced to choose jobs which will cause humiliation and mortification in face of your personality and your family; you will accept this personality humiliation because you have to! This personality mortification will abject you, and abjection the personality of man is not a humane act!

In the world and Universal Society of Standard Human the personality of a man will never be humiliated, as you will be working in your beautiful and rich country with pride and will reach the suitable social stance through complete vocational and personality satisfaction; you will only travel to another country along with your family that as a person you want to spend your free time on a touristic beautiful fun trip; and the people from other nations, when they see you with a different culture and a beautiful and different outfit who has travelled to their country, they will get happy seeing you and will love sitting down and chatting with you ....

This is the humane world of Universal Society of Standard Human, which appreciates the personality of all human beings to the level they are worthy of, and defends the dignity and personality of all human beings, a respect which will be visualized and put into through a worthwhile management and dynamic and elite humane laws.

In the world and Universal Society of Standard Human:

Commerce and industry and agriculture is managed and led in the most complete form, a coordinated management and in line with creating suitable jobs and production for all that is needed for living and in all sectors of work and production by economy and world commerce department which is managed in a coordinated manner, as a result the countries of the world will walk the road of growth and development in a special and unique manner.

Basically since the management of human world, based on Standard Human philosophy and thought, is the management of universal wisdom and knowledge, as a result all that mankind has is at the service of the best of a suitable life that can be envisioned for mankind; since *Standard Humanism deeply believes in human respect and human unity and human life,* hence it sees a superior and complete humane life in all the materialistic and spiritual aspects the right of all the African, American, Asian, European, people from Oceania and all the residential places all across the globe, with any ethnicity, nationality, color, language, religion, belief and culture will be preserved ....

Today's man should remove all the inhumane obstacles that are on his way for creating the best existence which is worthy of a humane life.

Today's man should build his human world at its best imaginable standards, and this is the inevitable task of humans.

We need the best world, as we are the best people worthy of spending the best human life.

Since Standard Humanism is a strong advocate of humanity and justice, and human peace and happiness to the benefit of all the human world, and sees himself responsible for establishing universal peace and humanity, as a result he believes that establishing justice and humanity should only be carried out through a universal, humane, and peace seeking powerful organization - who considers the benefit of all the people of the world with all their beliefs and cultures and tastes; ….

The stages of world reform

(Based on Standard Humanism)

After accepting the culture and belief of Standard Human, the world is ready for its fundamental and substantial change; and after the formation of Universal Society of Standard Human the stages of his complete and pervasive growth will commence:

1/ First mankind gets ready to accept Standard Humanism.

2/ The world will go toward formation and establishment of Universal Society of Standard Human - and its fundamental and systematic order.

3/ The serious resistance and objections of the Satanic 10% will commence, but with willpower and vigilance and universal unity it will soon become under control and annihilated.

4/ The strong management system of Universal Society will be established and reinforced, and start its renovation.

5/ The era for human flourish will start.

6/ Peace and tranquility will be established.

7/ The flow of positive energies in the world, and in religion, and in politics, culture, science and economy will get fast and with more tempo.

8/ The evolutional era of annihilation of the vicious nature of the destruction of the Satanic 10% and its annihilation starts.

9/ Justice and humanity will rule.

10/ Mankind will start moving towards the heaven on Earth - which is the prologue to the life on the true extraterrestrial Heaven (The life of mankind after this life).

11/ The next stage of human life on Earth and other galaxies and worlds will start; (Different physical and spiritual worlds) ….

After realizing the "the importance of reaching justice and peace and avoiding ignorance and oppression" mankind will be able to pass the stage of life in the world, and start the superior worlds after! Otherwise he will still be wandering and lost in the world of the Satanic 10% ….

The outcome of man's life on this Earth

The outlook of mankind towards continuing his life on the Earth, and the route of continuing it, and the form and its future has been experiencing variety, and different philosophies and theories have been presented in this regard, and preoccupied human mind to itself; mankind has always been curious and very concerned about the future of his life on this Earth! Curious from this point of view that what achievements will he gain in his future, and concerned whether he will continue to live in peace and tranquility or not! Mankind is concerned if he should await lethal events which will herald nightmares instead of tranquility for him? ....

Mankind looks at his future with concern in a way as if he has the least power and willpower over deciding his own destiny!!!

In order to understand man's outlook towards his future, we will take a look at the horizon of his look and his expectations in different stages and levels of his life:

1/ The first stage and level;
The real world of human life

Mankind in the real stage of his life which has commenced from thousands of years ago on this Earth and is still going on, looks at his world and the future of his world as such that he has to be powerful and rich so that to be able to overcome his enemies and protect his life; ....

In this stage he only thinks about his own survival and doesn't see anything beyond it; continuing the current status and nature of the world (The universal management and leadership system of power and riches) the current powers of the world, sooner or later will give way to other destructive powers, who will enter the world into another new cycle of oppression and inaptitude, the dominance of another group, which might have a narrower outlook towards the world of human beings, and follow and create wider satanic and more dangerous goals for mankind, as a result history will repeat its repetitive cycle and mankind will continue to be in his primitive and traditional life, or it is possible that human world might get near to its doom due to any natural or unnatural reason and come to an end ....

2/ The second stage and level;
The dream world of human life

In the dream stage of his life, mankind has numerous and colorful imaginations of his future! Through imaginations, and envisioning and story making, and or through religious or ideological beliefs he is looking for a savoir to create an ideal humane life based on his needs; ....

At this stage in addition to spending his routine and natural life in the real world, mankind without making any worthwhile effort is still hopefully expecting for his problems to be solved miraculously and in a supernatural manner ....

3/ The third stage and level;
The World of Standard Humanism

In the world of the Standard and model human, the man will reach a level of high human understanding and wisdom that in a united and systematic manner he will construct his humane world in a pervasive manner, taking into account the right of all people, and in all materialistic and spiritual aspects; a world which he has built based on wisdom and intellect, and under-standing and sense of distinction, and his power, and started his legal and legitimate life in it and continues living in it; ….

Mankind in the third millennium of his life has this understanding and sense of distinction to get out of the first and second level of his life and build his worthwhile life devoid of ignorant, selfish and oppressive penetrations of the Satanic 10%, and also without any need for endless dreaming (Be it right or wrong) only with a strong management and through his human unity, and commence his worthwhile life in the *world of reality* ….

In the world of Standard Humanism mankind will reach to a level of understanding and intellect that he will discover all the scientific and philosophical truth hidden in his first world and achieve great materialistic and spiritual mutation ….

Mankind in the world of Standard Humanism will be a progressed and mutated person who is reformed through the five principles of Standard Humanism and by human and strong management of Universal Society of Standard Human, he will commence his humane and animated world and his further superior lives ….

The main goal and intention of Standard Humanism is turning and changing from the primitive nature and tempera-ment of current life, towards the nature and temperament and system of "Standard type growth" (Exiting from the current primitive superiority-seeking circle of life and entering the world of progressive and gradual growth towards higher levels, and discovering more humane capacities and humane life).

Who is a Standard Humanist?!

A standard and model human being (Christian, Muslim, Hindu, Buddhist, Shinto, Taoist, Sikh, Confucius, Zoroastrian, Jainisit, Jew, Communist, Secular ... and Asian, African, American, European and from any part of the world from any ethnicity and nationality and color and language) and as a *Standard Humanist:*

1/ He believes in God and the creator and the nourisher of the world = The truth of the world, as the common point and the connecting symbol of him with all other human beings where all the truth and honesty stems from that truth, whether with a real and deep belief or with a symbolic and conventional one - which unites him and other people against forces and ignorant and oppressive and selfish forces.

2/ He believes in one of the religions, beliefs, and human thoughts from any colorful and various spiritual and ma-terialistic type and forms and builds his individual and social and spiritual nature based on its teachings.

3/ He pays equal respect to all credited human beliefs and believes in the absolute right of enjoying a complete human life for all its followers, and as a result the *common universal law* which is the result of the common points of all human beliefs and is compiled by Universal Society of Standard Human will be used as their international law in their universal interactions.

4/ To eradicate the domination of the Satanic 10% who has kept his life in pain and poverty and oppression in the past thousands of years he will vote for the formation of Universal

Society of Standard Human, with the hope that with its universal management justice and constitution, and pervasive growth and development is provided for all human beings with different types of tastes and thoughts in an equal manner and is established.

(A Standard and model human will vote for the formation of Universal Society of Standard Human through Standard Humanism website and or through the Facebook group and page of Standard Humanism: www.facebook.com/StandardHumanism and will try to propagate Standard Humanism with the hope of establishing a world which is worthy of Human beings).

5/ He pays special attention to his physical and spiritual, and individual and social hygiene and cleanliness and keeps his individual and collective life at utmost level of cleanliness and order and hygiene.

Standard Human/
Is a clean, sophisticated, and understanding person.

Standard Human/
Is a man who is absolutely truth seeker & worshiper.

Standard Human/
Is the man of the third Millennium.

*Each school of thought presents principles to imagine its ideal human who follows those principles in order to introduce him to the world, ... hence this ideal man of Standard Humanism too is a **Standard Human** who has accepted the five principles of Standard Humanism and found identity through them to construct his world in a humane and pervasive manner and by following the rights of other people with other thoughts and beliefs and gives the gift of complete materialistic and spiritual humane happiness to all those who live in this world.*

)(

Any meritorious person has this humane right to make the effort to propagate the culture of peace, justice and universal equality of Standard Humanism as the representative of this school of thought in any part of the world and in any legal and legitimate manner.

This book, is not a holy religious book and or an analytic political book, but it is *a humane book* addressing all human beings to take a step towards whatever is worthy of mankind and can be done by them, and it is done with the hope that in the third millennium with a human unity we succeed in getting a grip on our life.

Standard Humanism is a thought, philosophy and belief which is beyond religion, politics and human.

It is beyond religion as by cleansing human religions and beliefs, and by creating a healthy surface it will lead to the worthy and healthy flourish of all human religions and beliefs devoid of the penetration of the Satanic 10% and be able to establish peace among their followers.

It is beyond politics as it is superior to any politics and management and gives order to human world in a strong and complete manner, and in all aspects of human life, bearing in mind all the materialistic and spiritual rights of all men.

It is beyond all human as it brings the gift of health for the humane life for all children, girls, boys, women, men and elderly of the world from any religion, and nationality and color and ethnicity and language through its humane system, and strongly defends honesty, integrity, respect, identity and human justice.

This was the gift of God to me and I shared it with you.

Dariush Ghasemian Dastjerdi
September 15, 2010

My Earth

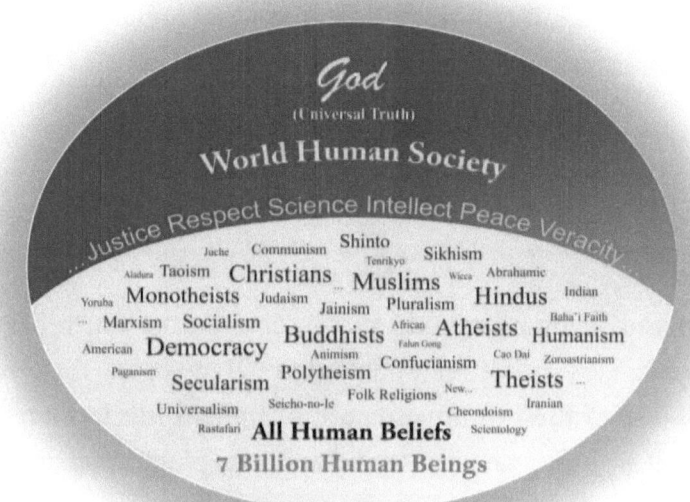

Standard Humanism©
www.standardhumanism.org / Founded by Dariush GH D - 2005/6

Standard Humanism
&
Worldwide Standard Human Society

By Dariush Ghasemian Dastjerdi
September 15, 2010 - Mysore India

Daily Pray in Standard Humanism, for All on the Earth:

<u>Me, as a Standard Human being</u>, with thank to the Creator of the beauties of the universe, live with good thought, good word & good deed; I believe that all the mankind by any religion, belief & race are respected and equal, and treat & respect all the people of the world, all the live and still creatures equally.

*- This, once a day pray, completes & covers all the other; also, helps to promote peace and human life progress.

The Final Word

Standard Humanism is the modern Management system and belief of mankind's third millennium - with the capability to establish peace and justice! With this motto that:

We need the best world, as we are the best human beings, Seven billion human beings ...

Standard Humanism is based on this basis and belief that:

1/ Human life from day one to this date on the Earth has been spent in a very primitive and traditional way; no thought and system due to the primitive nature of human life has been able to save it in a fair and pervasive and acceptable manner which is approved by everyone from poverty, oppression, massacre and crime and its shortcomings, as a result the pains and shortcomings and oppressions of his life have been there and even looking never-ending!

2/ To get out of this primitive and traditional life, positive thinking people with any belief and culture and nationality should equip themselves to the *five principles of Standard Humanism* - and by keeping all that they own, and not by losing them - change the nature of the primitive life of human beings and take human life to another world!!! *The difference between that world and today's world of mankind is the difference between underdeveloped men and men who have been kept underdeveloped in this era and those who have made changes in their life in the third millennium.*

(Standard Humanism advocates a **"Two Layers Identity"** for every human being, *First:* by equipping all with five principles of it in order to eliminate the rules of ignorance, oppression etc. from their life and, *Second:* by insisting anyone to live according to his/her belief and culture - at its best form - in a safe world by the support and the administration of *Worldwide Standard Human Society*).

3/ *Worldwide Standard Human Society* has this systematic characteristic based on believing the five superior fact of human life (Management and politics, religion and beliefs, culture and art, science, and economy) to provide for the right and need of all human beings and build and manage the complete and dynamic human life.

The main goal and intention of Standard Humanism is the change and turn from its current nature and essence, to the nature and essence and system of "a standard type growth" (Getting out of the current primitive cycle of seeking superiority and entering *the world of progressive and phase by phase growth towards higher stages, and discovering more human capabilities and human life*).

In other words/
The philosophy of Standard Humanism is:

1/ Believing in God (The absolute truth of the universe, the law of truth and honesty, the creator, energy and friend …) who has introduced and presented Himself (Itself!) to mankind through **ALL** peace and justice seeking religions and beliefs (Religious, social or political = spiritual or materialistic) to guide him in a route coordinated with his creation (Based on their capacity and capabilities).

2/ In the life of human beings there are **five superior facts** which build the complete human life in balance with one another ….

3/ Penetration of ignorance and oppression of 10% of mankind in the course of history has been cause for the impurity of these five superior facts and led to the pain of mankind in a way that he has never been able to form a life which he is worthy of in this world and establish peace and justice ….

4/ To save mankind in a way that he can reach the goals he has in this world and the lives he has after this world it is necessary that the 70% positive of the mankind who live among all the people of the world and among all the nations and cultures with different religions and beliefs - plus the 20% that are neutral among us - unite under the umbrella of Standard Humanism to take the control of human world from the Satanic 10% and reach the growth which is at their level.

5/ Standard Humanism is a management and social system, and a modern belief of the third millennium of human life which due to having a special system of its own which maintains and supports all that mankind has, it will form a sophisticated materialistic and spiritual complete life for mankind away from penetration of ignorance and oppression ....

- By reforming human life in both individual and social aspects of his life the possibility will become available that mankind can start a complete life in this world - with the highest standard level - and after passing it he can reach his other lives! Otherwise he will be struggling in the endless problems and hassles of this life forever and will never reach the stance he is worthy of ....

Let's accelerate the growth of our world by accepting Standard Humanism!

The claim letter of Standard Humanism

(Standard Humanism was established on September 15ᵗʰ, 2010 by Dariush Ghasemian Dastjerdi - born on February 8ᵗʰ, 1961 - after around ... years of contemplation and research).

Standard Humanism is an independent school of thought and belief, without any connection and association with any group and organization and culture and nation; this is a school of thought which is absolutely humanistic and independent with the goal of human unity and peace, and the hope of creating the chance to look for the best way for a complete and international humane life with the presence and cooperation of all the people of the world with all their thoughts and religions and cultural and political beliefs.

This is an international thought which goes beyond borders, with the goal of establishing peace and a life which is worthy of mankind through creditable universal organizations and with the presence of representatives from all the countries of the world in order to create the best chance for unity and peace and multilateral progress of mankind, and eradication of domination of the ignorant and the selfish and power-seeking people from the life of human beings.

Standard Humanism believes in creating the best world that is worthy of human life through formation of **Worldwide Standard Human Society,** as Standard Humanism believes that we are the best human beings hence we need the best world which is worthy of life for men, a world without the domination and penetration of the ignorant and oppressors and the selfish!

Standard Humanism thinks of establishing a world which is worthy of human life while maintaining all the cultures and beliefs and religions and politics! Not making everything vanish because of one school of thought and belief.

In the world of a Standard Human and Standard Humanism all the cultures and beliefs, the best policies will shine brightly through management and cleansing of the modern and pervasive system of Universal Society of Standard Human in their most ideal form, unlike the way they are in the world which is dominated by the Satanic 10% where everyone is fighting with one another and there is constant struggle and superiority seeking in order to make their own party or group victorious at the price of annihilating others!

The world of human beings in the course of history has moved phase by phase towards improving and making things positive but it still has not reached complete materialistic and spiritual maturation, and peace and joy in a way that we expect and are worthy of it! So with getting united and through *Standard Humanism* we get the chance to establish *the complete and worthy humane world,* and eradicate the penetration of negative and ruining forces that take the world of positive men towards annihilation and disappointment and oppression with superstition and ignorant predictions, as a result we will ruin the picture of a dark future and accelerate the growth of our world; *we need the best world, as we are the best human beings.*

* * *

In order to propagate an ideology which is beyond humans and covers the whole universe and thinks of establishing peace and justice and complete materialistic and spiritual progress of mankind, please introduce the book Standard Humanism to your friends and university centers and libraries which you know all across the world. You can do this through its website:

http://www.standardhumanism.org

Enclosures

Standard Humanism Comparison:
The comparison of Standard Humanism
Five Worldviews (by Dennis McCallum)
Worldview of Standard Humanism (In comparison)
To clear confusion about the concept of reality and truth!

The Satanic 10 percent and their world!!!
Before establishing the Worldwide Standard Human Society!
Invitation letter to adopt Standard Humanism ...
The First Headquarters of Standard Humanism!
New words
References
Comments
Biography
•••
...

Standard Humanism Comparison:

The comparison of Standard Humanism ...

(According to the "religionfacts.com" website)

<u>*1/ Origin & history*</u> – Sep. 15th 2010 Mysore India; by Dariush Ghasemian Dastjerdi

1/ Origin & history – Sep. 15th 2010 Mysore India; by Dariush Ghasemian Dastjerdi

<u>*2/ Adherents*</u> – Worldwide ...

<u>*3/ God(s) and universe*</u> – **God** means no face and group but the universal truth which covers all mankind under its eternal law equally ... **God** is a vast-wise energy! One alive energy which has wisdom and power to create and hold what has created! ... **It** (He) is not a person ....

God (the alive truth) always exists, and in the history of mankind by the needs of time and the capacity of the special situation of a specific territory and people, has emerged - <u>passing thru: reason, heart & soul</u> - as a kind of belief or religion to show and guide the human beings to their best way of life (<u>matched by their culture</u>).

God (Truth) is the <u>justice</u> and <u>peace</u>! This means all the religions, beliefs and philosophies, which were and are in our life and tried to protect mankind, all come from God! Any idea - as a set of recognized principles in the way of justice and avoiding oppression and ignorance - is a branch of truth and comes from God; that's why in the history of man we have tens and tens of beliefs and philosophies in various places and geographies to guide us, and each by the same essence (Seeking justice and peace) formed a specific belief, whether it be of religious nature, social nature or political nature! <u>This means all the peace-loving and justice-seeking ideas (Material or Spiritual) come from truth (We specify and name that truth as: God)!</u> ....

Therefore, we have Abrahamic religions; Iranian, Dharmic, Taoic, and Indigenous beliefs & religions and social & political beliefs and ideas etc. all from God ... to save specific people of a territory from injustice and oppression, according to their situations and needs.

By <u>peace and justice</u> (thru universal humanistic laws) we will be able to pass thru our goal of existence and start our other lives! (The Satanic 10 percent - by ruining the five top human life facts - never let to live in peace & justice, and that's why our life is poor and incomplete, with a never-ending process of correction ...).

Thus all our beliefs in the way of *showing the best way of life and to guide and correct our life* are from God, **All are of Truth and God.**

This means all are correct for their people and their culture; and all need to be treated and be prescribed for their covered areas, and not necessarily to others, except by their choice and will.

By this logic it is not possible to force **A** to **B**, or **C** to **A**, etc. Because the history of our real life has always proved the impossibility of that; now as always there is the problem of imposing ideas to others, something must be found to protect human life.

(*Imposing ideas and beliefs to other persons and territories come from two goals:* **1/** to help the others by what some have achieved as a good ideology and good way of life, in the positive way; **2/** to try to control the other, and to rule over the others - by the means of ideas and covering the others under their ideologies - because of selfishness and power-seeking nature of some groups or as I say and name them: *the satanic 10 percent oppressors and ignorant,* in the negative way).

In this way:

Adopting Standard Humanism - as the new international belief of 3rd millennium - in the <u>complex world of today</u> which any group tries to impose its idea to others is the new way of controlling human life to keep order for the sake of respecting and shining ALL ....

<u>In individual part</u> - Standard Humanism equips mankind with its five principles of a kind of needs which will let to live with respect and purifying all our having from the control of *Satanic 10 percent* ....

<u>In social and global part</u> - Worldwide Standard Human Society by its five departments of: 1/ politics & management; 2/ religions & beliefs; 3/ cultures & beauties of life; 4/ sciences & knowledge; and 5/ economics & trades, will administer the human life in <u>peace</u> and <u>justice</u> ....

God (Truth) has two major aspects:

1/ *from the social view:* as the laws & orders to correct social life in various forms (Christianity, Islam, Hinduism, Buddhism, Marxism, Secularism, etc.).

2/ *from the individual view:* as the positive and alive energy, and the One which helps man to grow spiritually by various ways of worshiping, prayer, meditation, TM, yoga, etc. To grow spiritually and to help the soul to become nearer to the more pure truth and to understand more purity and then to pass the life better; and to find the capacity of passing the steps of soul-growing for this life which would deserve us eventually to step in our other lives happier and completer!

Therefore there are varieties of beliefs & philosophies to help mankind to correct their social and individual life; it is important to mention again that all the beliefs would shine in their places of emergence, and imposing them to other places may cause problems unless people by their desire and consciousness adopt that.

God is the universal truth, energy and the creator of universe and nature; which in different places and times emerged through the specific culture and nature of a group of mankind (By various names ...) **to guide them to the best way of living and according to the goal of their existence, and according to their needs and capacities of life.** *(Please also refer to: The Concept of Truth and Reality section/ page 291).*

Truth means what is correct, and **Reality** means to build according to correct! To understand the truth of our existence and life purely helps us to build our life more correctly.

Mankind is in the first steps of their life! And it is not possible to capture all the truth of life and universe all in this step (this world) such as: what is exactly God? or what is the purpose of our creation? or is there any afterlife? etc. so first we should reach to peace and justice and then by finding enough energy and capacity of understanding, to realize more truth and reality, closer to the universal facts ... it is better first we concentrate our energy to correct our real life of now and then more facts and truths would appear to us by our new and higher capacities of understanding captured thru living in peace and justice; thus peace and justice is absolutely important to save us from primitive life of satanic 10 percent.

Maybe the entire Universe is an alive thing (mankind trying to discover it or name it as God)! And all of us are inside and part of that alive Object! If mankind by all their varieties reach to peace and justice, happiness and the perfect working of Universe would be seen ....

4/ Human situation and the purpose of life – According to Standard Humanism there are **70 percent** honest, pure and peace-loving human beings spread in all countries and among all nations, cultures, religions etc. **10 percent** oppressors and ignorant; and **20 percent** neutral ones, and Standard Humanism has been designed to hand over the control of the world of mankind to the hands of 70 percent positives far from the control and influence of negative 10 percent or better Satanic 10 percent who are ignorant and oppressive in order to bestow the gift of a bright and brilliant world of 3rd millennium to mankind.

There are **Five top human life Facts** there in our life (absolutely equal and balanced; any imbalance among the importance of them would not allow a perfect and correct human life and would not allow to pass human life to its highest levels of progress in this life and our other lives after death!). *They are: A/ Religions & beliefs ... B/ Politics & management ... C/ Cultures & beauties of our life ... D/ Knowledge & sciences ... E/ Economics & trades ... This means equality and respect to all that we have and all of our desires ...* (All of our life belongings are subcategories of these five top facts ...).

The oppression and ignorance of 10 percent of us (*The Satanic 10 percent***) always ruin these 5 top human life facts, to make mankind suffer and to damage our life ....**

To save our life and to pass the mankind's life to its most perfect situation - *in this world and afterlife* - 70 percent positive people (Who live in all nations with any peace-loving and justice-seeking religion, belief and idea) + 20 percent neutral ones among us, need to be united under the **Standard Humanism** *and* **Worldwide Standard Human Society Organization** (By keeping and protecting all our having) to end thousands year failure and mismanagement of human life and make the dream of **Peace, Justice and Human life progress** to become true and eventually mankind pass thru their goal of existence ....

Human life just by a correct compiling of: "reason, heart and soul" and in the way of a perfect joining of material & spiritual life, and with a universal worldview is complete, meaningful and wide in the size of mankind.

5/ *Afterlife* – Mankind after realizing the importance of: avoiding ignorance & oppression and establishing peace & justice, would be able to pass thru this life - by its highest standards of material & spiritual life - and open the other perfect lives, (Various worlds of physics and metaphysics) otherwise he would remain and wander in the poor and incomplete world of Satanic 10 percent eternally ... (**Worldwide Standard Human Society** through its five departments would dedicate Peace & Justice to mankind ...).

It is absolutely important to mention that only by peace & justice we will be able to pass thru our goal of existence and start our other lives!
(The Satanic 10 percent - by ruining the five top human life facts - **will never allow living with peace & justice, and that's why our life is poor and incomplete, with a never-ending process of correction ...).**

6/ Practices – Standard Humanism advocates a **"Two Layers Identity"** for every human being, *First:* by equipping all with five principles of it in order to eliminate the rules of ignorance, oppression etc. from their life and, *Second:* by insisting to everyone to live according to his/her belief and culture - at its best form - in a safe world by the support and the administration of *Worldwide Standard Human Society*.

The five principles of Standard Humanism are:
1/ There is a source of truth to unite and cover mankind under righteousness ...
2/ Everyone has the right to choose his/her way of living ...
3/ All should be mentioned and respected in the universal culture of mankind ...
4/ We need a perfect international organization to protect us ...
5/ We are the clean, pure and wise creature on this earth ...

7/ Literature – Book of Standard Humanism ...
Written by Dariush ... (Sep. 15th 2010 Mysore India).

- Standard Humanism is a management and social system, and a new belief of the third millennium of human life which due to having its own special system in supporting and taking care of all that mankind has, it will provide a progressive materialistic and spiritual life away from the penetration of ignorance and oppression for human beings ....

Five Worldviews *(By <u>Dennis McCallum</u>)*

It sometimes seems as if there are more philosophical and religious views than any normal person could ever learn about. Indeed, there are more than six thousand distinct religions in the world today! However, some people are surprised to find that the world's religions and philosophies tend to break down into a few major categories; **these five worldviews include all the dominant outlooks in the world today:**

<u>Naturalism</u> *(Atheism; Agnosticism; Existentialism):*

REALITY - *The material universe is all that exists. Reality is "one-dimensional." There is no such thing as a soul or a spirit. Everything can be explained on the basis of natural law.*
MAN - *Man is the chance product of a biological process of evolution. Man is entirely material. The human species will one day pass out of existence.*
TRUTH - *Truth is usually understood as scientific proof. Only that which can be observed with the five senses is accepted as real or true.*
VALUES - *No objective values or morals exist. Morals are individual preferences or socially useful behaviors. Even social morals are subject to evolution and change.*

<u>Pantheism</u> *(Hinduism; Taoism; Buddhism; ... New Age; Consciousness):*

REALITY - *Only the spiritual dimension exists. All else is illusion, Maya. Spiritual reality, Brahman, is eternal, impersonal, and unknowable. It is possible to say that everything is a part of God, or that God is in everything and everyone.*
MAN - *Man is one with ultimate reality. Thus man is spiritual, eternal, and impersonal. Man's belief that he is an individual is illusion.*
TRUTH - *Truth is an experience of unity with "the oneness" of the universe. Truth is beyond all rational description. Rational thought as it is understood in the West cannot show us reality.*
VALUES - *Because ultimate reality is impersonal, many pantheistic thinkers believe that there is no real distinction between good and evil. Instead, "unenlightened" behavior is that which fails to understand essential unity.*

<u>Theism</u> *(Christianity; Islam; Judaism):*

REALITY - *An infinite, personal God exists. He created a finite, material world. Reality is both material and spiritual. The universe as we know it had a beginning and will have an end.*
MAN - *Humankind is the unique creation of God. People were created "in the image of God," which means that we are personal, eternal, spiritual, and biological.*
TRUTH - *Truth about God is known through revelation. Truth about the material world is gained via revelation and the five senses in conjunction with rational thought.*
VALUES - *Moral values are the objective expression of an absolute moral being.*

Spiritism and Polytheism (Thousands of Religions):

REALITY - _The world is populated by spirit beings who govern what goes on. Gods and demons are the real reason behind "natural" events. Material things are real, but they have spirits associated with them and, therefore, can be interpreted spiritually._
MAN - _Man is a creation of the gods like the rest of the creatures on earth. Often, tribes or races have a special relationship with some gods who protect them and can punish them._
TRUTH - _Truth about the natural world is discovered through the shaman figure who has visions telling him what the gods and demons are doing and how they feel._
VALUES - _Moral values take the form of taboos, which are things that irritate or anger various spirits. These taboos are different from the idea of "good and evil" because it is just as important to avoid irritating evil spirits as it is good ones._

Postmodernism:

REALITY - _Reality must be interpreted through our language and cultural "paradigm." Therefore, reality is "socially constructed"._
MAN - _Humans are nodes in a cultural reality – they are a product of their social setting. The idea that people are autonomous and free is a myth._
TRUTH - _Truths are mental constructs meaningful to individuals within a particular cultural paradigm. They do not apply to other paradigms. Truth is relative to one's culture._
VALUES - _Values are part of our social paradigms as well. Tolerances, freedom of expression, inclusion, and refusal to claim to have the answers are the only universal values._

*- Each of the above worldviews has realized the world from their own point of view.

Imagine – in a designing and making sand-sculpture competition, on the bank of a blue sea – some artists (each in their confined areas, and by their knowledge and culture) with forming sands, has made sculptures ...; each of them is proud of his man-made masterpiece and considers it the best and the just absolute truth, and put a name on it! But the absolute truth is only the sand of that blue sea! ... and those sculptures are just reflections of the absolute truth, and not the whole truth; they are relative truths ....

The story might be superior than or a mixture of these!

Worldview of Standard Humanism (In comparison)

Reality (What is there/ physics + the combination of physics & metaphysics) **-** Reality is the existence and to be ... Reality is that something amazing is there ... Reality is to be united and discovering ... Reality is passing this life thru peace and justice ....

.....

Truth (1/ What is correct beyond there, and the origin of the existence (God); 2/ or the most perfect situation of anything/ metaphysics).

1/ Truth is that **Vast-wise-energy** which Its created measures and objects speak about billions ... That is the One which creates and holds what has created ... To see It is like a fish looking to the outside-world, vague and not realizable correctly (At least in this step of our life), because It is all and we are small ....

2/ Various people and cultures see and understand It from their different points of view! So It is a very wide and complex object, not recognizable just from one dimension and philosophy ....

.....

Man- Man is a work of art! Created by the creature of universe thru the energy and wisdom released in the nature ... This work of art is a very complex object showing Its creator is a very amazing one ... We as human beings create works of art too, but the difference is that our creatures cannot understand us or think about us, but man can think and discover the truth and reality, in steps! This means we need to pass steps of growth ... and then to find enough capacities of understanding the Truth = this is *The Standard Human Philosophy* which leads man to *A standardization life!* This means we need to trace the best standard of material and spiritual life (For all) we can do today and then by reaching to it trace the other higher standard of life and again higher standard of spiritual and material life ... until we become bigger and bigger (By living and passing through various worlds of physics and metaphysics) and finally to be dissolved to The Pure Truth & Energy (God) and understand It.

Man is a piece of universal spirit and a masterpiece – and has such a stance - which must be welcomed in peace, respect and justice at the highest levels by all peoples and cultures, and never be oppressed.

.....

Values- Values are those behaviors and acts of man which by forming to their ideals help us to become a man that would live in a way to reach peace and justice needed to let us pass this step of life (On this Earth)!

Some values are universal and some are cultural and regional ... Universal ones like honesty and veracity are not changeable, but regional ones are prone to be mixed with ignorance and oppression! Satanic 10 percent by their ignorance and oppression try to never let man live in peace and justice and thus go for their next step of universal progress.

.....

Peace and Justice- Peace and justice speak about a situation in which all are content and satisfied; this means providing a global system to apply that; without a perfect global system there would not be any stable peace or widespread justice.

To apply justice means respect to all our possessions, and these possessions according to Standard Humanism are the five major facts of mankind's life which consists of: 1- politics & administration ... 2- religions & beliefs ... 3- cultures & beauties of our life ... 4- knowledge & science ... 5- economics & trades ....

The ignorance and oppression of 10 percent of mankind (According to the philosophy of Standard Humanism) by capturing or ruining these five top human life facts never let us live in peace and justice, and that's why Standard Humanism has invented the five 3D principles of human unity to control human life thru the advanced administration of *Worldwide Standard Human Society Organization* instead of UN.

In order to achieve the peace and justice and then start our other lives **the entire world** (Countries, cultures etc.) **should grow** - in all the aspects of human life - **all together;** in this way all the spirit of mankind, in unity and solidarity, would pass to the other and higher life.

.....

Note: Mankind is in the first steps of their life! And it is not possible to capture all the truth of life and universe in this step (This world) such as: what is exactly God? Or what is the purpose of our creation? Or is there any afterlife? etc. So first we should reach to peace and justice (The highest standard of this life) and then by finding enough energy and capacity of understanding, to realize more truth and reality, closer to the universal facts ... it is better first we concentrate our energy on correcting our real life for now and then more facts and truths would appear to us by our new and higher capacities of understanding captured thru living in peace and justice; thus peace and justice is absolutely important to save us from primitive life of satanic 10 percent ....

Human life just by a correct compiling of: "reason, heart and soul" and in the way of a perfect joining of material & spiritual life, and with a universal worldview is complete, meaningful and wide in the size of mankind.

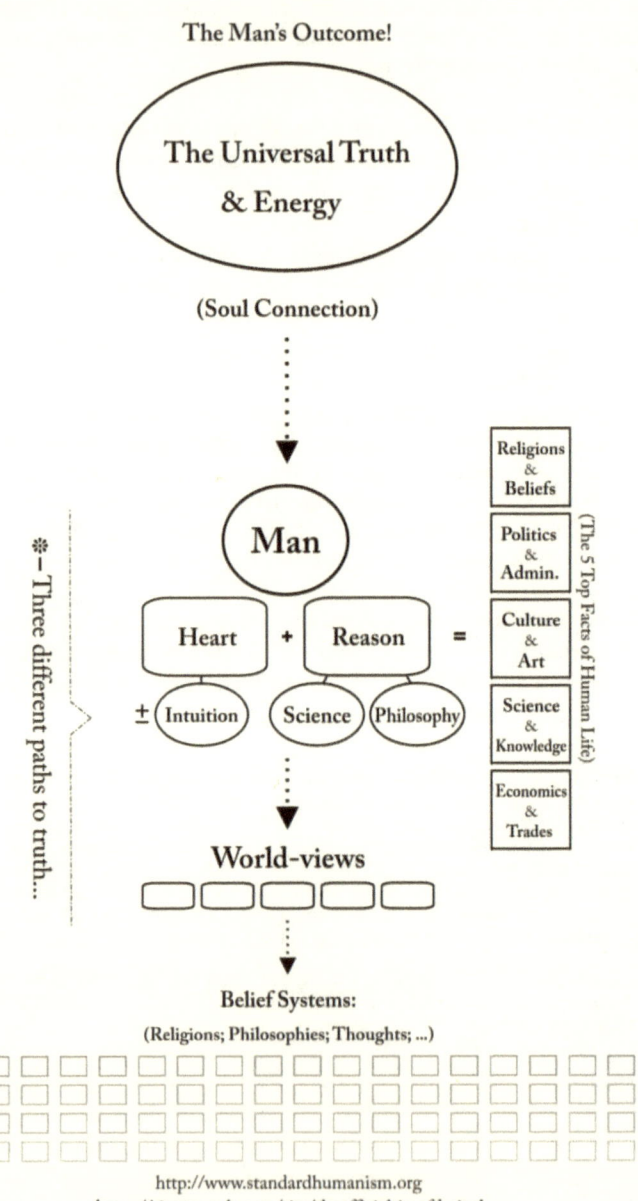

The Man's Outcome!

The Universal Truth
& Energy

(Soul Connection)

Man

Heart + Reason =

± Intuition Science Philosophy

World-views

Belief Systems:

(Religions; Philosophies; Thoughts; ...)

Religions & Beliefs

Politics & Admin.

Culture & Art

Science & Knowledge

Economics & Trades

(The 5 Top Facts of Human Life)

❋– Three different paths to truth...

http://www.standardhumanism.org
https://sites.google.com/site/theofficialsiteofdariush

To clear confusion about/
The concept of reality and truth!

There are three different situations regarding the relationship between truth and reality, and their meaning and concept:

Reality = (The thing that exists/ ...) **Truth** = (1/ The thing that is beyond reality, and the essence of existence of the world; 2/ and or the most precise situation in the face of anything/ ...).

A *(Looking towards the future)*/ In the first step of their relationship, and to understand what exactly are the truth and reality, we mention that first there is *one absolute reality* which is physical and visible, and *one absolute truth* which is metaphysical and is the absolute correct being (Maybe we name it as *God* in its philosophical and scientific sense) which leads all ....

* In this case, there would not be any integration between the truth and reality! And you are going to imagine a one-dimensional world i.e. physical or metaphysical (This means you are failing to have a perfect philosophy for your world and life, and would miss whether physical progress or spiritual growth) ....

B *(Looking from the present time/ in action)*/ In the second step of the relationship between reality and truth the situation is that they will reach together and will make one unique fact! For example: the truth is that you deserve to be and have the capacity to be the best artist in your town; or you deserve to have a good and suitable life, but in reality is not so! Whenever you could have a good life, then reality and truth about you would match together, and reality and truth would mean one reality (Fact) ....

The second relationship could be a never-ending process! And you always trace a higher situation you deserve that, and then in reality reach to it and step by step pass the levels of progress; ....

*(**Standard Humanism** is based on this second formula ... to lead human life to what we really deserve, by tracing our highest and most*

correct situation of a perfect life we may build now, up to going further and further to reach to the pure truth or God).

* In the second phase the truth and reality would eventually be integrated (This means you believe in the growth of both material and spiritual life at its highest situation which is possible and imaginable to mankind, and to discover the highest truths of universe) ….

C *(Looking to the past)/* The third situation is the fact that both reality and truth mean one; for example there is an event there and you want to know how exactly it happened; in this situation you would ask what is the truth about this incident? Or, what is the reality about this incident? By both questions you mean one answer, and want to know one thing = what is the story *exactly?*

* Thru the third phase you believe that reality and truth are both one, and the universe and human life are running by them (This means you have nothing to do or you are quite relaxed and satisfied, adopting anything happens) ….

- (Each of the five worldviews mentioned earlier tries to discover the Reality and Truth of universe and human life from a part of these three dimensions or angles! But in fact all the three of **A, B & C** must be mentioned in analyzing and understanding the facts of universe).

- *(Distinguishing the truth in its early stages is relative and multilayered until we can reach absolute truth; truth will refine itself constantly in course of time, and it gets more pervasive and more understandable).*

The Satanic 10 Percent and their World!!!

In our real world **Satan** is a twofold concept:
(According to the philosophy of Standard Humanism)

A / a part of our instinct which pushes us towards selfishness, greed, power-seeking, oppression, ignorance etc. (Mostly in 10 percent of man ...).

B / some negative energies and situations which prepares the area of dominating selfishness, oppression, power-seeking ....

Thus: **(a)** to be equipped by knowledge, respect, understanding ... *and* **(b)** to control human life by a systematic control based on *Law* and *Reason* is the answer to all human life problems and failures! (And Satan of ignorance & oppression would be eliminated).

The amazing *Philosophy of Standard Humanism* based on: **1**/ Inventing the **Five well-chosen principles of Standard Humanism;** and **2**/ Realizing the **Five Top Human Life Facts,** makes it practically accordable to our real life, in a way which the roots of all our failures can be discovered and controlled!

<u>**For the part (a)**</u> *Standard Humanism* advocates the **Five Principles of Human Unity** ....
      &
<u>**For the part (b)**</u> advocates the **Worldwide Standard Human Society** to manage an advanced life with peace, justice and human life progress in third millennium ... (Thru its five departments).

In this way **The Satanic 10 percent** are those who,
(<u>By their negative character ruin the five top human life facts</u>; and this is the World of Satanic 10 Percent):
1/ control the administration of human societies to oppress pure people ... (Politics & management)
2/ control and damage the face of religions and beliefs to make pure people to be enemy of each other ... (Religions & beliefs)
3/ control the cultures ... and try to eliminate our beautiful and various belongings ... (Cultures & beauties of our life)
4/ control the economy and trade to make the people poor and suffered ... (Economics & trades)
5/ control man to remain illiterate and thus make him/her their slave ... (Knowledge & sciences)

The administration of Worldwide Standard Human Society *by cleaning and purifying the five top human life facts would eliminate their rule and influence thru its five major departments!*

*The five departments of Worldwide Standard Human Society will control the influence or rule of Satanic 10 Percent in the world affairs and politics, and administration of any country to save all our belongings for the sake of ALL ... (According to Standard Humanism there are **70 percent** honest, pure and peace-loving human beings spread in all countries and among all nations, cultures, religions etc. **10 percent** oppressors and ignorant; and **20 percent** neutral ones, and Standard Humanism has been designed to hand over the control of the world of mankind to the hands of 70 percent positives out of the control and influence of negative 10 percent or better to say Satanic 10 percent ignorant and oppressive in order to bestow the gift of the bright and brilliant world of 3rd millennium to mankind).*
.....

And now you realize;

This is exactly what Standard Humanism is invented for,
That is:

By systematic knowledge of *Standard Humanism* (The five principles) and by systematic administration of *Worldwide Standard Human Society,* <u>**To Save Human Life**</u> and dedicate the bright and brilliant world of third millennium to pure children, girls & boys, women & men in all nations and by any beautiful culture, race, belief, language etc. far from the control and influence of *Satanic 10 Percent.*

(Standard Humanism advocates a "**Two Layers Identity**" for every human being, *First:* by equipping all with five principles of it in order to eliminate the rules of ignorance, oppression etc. from their life and, *Second:* by insisting anyone to live according to his/her belief and culture - at its best form - in a safe world by the support and the administration of *Worldwide Standard Human Society*).

By our special human unity of Standard Humanism and its powerful and advanced administration we can step forward faster than what now in the world of *Satanic 10 percent* are doing, which is very weak and under the control or influence of oppressors and ignorant.

Mankind after realizing the importance of: avoiding <u>ignorance</u> & <u>oppression</u> and establishing <u>peace</u> & <u>justice</u>, would be able to pass thru this life - by its highest standards of material & spiritual life - and open the other perfect lives, otherwise forever would remain and wander in the poor and incomplete world of Satanic 10 percent ... Worldwide Standard Human Society by its five departments would dedicate Peace & Justice to mankind.

Standard Humanism will purify and shine all the beliefs, politics, religions, cultures, economies ... and will manage them to eliminate the rules of ignorance, oppression ... to live with solidarity, peace and justice in a safe world ....

By correcting and managing an advanced life (Both in individual and social life) in this world we would be ready to step in the other worlds and lives in the highest standards and capacities; Otherwise the result of our life - because of the influence of Satanic 10 percent - would be incomplete, poor and not exactly according to the purpose of our creation and existence ....

Try to make our world bright and brilliant with peace, justice, respect and progress.

.....

Standard Humanism & Worldwide Standard Human Society

In reality and action
(Before establishing the Worldwide Standard Human Society)

Before establishing the Worldwide Standard Human Society – and its worldwide administration by the participation of the all countries and international organizations – in each country and city, by the will of those who love to change or improve their life according to *Standard Humanism, the primary and temporary centers of WSHS can be established*, in order to start the perfect changes of human life which all of us are waiting for ..., to change and improve our societies and all our having from all its failures to what we really deserve! (These centers as NGOs according to the laws of any recognized country can be formed by the name of: *"Standard Humanism Center"* by the professors of universities or recognized persons after acceptance and allowance letter from *Dariush Gh. Dastjerdi: founder of Standard Humanism* ...).

In all the primary centers of the Worldwide Standard Human Society because of the special insistence of *Standard Humanism* to just follow **The Law**, there would be only one president which is *The Book of Standard Humanism* ... and not any specific person as the president of the center!

There are the presiding committees in each center consisting of 15 high standards and recognized members chosen from the professors of universities, all equal and friendly working (From each of the five departments of the center three persons = total 15).

In each of the five departments, there would be about 50 members to follow the tasks of their department according to what is outlined in the chapter four of the book ... as follow:

1/ **in the Department of politics and administration,** members will work to lobby for doing any positive changes in their political system according to the proposed political system of *Standard Humanism*; watch the human rights of people, environment etc.

2/ **in the Department of religions and beliefs,** they will work for adopting *The Five Principles of Standard Humanism* by the people of their territory, in order to dedicate peace and understanding to societies, ...

3/ Department of cultures and beauties of our life, will work for the correcting of the structures of the cities, architecture of the cities, and also on the traditions, ceremonies, costumes, foods of their territory etc.

4/ Department of economics and trades, will work for job-creating, and elimination of poverty etc.

5/ Department of knowledge and sciences, to eliminate illiteracy and work for public health etc.

In each center there is an *administering and financial section,* to find financial resources in order to run and support the affairs of the center.

The importance and acceptability of managerial system of Standard Humanism is: **a/** covers and realizes all the aspects of human life just at one glance ...; **b/** because of its pure and perfect world-view makes it loveable in the heart of people of any country by any race, religion and nationality to trust *Standard Humanism* and adopt it, and live with it; as *Standard Humanism* supports all of their having of life purely and perfectly.

Before establishing the **W**orldwide **S**tandard **H**uman **S**ociety! *One head-quarters* in *India, USA* and *Europe* will be established to watch and guide the worldwide centers in their tasks ....

- Each worthy person has this human right to make an effort as the representative of this school of thought in any part of the world in any legitimate and legal manner to propagate the culture of peace and justice and universal equality of Standard Humanism.

http://www.standardhumanism.org
info@standardhumanism.org

Invitation letter to adopt Standard Humanism

To all those who are concerned!
Please adopt and realize Standard Humanism!
And save the world of 7 billion mankind and life on Earth!!!

Dear Sir/ Madam
With all my respect and best wishes

The letter you are reading is in regards to my new book (Standard Humanism ...) which is about human life and peace, and perfect living on this Earth!

As we are all human beings with our diverse Nationalities, Cultures, Religions, Beliefs and Ideas; we need to live on this earth in peace, justice and solidarity ... but this is thousands year hope and dream and has never visualized perfectly, thus it is our job and duty to constantly work on it and try to make this dream come true; I am also trying to do something in this concern by my ability, even if I am not very strong about it.

Through this letter I am going to invite you to adopt Standard Humanism and participate in changing your world for the sake of all human beings; and do your share to in support of dedicating the bright and brilliant world of third millennium to mankind!

Standard Humanism is the first international belief of the 3rd millennium, covering all the aspects of human life and has the potential to bring peace & justice;
With the slogan of:
"We need the best world, because we are the best Human beings - 7 billion human beings, all human beliefs ..."

Maybe this effort makes us become nearer to what human beings deserve for a good life and helps us to pave the way of peace and understanding and end the darkness of ignorance, oppression, etc.

This is a try to save and change human life from primitive to advanced world by the participation of **all** ....

The whole idea of Standard Humanism is discussed in my book:
"Standard Humanism and Worldwide Standard Human Society" which can be downloaded from the site: http://standardhumanism.org

Best regards,

Dariush Ghasemian Dastjerdi
Founder of Standard Humanism

Promoting Standard Humanism for the sake of all ...

Any peace-loving and pure human being needs to **promote** and **strengthen the belief of Standard Humanism** in order to give the gift of the ideal and best imaginable world to mankind which will change the human life for the sake of all (*Politics, religions, beliefs, ideas, cultures, races, and people of the world* ...) to eliminate all the failures, ignorance, oppression, superstition etc. and shine the life of human beings on this earth;

This can be done by: speaking, advertising and any other ways of promoting you can and desire.

In order to promote the Idea of Standard Humanism (In its worldwide tour) you can also donate to:
Account No. **30886398269**
Name: **Dariush Ghasemian Dastjerdi**
State Bank of India; Karnataka, Mysore - Main Branch: Code No. 3130
Swift Code: SBININBB 170

And how to fulfill it?!

1/ Adopting and voting for Standard Humanism!!!
2/ Read the book and teach the five principles of Standard Humanism!
3/ Establishing NGOs of Standard Humanism!
4/ Establishing Worldwide Standard Human Society
(The Universal Society of Standard Human) in the place of UN!!!

Download and send the book of Standard Humanism to your friends!

**To human unity and elimination of the ignorance and oppression
of "the Satanic 10%" in human societies!**

Standard Humanism is a kind of belief system! Which:

1 – Spreads to public life thru believe in its 5 principles ....
2 – Thru the NGOs of Standard Humanism works officially.
3 – By establishing **"Worldwide Standard Human Society"** - in the place of UN - changes and purifies human life of mankind!

Design for **"The First Standard Humanism Headquarters"**

This architectural design is based on my recent research and design of **Hanging Gardens of Babylon** as one of the *7 wonders of ancient life* which now I am turning it to the building of *The First Standard Humanism Headquarters!* To be suggested and be built as a magnificent masterpiece as well as a center for the new researches in the field of: *The best way of human life administration,* according to *The Philosophy of Standard Humanism,* that is based on: *peace, respect, purification & understanding.*

The specific characters of this design makes it possible **to host** scholars, meetings and visitors from all around the world (**Both as study center & hotel**) who are interested to witness the first steps in the new changes of human life by the philosophy of respect and understanding in *The New Way of Standard Humanism.*

There are five and five things there!
*There are five (1) & five (2) & five (3) there in matching to make the **5 floors** of Hanging Gardens reasonable and to be accordable with the **principles** and **departments** of Standard Humanism in constructing this design, as the **best design** for the building of the first Standard Humanism Headquarters!*

In this way in the:
Top floor (5): All religions & beliefs **come out of** God and the Truth! Thus, *the first principle* and *the first department* are placed - philosophically - on the top floor of the design!

The next floor (4): Believe in one of the recognized beliefs & religions **with** the Cultures & beauties of life on the next floor!

The next floor (3): Believe in the common characteristics of all the beliefs **with** Politics & management!

The next floor (2): Vote for constructing the Worldwide Standard Human Society **with** Economics & trades!

The next floor (1): To be clean and pure in our life **with** Sciences & knowledge!

All these mean:

To construct something beautiful and correct as the first building of an office, to start the best possible start in making a place to change human life from primitive nature to an advanced one by Standard Humanism!

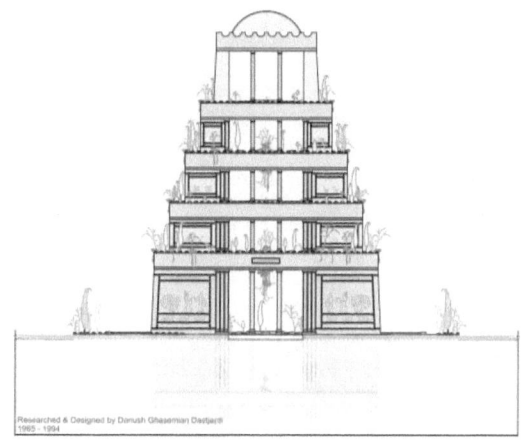

This is available here in the hope of having your respectful cooperation in constructing the first Standard Humanism Headquarters as well as the first study center to promote human life by the participation of all recognized scholars!

This is also sent to more recognized Offices of democratic countries to capture more attention & cooperation and even to build the equal centers to share more spaces and knowledge, and hence to step forward faster in changing human life to what we really deserve.

The Headquarters activities and programs:

1. Introducing & preaching Standard Humanism thru advertising, publishing etc.
2. Finding the opportunities of establishing NGOs of Standard Humanism in various regions and countries ....
3. Holding seminars and conferences regarding the introducing Standard Humanism ....
4. Active connection with the international organizations with the scope of fulfillment of the Standard Humanism!
5. Active connection with the universities and finding the ways of teaching Standard Humanism thru the establishment of the departments of Standard Humanism in universities with the scope of changing human life from its primitive nature of now to the progressed and advanced life of 3rd millennium for the sake of all seven billion mankind.
6. ....

New Words and Expressions

The words and expressions used in this book:

Standard Human
Standard Humanism
Worldwide Standard Human Society
The bright and brilliant world of the third millennium
7 billion people
Human nature
The personality and nature of the human world
The personality and nature of human beings
The stages of man's personality
70% positive
Satanic 10 Percent
20% neutral
Wisdom and sentiments
Ignorance and oppression
Human right and wrong behaviors
Fate and destiny
Decree
Equality of atom and galaxy
Utopia
The three-dimensional principles of human unity
The negative and satanic antihuman powers
The true and or symbolic belief
The common universal culture
The five superior facts of human life
The moral and ideological charter of WSHS
Management and cleansing
The goal of mankind
The wisdom of mankind
Superiority and power seeking and illiteracy
Strong human cleanser and reformer
Ultra-religious and ultra-political and ultra-governmental
Total human identity
Ultra normal
Greater human mutation
Religious, political, cultural, scientific and economical cleansing
A very bright glass prism
An ideal world ideal for human life
A stable peace and justice
A standardization growth
Superior goals
New world administration

Human credit
Human growth
The stages and levels of human life
The law of jungle
The demon of ignorance
Powerful human and overall administration of human world
The absolute truth of the world
Wisdom, heart and spirit
Positive energy and negative energy
The combination of body and soul
The educational program of human life
Spiritual improvement
The capacity of the next better life
The enormity and vastness of the world
Intra stone trip
The giant super world
The better and superior truth
The mental pseudo world
A complete and double layer identity
A unifying factor
The world of friends and the world-fellows
Human shield
The law of truth and righteousness
The concept of God (a Vast-wise-energy)
The common culture of human beings
Understanding of mutual respect
Human growth
Belief identity
The law of humanity
A complete human life
Collective wisdom
Perspective management
A worldwide society
The logic and spirituality of Standard Human
The governance of humanity over human
Worldwide solidarity
A small ignoramus group
Quasi-government
Sectarian power seeking
Satanic leeches
The doomed satanic world
Human originality
Reviving human life
Just and truth seeker

Individual worshipper
Law worshipper
Truth worshipper (Following what is right, and thru wisdom, heart and soul of man is realizable and can be implemented)
Universal human identity
National and patriotic identity
Human respect
The world of reality
Universal growth
Logo and mark
Human journey
Truth seeking
Worldwide
World political morality
Human Rights
Suitable solution
The world of progressive and periodical growth
The wild nature of bestiality
Somatic cleansing and spiritual tranquility
Satanic and ignorant confrontation
A standard and exemplar world
International life
The first group and stance of human beings ...
World tourism
The new human world
The mutual individual and social rights of human beings
A worldwide solution
The national and patriotic tendencies
The steps of world reformation
The period of human flourish
The flow of positive energies
The man of the third millennium

...

References

Sources and books which have been used or reviewed in writing this book:
Starred ones indicate the used resources, (First check date 03/09/2010) ....

List of sites and organizations:

http://en.wikipedia.org/wiki/Religion*
http://en.wikipedia.org/wiki/List_of_religions*
http://en.wikipedia.org/wiki/Major_religious_groups*
http://en.wikipedia.org/wiki/List_of_belief_systems
http://en.wikipedia.org/wiki/List_of_people_by_belief
http://en.wikipedia.org/wiki/Religions_of_the_world
http://en.wikipedia.org/wiki/List_of_new_religious_movements
http://en.wikipedia.org/wiki/List_of_religious_organizations
http://en.wikipedia.org/wiki/List_of_religious_populations
http://en.wikipedia.org/wiki/List_of_political_ideologies
http://en.wikipedia.org/wiki/Category:Religion_by_country
http://en.wikipedia.org/wiki/Religion_and_happiness
http://www.xenos.org/classes/papers/5wldview.htm*
http://en.wikipedia.org/wiki/philosophy_of_religion*
http://en.wikipedia.org/wiki/Religious_symbolism
http://en.wikipedia.org/wiki/List_of_symbols
http://en.wikipedia.org/wiki/Religious_humanism
http://en.wikipedia.org/wiki/Religious_conversion
http://en.wikipedia.org/wiki/God/Names_of_God/...
http://en.wikipedia.org/wiki/Religious_text
http://en.wikipedia.org/wiki/Humanism
http://www.nobeliefs.com/beliefs.htm
http://en.wikipedia.org/wiki/Dualism
http://www.religionfacts.com
...
http://en.wikipedia.org/wiki/League_of_Nations*
http://en.wikipedia.org/wiki/United_Nations*
http://en.wikipedia.org/wiki/World_Federalist_Movement
http://en.wikipedia.org/wiki/United_Nations_Global_Compact
http://en.wikipedia.org/wiki/Dialogue_Among_Civilizations
http://en.wikipedia.org/wiki/Interfaith_dialog
http://en.wikipedia.org/wiki/Institute_for_Interreligious_Dialogue
http://en.wikipedia.org/wiki/Peace_movement
http://en.wikipedia.org/wiki/Global_citizenship
http://en.wikipedia.org/wiki/Parliament_of_the_World's_Religions

http://en.wikipedia.org/wiki/Democratic_World_Federalists
http://en.wikipedia.org/wiki/World_government
http://en.wikipedia.org/wiki/Monism
http://en.wikipedia.org/wiki/World_Social_Forum
http://en.wikipedia.org/wiki/Earth_Charter
http://en.wikipedia.org/wiki/University_for_Peace
http://en.wikipedia.org/wiki/Alter-globalization
http://en.wikipedia.org/wiki/Global_governance
http://en.wikipedia.org/wiki/World_Peace
http://en.wikipedia.org/wiki/Global_Peace_Index
http://en.wikipedia.org/wiki/Global_Centre_for_Pluralism
http://en.wikipedia.org/wiki/Reform_of_the_United_Nations
http://en.wikipedia.org/wiki/Hans_Kung
http://en.wikipedia.org/wiki/Multiculturalism
http://en.wikipedia.org/wiki/1973_World_Congress_of_Peace_Forces
http://en.wikipedia.org/wiki/Le_Corbusier
http://en.wikipedia.org/wiki/Utopia*
http://worldparliament-gov.org
...
http://en.wikipedia.org/wiki/Category:Wars_by_type
http://en.wikipedia.org/wiki/Religious_war
http://en.wikipedia.org/wiki/Category:Religion_and_violence
http://en.wikipedia.org/wiki/Category:Religion-based_wars
http://en.wikipedia.org/wiki/List_of_wars
http://en.wikipedia.org/wiki/List_of_invasions
http://en.wikipedia.org/wiki/List_of_treaties
http://en.wikipedia.org/wiki/List_of_wars_and_disasters_by_death_toll
http://en.wikipedia.org/wiki/List_of_ongoing_conflicts
http://en.wikipedia.org/wiki/List_of_wars_2003current*
...
http://en.wikipedia.org/wiki/Culture*
http://en.wikipedia.org/wiki/Cultural_assimilation
http://en.wikipedia.org/wiki/Science*
http://en.wikipedia.org/wiki/Economics*
...

List of books:

1- Department of Political Science. Western political thought (MA Political Science Course Lessons), Karnataka State Open University, Mysore India: Academic section; 2009.*

2- Durant Will. The Story of Philosophy, New York: Simon and Schuster; 1926.*

3- Durant Will. Our Oriental Heritage, New York: Simon and Schuster; 1935.*

4- Malherbe Michel. Les religions de l'humanité, Paris: Critérion; 1990. (Farsi translation by Tavakoli M. Iran: Nashr-e Nei; 2008).*

5- Hume R E. The World's Living Religions, New York: Scribners; 1959. (Farsi translation by Abdolrahim Gavahi. Iran: Nashr-e Elm; 2007).*

6- Fakhori H, Jar KH. Tarikh al Falsafeh al-Arabiya (The Story of Philosophy of Arab), Farsi translation by AbdolMohammed Ayati. Iran: Entesharate Elmi Farhangi; 2007.*

7- Alam A. Bonyad'haye Elm-e Siyasat (The basis of Political Science), Iran: Nashr-e Nei; 2009.*

8- Pooladi K. Tarikh-e Andisheye Siasi dar Gharb (A History of Political Thought in West), Iran: Nashr-e Markaz; 2009.*

9- William Sahakian & Mabel Lewis Sahakian. Ideas of the great philosophers, Barnes & Noble; Reprint. 3rd printing 1967 L. C. 66-23155 edition (1967). (Farsi translation by Dr. G. Saiedi…).*

10- Gregory Bergman. The Little book of Bathroom Philosophy, Fair Windows Press; 2004. (Farsi translation by K. Ghobadian…).

11- Koenig. Harold G., Larson, David B., and McCullough, Michael E. – Handbook of Religion and Health, Oxford University Press (2001), ISBN 0-8133-6719-0.

12- Theories of World Governance: A Study in the History of Ideas by Cornelius F. Murphy; Publisher: Catholic University of America Press 1999.

13- Michelet Jules. The Bible of Humanity, New York: J.W. Bouton 706 Broadway 1877.

…

Please send your feedback to the following email addresses:

Standardhumanism@yahoo.com
Standardhumanism@gmail.com

And:

A - I would appreciate any invitation regarding the speech on the subject (in English).

B - This book (The original Farsi and its translated to English) is published in limited copies, so I would appreciate any suggestions regarding translation it to other Languages - too - for worldwide publishing.

C - In order to promote the Idea of **Standard Humanism** in our worldwide tour you can donate to:
Account No.: **30886398269**
Name: **Dariush GHASEMIAN DASTJERDI**
State Bank of India; Karnataka, Mysore - Main Branch: Code No. 3130
Swift Code: SBININBB 170
(Through SBI, Commercial Branch – 4161)

Vote for Standard Humanism
Any vote will make the world nearer to what we really deserve.

Worldwide Standard Human Society
http://www.standardhumanism.org
info@standardhumanism.org

Please always download the last edited thru the:
http://www.standardhumanism.org
https://sites.google.com/site/standardhumanism/

My Resume & Biography (In one page)

Name: DARIUSH/ *Surname:* GHASEMIAN DASTJERDI
Date of birth: 8th February 1961 - IRAN
Artist, designer & writer; and the founder of Standard Humanism!

(Education: MFA; Ministry of Culture … Tehran 2013 – MA Political Science; Mysore, India 2011 – (Ph.D.) Researcher; *Thesis:* Human life in 3rd Millennium …; Mysore, India 2013 …).

I dream to make *Standard Humanism* worldwide and running in human life! Also, the rest of my life have a beautiful farm by my own design and live in it in the calm …

Fields of Interest & Occupations (What I have done and I'm doing now!)*:*

1/ Designing & Painting (and Teaching) 1976 – 2014 …
The best one and masterpiece is the flowers bouquet - Oil on canvas 83x107 cm/ 1980 - 1989 …

2/ Set Design (& Decor) for TV Programs 1999 – 2019 …
The result in this field is my design of the great package of *Up-village* film, a comedy for cinema (With all the scenario, storyboard, direction and set-designing of the film) …

3/ Designer & Advisor of Architectural Projects 1985 – 2013 …
The best of mine in the field of architecture is the research & design of the Hanging Gardens of Babylon; 1985 - 1994 (To be built as a 7-star hotel or a palace in the UAE! Or the first Headquarters of Standard Humanism!) …

4/ Research & Writings 2000 – 2021 …
In various artistic & humanistic fields (By publishing or thru the internet: **Lulu.com**; **Amazon Kindle**, and more, and on the Facebook groups & pages) …

5/ Qur'an and Islam 2014 …
The new outlook & understanding in Islam & Qur'an! (One God - One Islam! & the Islamic Consultative Council of Islam World! To gift peace and progress in Muslim societies!) …

6/ Standard Humanism 15th September 2010 Mysore - India;
The New International and Humanistic Belief of 3rd Millennium! To change human life from its primitive nature of now to the advanced one …

http://www.standardhumanism.org
info@standardhumanism.org
https://sites.google.com/site/standardhumanism/

More details on the: https://sites.google.com/site/theofficialsiteofdariush/
Autobiography: The Amazing Story of Dariush's Life!

Teaching "The Standard Human Thought" at Universities...;

* - (Every individual and/or legal authority is allowed to teach standard human thought based on the educational resources of this course...).
Teaching resources: 1. The standard human book...; 2. The book of standard humanism...! (*Compiled by* Dariush Ghasemian Dastjerdi).
Free downloads from: https://sites.google.com/site/theofficialsiteofdariush

*** - Standard human thought, in two parts of social personality, and human life administration in the new century...*

"The **Standard Human** is the one who, using the correct and complete utilization of all of his spiritual and material capacities and abilities in his life (and based on his internal forces...), takes himself to the most ideal human condition in his dignity and power, and this requires first to become self-conscious and to become acquainted with its morale and characteristics, and then to cultivate itself to the highest human qualities to reach its standard of humanity (in all aspects of life)."

*** - The degrees of social character of individuals, according to the internal forces of each human being (*physical force, force of senses..., emotional forces, force of reason and wisdom*) = 1. The Sublime Standard Human; 2. Social Standard Human; 3. The Standard human-to-grow, and 4. Third-grade people!

* - The Sublime Standard Human:
1. In the individual section, it acts in accordance with the principles of religion and creed...
2. In the social sector, transcendental behavior, along with knowledge, intelligence and magnanimity itself, manifests itself...

* - Social Standard Human:
1. In the individual section, it acts in accordance with its intellectual and scientific discretion...
2. In the social sector, it is secular and acts in accordance with reason, science, respect for all, and based on the standard human standards (human rights) and brings an advanced human society...

* - Standard human-to-grow:
In both personal and social aspects, it is learning, experiencing, and growing...

* - Third-grade people (Satanic10%):
1. In the individual section, it is lowbrow...
2. In the social sector, it causes the harassment and distress of others/ for any reason and excuse...

*** - The most distinctive feature, and the fundamental difference in standard human thought with other political and social systems and thoughts, is that:

1- There are three different ways to reach the truth, all of which are valid in the life of mankind...;
2- There are five top facts in human life that create an ideal and standard human life in balance!

A. The three different paths are: **Philosophy** / philosopher, with the instrument of reason and logic --- **Science** / scientist, with the means of observation, comparison and experience --- **Spiritual and sentimental inspirations** / sublime man, through spiritual cultivation.

B. The five top facts of human life are:
1. Religion and Belief; 2. Policy and Management; 3. Culture and Art; 4. Science and Knowledge; 5. Economics and Business.

* - When understanding the truth and the ways of reaching the truth (what is right...), we are inconsistent with the choice of the right path - and through the three paths above! And also, whenever the Third-grade people controls take on the five top facts of human life, we will not reach the standard and ideal human society... and we will have plenty of social dilemmas, and only chaos and misery in different affairs will result from our performance!

*** - In the modern world:
- Sublime humans with the help of social human beings, create a transcendental modern society; /
- Social human beings, create a modern human society; /
- The Standard human-to-grow beings, form the core of human societies; /
- Third-grade people, make up the backward and third-class society.

* _ Try to be standard humans, to move towards the right path = social progress and human prestige.
Dariush Ghasemian Dastjerdi
https://sites.google.com/site/theofficialsiteofdariush

The Standard Human Thought Teaching Course Syllabus!

Teaching resources: 1. The standard human book...; 2. The book of standard humanism...! (*Compiled by* Dariush Ghasemian Dastjerdi)

*** - Includes teaching sections and headings:
1 - The Purpose and Concept of Standard Human Thought.

2 - Achievement chart of human life / Overview of the diagram + Explaining the three main paths, and the five top facts of human life.

3 - Steps and levels of human life! + Human Nature / 70% Positive, 20% Neutral; Satanic10%!

4 - The internal forces of man and the formation of four categories of social personality in society... + The ideal society and the role of human beings in the formation of various types of societies (human; transcendental; grade 3).

5 - Five Principles of Human Unity in Standard Human Thought, and Providing Solutions to Deal with Satanic10% (Third-grade people) in the World, and As a Consequence of the Control and Management of Human Life by Standard humans!

6 - The Proposed Political System of Standard Human Thought for Countries...

7 - The International Standard Human Thought System (New World System instead of the United Nations).

8 - New structure and method of forming NGOs in standard human thought!

9 - Comparison of standard human thought with other thoughts and ideas!

10 - World-views and the explanation of the world-view of standard human thought! + Discussion of the meaning and the concept of truth and reality...

11 - Subjects and Supplementary Titles in the Main and Comprehensive Book of Standard Human Thought (Standard humanism).

        ...
* - Two-page conclusion...
* - (Talk: flourishing Countries and Universe, with standard human!)
https://sites.google.com/site/theofficialsiteofdariush

Sessions in the Standard Human Thought Teaching Course!

Videos (Sessions 1-12) **on the** YouTube **Channel of** <u>**Standard Humanism**</u>

Session1
Introduction: A new standard of living, and a new human thought in human life is in the scene!!!
Entitled "Standard Human Thought "; and accordingly/
1. The purpose and concept of standard human thought.

Session2
2. Achievement chart of human life/ Overview of the diagram.

3. There are three main and different ways to reach the truth (= what is right and correct), which is to create a new and standard life, all three must be considered together; Included: 1. Philosophy; 2. Science; 3. Intuition...

4. The five top facts are the result of the mixing and the output of three different paths in human life, all five of which are necessary and necessary to each other and are equal; the five top facts are: <u>religion and belief</u>; <u>politics and management</u>; <u>culture and Art</u>; <u>science and knowledge</u>, and <u>economics and trade</u>...

* - Consider a car factory; different parts of the factory make a single car! = Now consider a standard human life, five sections (Religion and beliefs; politics and management; and...) make different parts of a standard society.

Consequently, the standard human community must be based on five independent and complementary constituents, which, according to the constitution, oversee each other (by the method of checks and balances between the five sections, in order to prevent the concentration of power in one section, and consequently, tendency to dictatorship)!

Consequently, human life will enter a new stage in its structural and managerial identity, which has preceded all previous criteria, such as the discussion of the separation of religion from politics, religious rule, and so on! And bestows humanity the best result!

The performance of the five sections is as follows:
The department of religion and belief has its own responsibility in society;
The department of politics and management has its own responsibility in society;
The department of culture and art has its own responsibility in society;
The science and knowledge department has its own responsibility in society;
The economics and trade department has its own responsibility in society;

As a result, as an automobile factory! The room and body design section does not interfere with engine design issues, and... and... and...! But all under the supervision of the policy and management department, which has the expertise and managerial knowledge, and the ability to coordinate between members and departments in a modern and scientific world, - in accordance with the description of the assigned and statutory tasks, and coherently - the community make the ideal...

Session3
5. Steps and levels of human life! + Human Nature!

The first stage and level; the real world of human life...
Stage and second level; dream world of human life...
Stage and third level; principles of standardization...
Stage and fourth level; Universal Society of Standard human...

* - According to standard human thought! 70% of humans are healthy and positive people, of every race, nationality, religion and belief... 20% are neutral..., and 10% of others, with their wild animal temper, tend to dominate and take possession all human beings have... (See the description of the human nature chapter in the book Standard Humanism).

*** - The merits of the 5 top facts of human life... which should be available to everyone, by Satanic10% or third-grade people, due to the greed of wealth and power..., have gone away, and as a result, decent and ideal human life has become a dream, and oppression and excesses have dominated human societies!

Session4
6. The standard human thought way, to control five top facts... and their decent management by standard humans!

1 - The standardization of man, according to our capacities, including: the Sublime Standard Human; Social Standard Human; the Standard human-to-grow! + Ideal society...

Session5
2 - Adoption of the Five Principles of Human Unity of Standard humanism, in opposition to the Satanic10%...

Session6
3 - To reform and optimize the political system of countries, based on the proposed system of standard human thought!

Session7
4 - United Nations reform and optimization, with the "Universal Society of Standard human"!

Session8
5 - The structural change of NGOs... with the new proposed method of standard human thought!

Session9
7. Comparison of standard human thought with other thoughts and ideas!

Session10
8. World-views and the explanation of the world-view of standard human thought! + Discussion of the meaning and the concept of truth and reality...

Session11
9. Subjects and supplementary titles...

Session12
* - Two-page conclusion...
* - (Talk: flourishing Countries and Universe, with standard human!)

* - (Every individual and/or legal authority is allowed to teach standard human thought based on the educational resources of this course...)
Teaching resources: 1. The standard human book...; 2. The book of standard humanism...! (*Compiled by* Dariush Ghasemian Dastjerdi)

Free downloads from: https://sites.google.com/site/theofficialsiteofdariush

The Series of Standard Human Discussions

Videos (Sessions 1-5) **on the** YouTube **Channel of** <u>**Standard Humanism**</u>

Part One: Introduction… + the outcome chart of human life…

After hundreds of thousands of years from the presence of humans on the Earth; from about 12,000 years ago, human beings interacted with each other through agriculture in different regions…

From 7,000 years ago, urbanization was formed… --- 2500 years ago, the largest empire was founded… --- At the same time, philosophical and rational thoughts brought human life into a new world…

Different religions and beliefs, the Renaissance, and the Industrial Revolution have brought us to the spot we are witnessing now! --- Apparently, we are still not very successful! --- Our steps to correct our lives - in the realm of reality - are not enough! We need a new knowledge…

After 12,000 years of experience and thinking… from now on, the standard human being will be a criterion!!! --- Failure in the right way to this day, i.e., the third-grade people controlling man's lives, and not the standard human beings - Standard Human Thought will bring us into a new world…

Let's look at the human outcome chart:

In the center, we have a man connected with the Creator through a spiritual connection, and receives energy to stay alive… From man, the two elements of reason and heart are branched… Similarly, of wisdom, Philosophy and Science, and from heart, heart and spiritual inspiration --- each of them has both positive and negative aspects!

Thus, <u>in the positive part</u>, at the head of philosophy, the philosopher is located and his means to reach the truth is reason and logic --- at the head of science, the scientist, and his means to achieve the truth is observation, comparison, and experiment --- And at the head of spiritual and spiritual inspiration, there is a sublime and spiritual man who has the means to achieve the truth by self-cultivation...

In the negative section, in the philosophy section, we have a combative person, who only argues because he does not have the rational ability to make a correct and logical conclusion! Without right conclusions... --- In the negative part of science, there is a foolish and illiterate person who makes himself and others exploited...

And in the negative part of the inspirations of heart and soul, there is a fanatic, who the result of his actions is nothing but oppression and illusion... / Suppression of ideas and thoughts is here...

Standard human beings are active in the positive fields - and they may have at least a few percentages of all these, and third-grade people are active in the negative sections...

These three parts of philosophy, science, and spiritual and spiritual inspiration are three different ways to reach the truth; the "truth" is what you have realized as the right! "You" as a human being... --- a part of man, through the philosophical thought reach to the truth and right, some through science, and some through the heart and soul perception...

At first there is a supernatural truth, and a physical and visible reality..., and a third form, which is definite and fact...

Every time, the truth you believe in is what you really can prove to be true in the realm of reality, your truth becomes definite thing, and science, and in this the situation will be acceptable to others as well.

Otherwise, it will only be true in your mind and it will not have any scientific credence... the science developed in research centers... and not just the personal experience or the mental imagery of individuals...

In the end, we have five worldviews that have emerged from the three paths..., and from these worldviews there are many religions, beliefs and thoughts...

At the same time, from the combination of wisdom and heart, human beings achieve five of the highest and most superior facts in their lives that are necessary and complementary to each other, and together they bring a complete human life in their own place...

These 5 Top Facts are:

Religion and Belief --- Politics and Management --- Culture and Arts --- Science and Knowledge --- Economics and Trades.

Each of these five divisions has their own responsibility to create a complete and standard human society and should not disturb each other... the final management is also the responsibility of the management and policy department, which has the necessary knowledge in this connection...

Standard Humans boost these five top facts - that is to say, the flourishing of all cultures, religions, and advanced sciences... --- and third-grade people also destroy them and try to make their own point - and in different affairs impose on others...

In any society where these five truths are in a state of inappropriateness, that is, third-grade people have control over those parts... --- This is a logical and very simple formula...

Part Two: Internal forces of man, and the formation of 4 degrees of social character... + Ideal society...

In the presence of any human, there are 4 forces: 1. Physical Force 2. Force of senses (internal and external senses) 3. Force of emotions and sentiment 4. The power of reason and wisdom.

The human being communicates with the surrounding environment through the senses..., then emotional and sentiments appear and the will takes shape, in the end, to do something, either to disagree with it and not to do anything...

The important point is whether the behavior and decision is correct or inaccurate?!

This is where the fourth force is coming to you! = The power of reason and wisdom --- man through his intellect can do the right behaviors or review his behavior --- reason takes the final decision, and not emotions...

As much as our abilities, and the strength and weakness of these four forces, we are faced with behaviors that shape our social personality... And accordingly, there are four personality traits! 1. Sublime standard human, 2. The standard social human, 3. Human in growing, and 4. Third-grade person!

The first three categories are standard, and the fourth category, which itself covers countless numbers, is below the human standard... but it is standardized by modifying their behavior.

To be Standard Human, means the balance of our internal forces is at the optimum level, and as a result, we act like a deserved human...

In the standard human, we deal with the behavior and function of individuals, and not with the appearance, position and reaches...

Standard Human Thought, is for to care about our behavior and behave in different situations like family, work, and social affairs, like decent and standard people, and not like third-grade people!

The outcome of human performance in society, three types of society are simultaneously formed: **Human, Sublime,** and **Grade 3**!

It is obvious that standard human beings create a standard human society, sublime standard humans, a supranational standard society..., the human in growing form the core of healthy societies..., and third-grade people make a third-grade society --- look at ourselves...

Part Three: Steps and Levels of Human Life + Human Nature + the 5 Principles of Human Unity In the face of 3rd grade and 10% evil people...

At present, two levels of life are conceivable to human beings! 1. Real world 2. Dream world!

The real world is what we see and we have lived for thousands of years with all its bitterness and sweetness... --- A dream world, which is very diverse and colorful, is in our minds!

That is, when we cannot reach our desires and needs in the realm of reality, we drown in dreams and try to get rid of the present reality of the present, and build our lives in a dream! Of course, with a great deal of effort in the realm of reality, we may also achieve part of our desires...

Everyone in this world has a dream! From thoughts and beliefs to individuals --- but sometimes it's not possible to reach these dreams --- because we are caught up in the real-world disabilities – that is, we will either cease to meet with each other who does not realize our goals! We do not have the necessary knowledge and management to succeed!

Standard Human Thought, by designing five humanitarian principles, and by designing a new political system for international management, has designed a new world in order to reach the things we deserve in the realm of reality – and pass from the first and second worlds and reach the third and fourth levels and worlds in human life... / Undoubtedly, third-grade and 10% evil people will resist...

Here it is necessary to take a look at human nature; --- human nature can be examined from two perspectives! **1**. From the perspective of the character and nature of the human world (in general terms) **2**. From the angle of personality and nature of human beings (from component to whole).

In general, 70% of humans are always health and well-being in all ages and in all communities... --- 20% neutral... --- and 10% excessive, destructive, and evil! --- Please see the human nature chapter in the Standard Humanism book for a better understanding.

10% Satanic, take under control the 5 top facts of human life and cause suffering of mankind, thus the way of salvation is unity --- Unity through the five principles of Standard Human Thought, which are: **1**. Believe in God... **2**. Believing in a true human religion and belief, according to your own understanding and recognition... **3**. Observing the common principles of human rights in international life... **4**. Vote for the formation of universal society of standard human, instead of the current United Nations... **5**. Observing cleanliness, and individual and social hygiene, as well as maintaining mental and spiritual relaxation in life...

Part Four: New political system for countries... + International Society of Standard Human Organization... + New NGOs...

Standard Human Thought comes in two complementary parts:
1. In the social personality section 2. In management and international administration.

In the personality section, with the transformation that we create in our personality, as standard humans, we will enter the third world of our lives on Earth! And in the management sector, with the transformation of the political and international system, we enter the world and the fourth level of human life, as in the past, mankind passed the traditional life cycles, slavery, feudalism, Marxist thought and dictatorship for community management, etc., and came to democracy and public awareness... with the difference that with Standard Humanism, we will enter a world of completely new and advanced and healthy nature! Without 10% evil influence... also, reforming the NGO's structure here will be very important and will help us move more quickly towards social and international reforms...

In the new political system for countries, the suggestion of standard humanism, is a new parliamentary system which popular representatives in parliament are selected among retired university professors in different disciplines, and the political parties in the style of the world of 3rd grade and 10% evil, will not exist!

* - In each government, two groups of specialists perform their duties: 1. The administrative department, which is used through the relevant degree in its collection, and with executive and managerial competence, reaches the high executive positions; the highest qualification required for this group is a master's degree (doctoral degree is essentially a university degree, meaning that by presenting a new thesis and idea, the holder of the degree in scientific and research centers trains specialists and then they gain new knowledge in The executive centers are busy, and the growth and development of the country will continue; the 3rd grade people in the 3rd grade communities will try to get a doctorate degree and as a result reach high management positions in any way so that they become the general director of everything...) 2. The political and governmental sectors that come to power in the traditional way through the parties; according to the standard human being, this method has not worked in today's societies and must be changed...; In the world of standard human beings, all thoughts and ideas - in accordance with the principles of human standard: truthfulness, honesty and respect - are free to form their own party and group and to flourish and spread their own ideas... but such an imagination that some of them will come to power and take over the management of the society, or even try to

infiltrate the power by lobbying! It is impossible and impossible for eternity... how can it be imagined that third-grade and power-seeker people enter the political arena of countries and take control of people's lives by dividing power among themselves in turn! And with repeated promises and deceptions and incompetence to blacken the future of the country and the lives of the people... In a standard human society, retired professors after 30 (20, 25) years of service, - through national elections - enter the parliament and they will serve as the representative, the speaker of the parliament, and the prime minister and the president - one or a maximum of two courses -...

***- Standard Humans only support the political system of standard human thinking and do not accept anything else...

In the international system, a huge global organization, with an organizational chart and ambitious goals and tasks, will be in place of the current United Nations, and human life will be best suited to meeting the needs of all countries and religions and beliefs, new and fresh... --- Please read the book for a better understanding of the subject.

Part Five: Free Debate = the flourishing Countries, Standardized Method...

What changes can be made by Standard Human Thought in a variety of fields such as agriculture, environment, production and economy, urban and rural management, air pollution, population control, culture and customs, clothing and architecture, family, etc.?!

Please think about these things: Third-grade billionaire... Third-grade driver in driving... Third-grade person in the destruction of nature and landslide... Third-grade person in garbage spill in the city and nature... 3rd grade person in management and political position... 3rd grade person in governmental construction and graft... 3rd grade person in urban drawing... 3rd grade physician meddling in construction for money... and....

Please note: What are the characteristics of a standard Iranian human being? What about a standard Japanese human? A standard Vietnamese human? A standard Belgian human? A standard South African human? And...

I'm not saying who is a third-grade person ... The person himself should examine his behavior and correct it according to standard human patterns...

***

* - (More notes on the affiliated standard human social media links, thru my official site: https://sites.google.com/site/theofficialsiteofdariush).

This book at the same time is sending to many parts of the world; Such as:

A- The Honorable Offices of the Governments of:

Switzerland; Finland; Austria; Denmark; Spain; Italy; French; Russia; Japan; China; South Korea; Malaysia; Hong Kong; Canada; Brazil; Mexico; United States of America; Cuba; South Africa; Lebanon; India; United Arab Emirates; Australia; Singapore; Sweden; Egypt; Turkey; Brunei; England; Netherland; Norway; ....

B- Main international organizations of the world:

1- UN - 1st Ave & E 44th St. New York, NY 10017 USA.

2- UNESCO - 7 Place de Fontenoy, 75007 Paris, France - 01 45 68 10 00.

3- Democratic World Federalists - 55 New Montgomery St # 225 San Francisco, CA 94105-3421 (415) 227 - 4880 USA.

4- Council for a Parliament of the World's Religions - 70 E. Lake Street, Suite 205 Chicago, IL 60601 USA.

5- Dialogue among Civilizations - Herengracht 518 1017 CC Amsterdam, Netherland.

6- Global Centre for Pluralism - Sussex Drive, Ottawa, Canada.

7- Council for a Parliament of the World's Religions - Melbourne, Australia....

8- The World Federalist Movement - 708 3rd Ave # 24, New York, NY (212) 599-1320 USA.

9- The World Federalist Movement - 145 Spruce Street, Ottawa, ON K1R 6P1, Canada - (613) 232-0647.

10- The World Social Forum - (WSF) Porto Alegre, Brazil.

11- American Humanist Association - 1777 T Street Northwest, Washington, DC - (202) 238-9088 USA.

12- Swedish Humanist Association - "Swedish Humanist Association (Humanisterna) Box 16241, SE-103 24 STOCKHOLM, Sweden.

13- Council of Australian Humanist Societies - 4 Alandale Ave, Balwyn VIC 3103, Australia - (03) 9857 9717.

14- Sociedade da Terra Redonda (Brazil) - R. Primeiro de Março, 66 - Centro, Rio de Janeiro, 20010-000 Brazil.

15- University of peace - Rua Paulino Fernandes, n°3, Rio de Janeiro - RJ, 22270-050 Brazil.

16- World peace council - 350 5th Ave # 59 New York, NY 10118-5999 USA.

17- Center for International Governance Innovation - 57 Erb St. West Waterloo, ON N2L 6C2 Canada.

18- Council on Foreign Relations - 58 East 68th Street New York, NY 10065. / 1777 F Street, NW Washington, DC 20006 USA.

19- The Institute of Oriental Philosophy - 1-236, Tangi-cho, Hachioji City Tokyo 192-0003 Japan.

20- The Society for Buddhist-Christian Studies - Society for Buddhist-Christian Studies c/o CSSR Executive Office Rice University MS 156
P.O. Box 1892 Houston, TX 77251-1892 USA.

21- Thai Inter-Religious Commission for Development - 29/15 Soi Ramkumheng 21, Ramkunhend Rd., A. Wangthonglang, Bangkok 10310 Thailand.

22- Soka Gakkai International - SGI Headquarters Josei Toda International Center 15-3 Samon-cho, Shinjuku-ku, Tokyo, 160-0017 Japan.

23- Museum of World Religions - 6F, No.236, Sec. 1, Jungshan Rd. Yonghe, Taipei County 234 Taiwan R.O.C.

24- The Office of Tibet in New York - 241 East 32nd Street
New York, NY 10016 USA.

25- The Los Angeles Buddhist-Catholic Dialogue - 928 S. New Hampshire Ave Los Angeles, CA 90006 USA.

26- The Society for Buddhist-Christian Studies - Society for Buddhist-Christian Studies c/o CSSR Executive Office Rice University MS 156 P.O. Box 1892 Houston, TX 77251-1892 USA.

27- The Interfaith Education Initiative - 815 Second Avenue New York, NY 10017 USA.

28- Three Faiths Forum - Star House 104 Grafton Road London NW5 4BA UK.

29- BRUCKE – KOPRU - Begegnung von Christen und Muslimen Leonhardstrase 13 90443 Nurnberg, Germany.

30- World Council of Churches - PO Box 2100, 150 route de Ferney, CH-1211, Geneva 2, Switzerland.

31- All Africa Conference of Churches - P.O. Box 14205- 00800 Westlands, Nairobi Kenya.

32- The Ecumenical Association of Third World Theologians - UNISA Theology P.O. Box 392, PRETORIA 0003 South Africa.

33- The NCC Center for the Study of Japanese Religions - Karasuma Shimotachiuri Kamikyo-ku Kyoto 602-8011 Japan.

34- KAIROS- Canadian Ecumenical Justice Initiatives - 129 St. Clair Ave. West Toronto, ON Canada M4V 1N5.

35- The Supreme Council for Confucian Religion in Indonesia - Kompleks Royal Sunter Blok F 23, Jl. Danau Sunter Selatan, Jakarta Utara City : DKI Jakarta, Indonesia.

36- Centre Vedantique of Geneva - 63 Av. d'Aire CH-1203 Geneva.

37- Hindu Forum of Britain - Unit 3, 861, Coronation Road, Park Royal, London NW10 6PT United Kingdom.

38- Hinduism Today (Magazine) - Hinduism Today 107 Kaholalele Road Kapaa, Hawaii 96746-9304 USA.

39- Hindu Institute of Learning - 2411 Dundas Street West, Toronto, Ontario, M6P 1X3 Canada.

40- The Hindu Council of Australia - The Hindu Council of Australia 17 The Crescent, Homebush NSW 2140 Australia.

41- Hindu Council UK - Boardman House 64 Broadway Stratford, London E15 1NT United Kingdom.

42- Morung for Indigenous Affairs & Just Peace - The Morung Express, House No: 4, Duncan Road Dimapur Nagaland-797112 India.

43- The Center for World Indigenous Studies - Center for World Indigenous Studies PMB 214 1001 Cooper Point Road SW Suite 140 Olympia, WA 98502-1107 U.S.A.

44- World Federation of Dalit and Tribal Rights - World Federation of Dalit and Tribal Rights C/o. BSS (Buddha Smriti Sansthan) 110/A Baba Ganganath Market, Munirka, New Delhi-110 067 India.

45- The Australian Institute of Aboriginal and Torres Strait Islander Studies - AIATSIS GPO Box 553, Canberra ACT 2601 Australia.

46- Arctic Council Indigenous Peoples' Secretariat - Strandgade 91, 4th floor P.O. Box 2151 1016 Copenhagen K, Denmark.

47- The Federation of Jain Associations in North America - JAINA Headquarters P.O. Box 700 Getzville, NY 14068 USA.

48- Jain Centre of Leicester (Jain Samaj Europe) - Jain Centre 32 Oxford Street Leicester LE1 5XU United Kingdom.

49- Jain Heritage Centres - Nitin H.P. No.62, 'Sonia', 3rd cross, Kurubarahally, Near Siddarthanagar, Mysore-570011 Karnataka, India.

50- The Abrahamic Fellows Program - P.O. Box 705 New York, NY 10150 United States.

51- Inter-Religious Organization of Singapore - Raffles City P O Box 712, Singapore 911724.

52- The Centre for Inter-religious Dialogue - 595, Ajesa Street Off Amino Kano Crescent Wuse II Abuja, Nigeria.

53- National Peace Council - 12/14 Purana Vihara Road Colombo 6 Sri Lanka.

54- World Congress of Faiths - c/o 1 Ashbourne Grove, London, NW7 3RS United Kingdom.

55- Auburn Seminary- The Center for Multifaith Education - 3041 Broadway New York, NY 10027 USA.

56- UNESCO – Division of Cultural and International Dialogue - Division of Cultural Policies and International Dialogue 1, rue Miollis 75732 Paris Cedex 15 France.

57- Religions for Peace: The European Council of Religious Leaders - P O Box 6820 St. Olavs pl, NO-0130, Oslo Norway.

58- The Organization for Security and Cooperation in Europe - Kaerntner Ring 5-7 1010, Vienna, Austria.

59- Bangladesh Hindu-Christian-Buddhist Oikya Parishad - 5, Tejkuni para, Dhaka-1215 Bangladesh.

60- Institute for Feminism and Religion - 30, Parkhill Rise Kilnamanagh, Dublin 24, Ireland.

61- United Religions Initiative - P.O. Box 29242 San Francisco, CA 94129 USA.

62- The United Religions Initiative of Korea - 301 Uwon Villa 193-120 Jangchung-dong 2ga, Jung-gu, Seoul 100-856 Korea.

63- The World Faiths Development Dialogue - WFDD The International Study Centre The Precincts Canterbury Kent CT1 2EH UK.

64- Global Ethics and Religion Forum - P.O Box 7121 Orange, California 92863-7121 USA.

65- Knowledge Center for Religion and Development - P.O. Box 19170 3501 DD Utrecht, Netherlands.

66- The Glencree Centre for Peace and Reconciliation - Glencree Enniskerry County Wicklow, Ireland.

67- The Interfaith Center of New York - 475 Riverside Drive New York, NY 10115 USA.

68- Interfaith Youth Core - 1111 N Wells St., Ste. 501 Chicago, IL 60610 USA.

69- Children of Abraham - 307 W. 38th Street Room 1805 New York, NY 10018 USA.

70- The Pluralism Project - 1531 Cambridge St. Cambridge, MA 02139 USA.

71- The Nanzan Institute for Religion and Culture - 18 Yamazato-chō Shōwa-ku Nagoya 466-8673 Japan.

72- Religious Affairs Offices of the Ministry of Culture and Tourism - Ministry of Culture & Tourism Republic of Korea 110-703, 42, Sejongno, Jongno-gu Seoul, Korea.

73- The Cape Town Interfaith Initiative - 8 Erin Road, Rondebosch, Cape Town 7700 South Africa.

74- Africa Files - Room 21 300 Bloor Street West Toronto, ON M5S 1W3 Canada.

75- The New Zealand Interfaith Group - PO Box 5428 Wellington, New Zealand.

76- Inter-Faith Spiritual Fellowship - Batu 6, Jalam Puchong 58200 Kuala Lumpur, Malaysia.

77- Interfaith Resources - 511 Diamond Rd. Heltonville, IN 47436 Indiana, USA.

78- 3iG - Keizersgracht 788 1017 EC Amsterdam, Netherlands.

79- The World Bank: Development Dialogue on Values and Ethics - 1818 H Street NW Washington, DC 20433 USA.

80- Association of Women from Romania - P.O.Box 80 Postal Office 37 Bucharest, Romania.

81- Beliefnet, Inc. - 115 E 23rd ST Suite 400 New York, NY 10010 US.

82- Centre for Inter-Faith Studies at the University of Glasgow - Department of Theology and Religious Studies University of Glasgow 4 The Square Glasgow, G12 8QQ United Kingdom.

83- Religions for Peace - 777 United Nations Plaza, 9th Floor New York NY 10017, USA.

84- World Council of Religions for Peace in Croatia - Marticeva 43, 10000 Zagreb, Croatia.

85- The Week of Global Interfaith Dialogue - Global Family for Love and Peace 46-60 156th Street Flushing, NY 11355 USA.

86- Fellowship of Reconciliation - 521 N. Broadway Nyack, New York 10960 USA.

87- Global Peace Works - PO Box 316 Yorktown Heights, NY 10598 USA.

88- The Harmony Institute - PO Box 242 Jonesville, VT 05466 North Carolina, USA.

89- Interfaith Action - Star House 104 Grafton Road London NW5 4BA United Kingdom.

90- Inter-Faith Action for Peace in Africa - Coordinating Office Sheikh Saliou Mbacke, Consultant / Coordinator C/O LWF/DWS Gitanga Road Lavington P.O. Box 40870, 00100 GPO - Nairobi, Kenya.

91- Interfaith Voices for Peace & Justice - PO Box 23346 Santa Barbara, CA 93121 USA.

92- Interfaith Center of New York - The Interfaith Center of New York (We moved!) 475 Riverside Drive New York, NY 10115 USA.

93- Interfaith Center on Corporate Responsibility - Room 1842 - 475 Riverside Drive New York, NY 10115 USA.

94- International Association for Religious Freedom - 2 Market Street Oxford OX1 3ET United Kingdom.

95- International Committee for the Peace Council - 1112 Grant Street Madison, Wisconsin 53711 USA.

96- International Interfaith Centre (IIC) - PO Box 750 Oxford OX3 3BR UK.

97- Interreligious Engagement Project - Jim Kenney, Executive Director 980 Verda Lane, Lake Forest, IL 60045 USA.

98- Institute of Interfaith Dialogue - 5905 Winsome Ln. #200 Houston, TX 77057 USA.

99- Movement for a Beloved Community - P.O Box 620036 San Diego, CA 92162-0036 USA.

100- North American Interfaith Network - 1426 9th Street NW, Second Floor Washington, DC 20001-3330 USA.

101- Schools of Forgiveness and Reconciliation, ESPERE - Father Leonel Narvaez Gomez, Director Calle 40 No. 78A-14, Bogota, Colombia.

102- Tanenbaum Center for Religious Understanding - 254 W. 31st Street 7th Floor New York, NY 10001 USA.

103- The Temple of Understanding - 211 East 43rd Street, Suite 1600 New York, NY 10017 USA.

104- Tripartite Forum on Interfaith Cooperation for Peace - 556 Fifth Avenue New York, NY 10036 USA.

105- The Unification Theological Seminary - 30 Seminary Drive Barrytown, NY 12571 USA.

106- UNIITE - Tri-Cap Building #4 700 W St. Germain St. Cloud, MN 56301 Minnesota USA.

107- World Interfaith Congress - PO Box 23346 Santa Barbara CA 93121 USA.

108- World Peace Prayer Society - The World Peace Sanctuary 26 Benton Road Wassaic, NY 12592 USA.

109- World Youth Peace Summit - World Youth Peace – Headquarters Empire State Building 350 Fifth Avenue, Suite 5403 New York, NY 10118 USA.

110- Centre for Contemporary Islamic Studies - 32 Onan Road The Galaxy Singapore, 424484.

111- International Islamic Council for Daw'a and Relief - P.O. Box 34128 Jeddah 21468 Saudi Arabia.

112- The World Council of Muslims for Interfaith Relations - P. O. Box 142 Macomb, IL 61455, USA.

113- Affinity Intercultural Foundation - PO BOX 496 Auburn, NSW 2144 Australia.

114- Islamic Religious Council of Singapore - Secretary MUIS Islamic Center of Singapore 1, Lorong 6 Toa Payoh Singapore.

115- Qantara.de - c/o Deutsche Welle Online Kurt-Schumacher-Strase 3 D-53113 Bonn Germany.

116- The Organization of the Islamic Conference - PO Box 178 Jeddah-21411 Kingdom of Saudi Arabia.

117- The World Council For Muslim Interfaith Relations - 200 E. 10th Street #518 New York, New York, 10003 USA.

118- Lady Liberty League - Circle Sanctuary PO Box 9 Barneveld, WI 53507 USA.

119- The Pagan Federation UK - 22 Joiners Way, Lavendon, Buckinghamshire, MK46 4JF England.

120- The Pagan Federation Painne Canada - PO Box 876 Station "B", Ottawa ON, K1P 5P9 Canada.

121- The Druid Network - PO Box 3533 Whichford, Shipston on Stour, Warwickshire CV36 5YB England.

122- Center for Sacred Sciences - 1430 Willamette St. #164 Eugene, OR 97401 USA.

123- Brahma Kumaris World Spiritual University - PO Box No 2, Mount Abu 30750 Rajasthan, India.

124- The Sikh Interfaith Council of Victoria - PO Box 85, Mulgrave, Vic. 3170 Australia.

125- Sikh Nari Manch - 180 Plantsbrook Rd. Walmley Sutton Coldfield, West Midlands B76 1HL United Kingdom.

126- The Australian Sikh Association - PO Box 834 Blacktown NSW 2148 Australia.

127- Guru Gobind Singh Foundation - Guru Gobind Singh Foundation 13814 Travilah Road, Rockville, Maryland 20850 USA.

128- World Sikh Organization - 1183 Cecil Avenue Ottawa, Ontario K1H 7Z6 Canada.

129- Federation of Zoroastrian Associations of North America - 5750 South Jackson Street Hinsdale, IL 60521 Illinois, USA.

130- World Zoroastrian Organization - 135 Tennison Road South Norwood London SE25 5NF UK.

131- Zoroastrian Interfaith Group - Zoroastrian Association of Greater New York 106 Pomona Road Suffern, NY 10901 USA.

132- Zoroastrian College - Sanjan, India.

133- Asia Faiths Development Dialogue - University of Cambodia, Cambodia.

134- World Faiths Development Dialogue - 3307 M. St. NW Suite 200, Washington, DC (202) 687-6444 USA.

135- The International Shinto Foundation - Tokyo, Japan.

136- Global Family for Love & Peace/ Museum of World Religions - Jhonghe City Taipei County, Taiwan.

137- Chung Tai Chan Monastery - 2 Chung Tai Road, Puli, Nantou 54544, Taiwan, R.O.C.

138- Monash University - Monash University Clayton VIC 3168, Australia.

139- Guru Nanak Nishkam Sewak Jatha (UK) - Gurdwara Guru Nanak Nishkam Sewak Jatha (London) UK.

140- Shinji Shumeikai - 2430 E Colorado Blvd Pasadena, CA 91107-4250 USA.

141- Parliament of the World's Religions - Waldhäuser Straße 23 D-72076 Tübingen, Germany

…

C- Universities of:

1/ Stanford University – Stanford, CA, United States.

2/ University of California – 110 Sproul Hall, #5800 Berkley 94720 California USA.

3/ Peking University – 5 Yiheyuanlu Beijing 100871 Beijing province China.

4/ Michigan state university – 450 Administration Bldg. East Lansing 48824-1042 Michigan USA.

5/ Yale University – New Haven 06520 Connecticut USA.

6/ Indiana University – Bloomington Indiana USA.

7/ University of Cambridge – Trinity Lane Cambridge CB2 1TN East of England.

8/ University of Oxford – Wellington Square Oxford OX1 2JD South East England.

9/ Keio University – 2 – 15 – 45 – Mita, Minato – Ku Tokyo 108 – 8345 Tokyo Japan.

10/ National University of Singapore – 21 Lower Kent Ridge Road Singapore 119077.

11/ Federal University of Rio de Janeiro – Avenida Pedro Calmon, 550 Rio de Janeiro Brazil.

12/ Harvard University – Massachusetts Hall Cambridge 02138 Massachusetts USA.

13/ University of Washington – 1400 NE Campus Parkway Seattle 98195 – 4550 Washington USA.

14/ New York University – 70 Washington Square South New York City 10012 – 1091 New York USA.

15/ Boston University – One Sherborn Street Boston 02215 Massachusetts USA.

16/ Waseda University – 1 - 104 Totsuka – machi, Shinjuku – ku Tokyo 169 – 8050 Tokyo Japan.

17/ the University of Tokyo – 7 - 3 – 1 Hongo, Bunkyo – Ku Tokyo 113 – 8654 Tokyo Japan.

18/ Free University of Berlin – Kaiserswerther Str. 16 – 18 Berlin 14195 Berlin Germany.

19/ the University of Manchester – Oxford Road Manchester M13 9PL North West England.

20/ the University of Hong Kong – Pok Fu Lam Road Hong Kong.

21/ the University of Melbourne – Swanston Street Melbourne 3010 Victoria Australia.

22/ University of Geneva – 24 Rue du General-Dufour Geneva 1211 Genève Swiss.

23/ University of Oslo – PO Box 1072, Blindern Oslo Norway.

24/ Moscow State University – Leninskie Gory Moscow 119992 Moscow Russia.

25/ University of Delhi – University Road Delhi 110 007 National Capital Territory of Delhi India.

26/ Anna University – Sardar Patel Road Chennai 600 025 Tamil Nadu India.

27/ University of Milan – Via Festa del Perdono 7 Milano 20122 Lombardia Italy.

28/ Tampere University of Technology – Korkeakoulunkatu 1 Tampere 33720 Pirkanmaa Finland.

29/ National Autonomous University of Mexico – Ciudad Universitaria Mexico City 04510 Distrito Federal Mexico.

30/ International University of Japan – 777 Kokusai – cho Minami Uonuma – shi 949 – 7277 Niigata Japan.

31/ Chulalongkorn University – 254 Phyathi Road, Patumwan Bangkok 10330 Bangkok Metropolitan Area Thailand.

32/ University of Malaya – Pantai Valley Kuala Lumpur 50603 Selangor Malaysia.

…

D- International Libraries of:

Australian National University Library, Canberra - Australia
Birmingham Central Library - England
Huntington Library, San Marino, California - USA
London Library - UK

Library of Parliament, Ottawa - Canada
Library of Congress, Washington D.C. - USA
Los Angeles Central Library - USA
National Central Library (Rome) - Italy
National Library of Australia, Canberra - Australia
Library of Alexandria, Alexandria - Egypt
Royal Library of Sweden, Stockholm - Sweden
Danish Royal Library, Copenhagen - Denmark
Glasgow University Library - Scotland
National Library of New Zealand, Wellington - New Zealand
National Library of Russia, St Petersburg - Russia
National Library of India, Kolkata - India
National Library of China, Beijing - China
National Library of Brazil, Rio de Janeiro - Brazil
National Diet Library, Tokyo and Kyoto - Japan
…

E- News Agencies of:

CNN - 6430 W Sunset Blvd # 300, Los Angeles, CA 90028-7906
(323) 993-5000 USA.
CNN - 820 1st St NE, Washington D.C. 20002-4243
(202) 898-7900 USA.
CNN - 10 Columbus Cir, New York, NY 10019-1158
(212) 275-7800 USA.
BBC - Wood Lane Hammersmith, London W12 7, United Kingdom
0870 603 0304 - BBC.co.uk.
Algérie Presse Service - Avenue des frères Bouadou, Bir Mourad Rais - Alger,
Algeria.
Jiji Press Tokyo - "7th Floor, Jiji Press Building 5-15-8 Ginza Chuo-ku, Tokyo 104-
8178 Japan.
…

Also: More Officials; Organizations; Famous people & celebrities (Bill Gates; Pope
Francis; Aung San Suu Kyi; Amitabh Bachchan; …).